ANDY MCILREE

Men God Moved - Books 1-3

HAYES
PRESS Christian Publisher

First published by Hayes Press 2019

Copyright © 2019 by Andy McIlree

First edition

This book was professionally typeset on Reedsy.
Find out more at reedsy.com

Contents

I

Grace in First Peter - The Many-Splendoured Grace Revealed To An Ungracious Man

"Tracing the grace of God in Peter's first letter is like seeing the glory of God in Romans and the greatness of God in Hebrews."
In this deeply practical book, Andy takes us through each of Peter the rough fisherman's 5 chapters, and introduces us to the manifold (the many-splendoured) grace of God expressed in at least 11 different aspects.

1.1 GRACE REQUIRED IN AN UNGRACIOUS MAN

It's unlikely that you have ever received a letter without your first question being, "Who is it from?" It should be the same when we begin to read the letters in the New Testament of our Bibles. We really ought to know who the penman is behind the writing. We know, of course, that it has come from God, but behind each one is a man whom God shaped for the purpose. Peter, who has been called 'the big fisherman,' was an unlikely candidate for letter writing. If he had been told, while hauling in his nets, that he would write letters some day, he probably would have said, "In your dreams!"

As we start to think of him, we need to link him with others who were given the same privilege. Paul's letters, for instance, cause us to realise the kind of company that Peter knew he was in, yet there's no hiding that he had the advantage of walking with the Lord throughout the days of His ministry, of being at Calvary to see the way his Saviour died, and of meeting Him in resurrection. Paul missed all that, but was compensated in other ways during the three years following his conversion, as we read in Galatians 1:11–18.

Tracing the grace of God in Peter's first letter is like seeing the glory of God in Romans and the greatness of God in Hebrews, but this doesn't suggest at all that these other letters don't have what Peter has in his. When we think of the glory of God in Romans, we are very much aware that His glory is associated with His greatness and grace. Likewise, when we step into Hebrews to consider the greatness of God, we soon realise that it expresses His glory and grace; and now, as we focus on the grace of God in Peter's five chapters, we become just as conscious that it is seen in His glory and greatness. Taking these altogether, we rejoice that each one is expressed in Christ, and this is the beauty of studying them.

It was vital before Peter dipped his pen into the ink that God would reveal much to him as he drank deeply from the wells of salvation. God was about to use him to speak to others, so firstly He must speak to him. Let's not deceive ourselves; we will never be able to speak to others about our Lord Jesus Christ unless the Spirit of God has fulfilled His ministry by speaking first to us about Him. As Peter took up his pen and thought of how far-flung his readers were, he must have felt it strange for a man who hardly knew the outside of a boat, yet this was the plan God had in mind when he called him. When the Saviour paused on the beach to call him and Andrew from the fishing boat,[1] he had no idea of what lay ahead. Their stepping out reflected Abram's faith and obedience as he *"went out, not knowing where he was going"*[2]; and *"the Lord of glory"*[3] appeared to them just as *"the God of glory"*[4] appeared to him.

Peter was probably within earshot when Jesus told the Pharisees, *"Your father Abraham rejoiced to see My day, and he saw it and was glad."*[5] What a contrast, that they saw Him up close and rejected Him! Abraham was unusual for he knew more about predestination than he knew about destination. Years later, it was very different for Ruth as she left Moab. She knew that she was going to Bethlehem, but had no idea that she was destined for Matthew 1:5 to be a vital link in the royal line that led to the Lord Jesus. She was the opposite of Abraham for she knew about her destination, but didn't have the slightest clue about predestination.

As for Peter, God in His wisdom had a plan for him, which included writing two letters that would find their way into His written Word to sit side by side, and in absolute agreement, with the writings of Paul; but before we read any more from his letter we need to explore the first word:

Peter

Paul and Peter had a major disagreement, yet two points should be clarified right away. Yes, they had a dispute, of which Paul wrote, *"I withstood him to his face."*[6] No, it didn't mean that this led to a divergence in their beliefs and teaching. These two men had been at loggerheads with each other, and there was good reason why they had stood toe to toe, face to face, and eye to eye, for Paul recognised that Peter had compromised himself before God and before Gentile believers.

Peter had heard that men were coming from James, and he panicked. He took fright, because he had been saying things among the Gentiles that he shouldn't have said. It wasn't simply that he was eating with them, he had made adjustments to the gospel for them, but when he heard these men were coming he *"withdrew and separated himself."*[7] He put them out of sight and distanced himself from them, as if they never existed. In his mind, they were gone. He had shunned them and completely shut them out, so that he excluded and no longer countenanced them.

He had gone into reverse mode, which Paul called *"hypocrisy"*[8] and *"withstood him to his face"*[9] for the problem was doctrinal and serious. Peter's compromise had misrepresented the truth of the gospel and was so influential that it misled Barnabas. Paul wouldn't tolerate this and confronted Peter in a way that could be translated as "he opposed him and faced him down." Weakness would have stepped back, but with appropriate spiritual strength Paul stepped up to the challenge. It may sound as though Paul was being ungracious, yet it's even more direct in the Greek language, which says, *"kata prosōpon"* – he faced him down. Yes, he was gracious enough to tell his brother that he was a hypocrite, which was hardly the qualification for a man of God, an apostle, for a disciple or a writer.

Their dispute didn't last, for both of them knew that they had such an affinity with each other that caused them to be mightily used of God, since they knew that the Spirit of God was at work in each other's ministry, resulting in an overlap in what they taught. These dear men were not out of synchrony. An indication of harmony in what they communicated is seen in Galatians 2:8, where Paul summed up the harmony of their commission by saying, *"For He who worked effectively in Peter for the apostleship to the circumcised also worked effectively in me toward the Gentiles."* This is a tremendous acknowledgement from Paul and it confirms:

· **Harmony of calling** - Their call from God as apostles;
· **Harmony in commission** - Their ministry was according to the mind of the Holy Spirit;
· **Harmony in communication** - Their teaching corresponded.

Peter reciprocated Paul's genuine, and generous, acknowledgement of his ministry by adding, *"consider that the longsuffering of our Lord is salvation—as also our beloved brother Paul, according to the wisdom given to him, has written to you, as also in all his epistles, speaking in them of these things, in which are some things hard to understand, which untaught and unstable people twist to their own destruction, as they do also the rest of the Scriptures."*[10] If there had been any lingering doubt or discomfort in Peter's mind, he could easily have re-phrased this to 'your beloved brother Paul,' and not everyone would have noticed his evasion. Instead, he thought of the brother who faced him down, looked him in the eye and told him that he was a hypocrite, and called him *"beloved."* That took grace!

Perhaps we should pause here to listen to Peter the fisherman talking about the *"Hebrew of the Hebrews"*[11] and learn how God takes up servants from different backgrounds and ability to produce their mutual regard for one another. John and Peter shared the same upbringing and occupation in Galilee and were described as *"uneducated and untrained,"*[12] which meant their schooling wasn't from rabbis and that they were mere layman whose confidence and plain speaking came from being in Jesus' company. Peter thought highly of Paul's delight and reasoning in the Old Testament Scriptures, but Peter must have done this too. Would God not have us assume that, since Simon was the one to whom Andrew made a beeline when he *"found the Messiah,"*[13] that he was among those who were *"waiting for the Consolation of Israel"?*[14]

At the time of his calling, Simon may have been less academic than Saul of Tarsus, but more devout. In his on-going devotion, he had an appreciation of divine things revealed through Paul that were *"hard to understand,"* things that others would twist. He knew there were twisters around, and so did other writers like Paul, John, James and Jude.[15] Even so, it's not only that he ascribes high regard for Paul's spiritual ability. He goes much farther by recognising that Paul's writings form part of Scripture, which is clearly implied in his condemnation of those who perverted his reasoning – Gr. *hōs kai tas loipas graphas* – *"as they do also the rest of the Scriptures."*[16] What a marvellous acknowledgement that Paul's letters are equated with the other Scriptures!

Some readers may be inclined to respond to him by saying, 'Hold on Peter, do you know what you are saying?' and his reply would be, 'Yes, of course I know! He is my *"beloved brother"* and I am speaking of *"all his epistles."* I love the man, I laud his ministry; and, above all, I have learned that his letters are part of the sacred Scriptures.' In saying, *"as they do also the rest of the Scriptures,"* he linked them with other Old Testament writings as the revealed Word of God. How well he knew that what others twisted and bent out of shape was nothing less than the inspired Word of God.

Earlier, in 2 Peter 1:20-21, Peter confirmed that *"no prophecy of Scripture is of any private interpretation, for prophecy never came by the will of man, but men of God spoke as they were moved by the Holy Spirit."* This was his way of re-wording and expanding Paul's statement that *"All Scripture is given by inspiration of God"*[17] – Gr. *theopneustos* – meaning it is *"breathed out by*

God,"[17] thus acknowledging that Paul's letters are part of God's inspired and inerrant Word.

Wherever each New Testament letter went, to an individual church or groups of churches, it was shared with believers, and we might well ask, 'How did they take it in the first time they heard it?' It's much easier to conclude that these early Christians must have gathered many times to search out the teaching that God the Inspirer wanted them to enjoy. What a vital example for us: for if present-day believers are so busy that they have no time to fit in regular teaching of God's Word, then the truth is they are too busy; and their churches are dying, even if they also are busy! We need to beware of the Sardis syndrome: reputed to be lively, but dead.[18]

As Peter thought on all that Paul had written, he must have had the longing that the grace of God would do the same through him; that he also would be so beloved that the Inspirer would breathe out His Word through him. It's not that Paul and Peter wrote words and God breathed into them. He breathed out the words, and Peter's concern was that men were twisting God's out-breathed Word.

Sadly, what they did with the Old Testament, others do with the New. There is no end of theories that contradict sound theology and they come from twisters who by nature oppose the straightness of His truth. When God used the Hebrew word *torah* to describe His Old Testament law, He had its root meaning from the word *yarah* in mind, and nothing could be straighter for it depicts an archer shooting an arrow. He sends it on its course toward its target by the corresponding straightness of the Holy Spirit's work, while twisted minds attempt to deflect it by twisting what it means. Peter's earlier inconsistent behaviour didn't lead to his being numbered with untaught and unstable twisters, but Paul was used by God to correct him after he had been guilty of misapplying the gospel and misleading his Gentile hearers.

How thankful we can be that God spoke so openly about disagreements between His workers and didn't ignore them or sweep them under the carpet. Differences of opinion aren't hard to find in the Bible, but it's wonderful to see how He helped divided minds get back together again, whether it happened in the Old Testament or in the New. Our minds go back to a much earlier dispute between Moses and Aaron. There's a great lesson in how Moses handled the problem in Deuteronomy chapter 9, especially when he came to verse 20, where he said, *"so I prayed for Aaron also at the same time."* What a great attitude!

God's openness about all these matters shows that He provides the way to put things right. It's not wrong to disagree, but reaching agreement has to be done His way. I started off by talking about Moses and Aaron, and I'll finish by going back to another example of Moses' ability to help him. It's in Leviticus 10 and, once again, he was really concerned about a mistake Aaron had made. The good thing is, that having shown him how troubled he was about it, he then let him explain himself, and the chapter ends by saying, *"So when Moses heard that, he was content."*[19] It was a great way to round off a disagreement about how the Lord should be served, and our prayer is that what we have been talking about with you will end in exactly the same way.

In Psalm 45, David wrote, *"My tongue is the pen of a ready writer."* Peter could talk, and we will think later of how saying the wrong things landed him in trouble. He was a talker. There were men in the Old Testament called Amorites, and the word *'amar* includes the thought that they were talkers. When David thought about the ministry of the Holy Spirit through him he said, *"The Spirit of the LORD spoke by me, and His word was on my tongue."*[20] This is where Peter wanted to be, if he ever was going to be among God's writers, and he could have said, *"For there is not a word on my tongue, but behold, O LORD, You know it altogether."*[21] There were things that he had said to the Lord Jesus Christ that were wrong.

We are thinking of grace that was required by an ungracious man for that's what Peter was. It's also what we were and, to some extent, still are. We are perfectly capable of saying something out of place. As we read through the five chapters of this letter, we will discover that this man is in harmony, not only with Paul but also with the Inspirer. He is moved by the Inspirer and assures us that no prophecy of scripture is *"of private interpretation, for ... men of God spoke as they were moved by the Holy Spirit."*

Paul had summed this up in a word – *theopneustos* – but the fisherman's mind wanted to know the practical outworking of its meaning. No one else in the Bible ever used Paul's word, so perhaps it was an academic's appreciation, whereas Peter wanted to describe how the word worked by telling us that *"men of God spoke as they were moved by the Holy Spirit."* They were carried along by His divine presence and power. That is, they were carried by the Holy Spirit from where they were to where God wanted them to be, since they were incapable of carrying themselves.

Let's ask ourselves if we are living in the enjoyment of being carried along by the Holy Spirit. We are not going to be inspired, but we have the inspired Word to share and we need to be carried along by Him. There are wrong ways to handle the Word of God. We can speak ungraciously.[22] We can speak unadvisedly.[23] We also can speak wickedly for God[24] by misrepresenting what He says and means. We should mean what we say by saying what He means, and not resort to false notions to support what we think He means! We can defend things we think we see in the Word that are not there at all, and end up speaking ungraciously, unadvisedly, and unrighteously for God. As Peter began his letter, he was waiting for the Inspirer to breathe out His spoken Word as He had done with Paul. All we need to do is step into the first chapter and we will think we are in Romans 8. Note how he showed this in the way his first chapter mirrors it by emphasising its well-constructed gospel themes. Listen to him and trace the similarity as he echoes the great truths of:

- v.2 election and foreknowledge - Romans 8:29

- v.3 hope - Romans 8:24
- v.3 resurrection - Romans 8:11
- v.4 inheritance - Romans 8:17
- v.5, 9 predestination - Romans 8:29-30
- v.7 glorification - Romans 8:30
- v.15 called - Romans 8:30

All these are included in his masterly introduction and present a wonderfully coinciding overlap with all Paul has shared, and we catch the distinct sense that Peter has much more to develop. As his letter progressed, he introduced other aspects of truth that correspond with Paul's teaching in his letters. For example:

- Chapter 1: **Salvation**
- Chapter 2: **Service** – the house of God, and priestly service
- Chapter 3: **Submission** – compassion, and sanctification
- Chapter 4: **Supply** – its glory, its grace, its gifts
- Chapter 5: **Shepherding** – the Elderhood, and the little flock

How good it is for us to see that the man, who on some occasions had been so out of step, by the time he dipped his pen in the inkwell was ready to open with the first word, "Peter." It's such a contrast from our habit of signing letters with our name as the last word. Paul adopted the same practice as Peter. In fact, in 2 Corinthians 10:1, Paul triples the reference to himself by saying, *"Now I, Paul, myself."* Was this the promotion of self? No, these were gracious men. The God of glory who worked through Paul in his letter to the Romans is the God of grace who worked through Peter as he wrote to Pontus, Galatia, Cappadocia, Asia, and Bithynia. By His help, we will see more evidence of this as we continue.

1.2 GRACE RESTORED IN HIS MISTAKES

"Peter, an apostle of Jesus Christ, to the pilgrims of the Dispersion in Pontus, Galatia, Cappadocia, Asia, and Bithynia ..." (1 Pet.1:1).

"And the Lord said, Simon, Simon! Indeed, Satan asked for you, that he may sift you as wheat. But I have prayed for you, that your faith should not fail; and when you have returned to Me, strengthen your brethren" (Lk.22:31,32).

* * *

Many thoughts probably went through Peter's mind as, in the wisdom of God, he began his letter by writing his name to introduce himself to those who may never have met him in their far-off new homeland now known as Turkey, far from where he had grown up in Galilee. We have thought of the grace that was required by an ungracious man, and can imagine his mixed feelings as he joyfully began to represent the Inspirer while sadly recalling how he disappointed his Saviour. As we consider the ups and downs of his life that lie between the lines of the opening verse, we can only begin to gauge what it meant to him when God asked him to write, like Paul, as an ambassador on *"Christ's behalf."*[1]

Thirty years had passed before the Lord Jesus Christ had gone from Bethlehem, the house of bread, via Egypt to Nazareth[2], then on to Bethsaida, the house of fishing, the birthplace of Simon and Andrew. Walking on the beach near Capernaum where they were now living, He had called them from their boat, as they were actively *"casting a net."*[3] He was interested in what we would call 'busy men,' for God never calls the idle. The call that came from the Man on the shore didn't reach Peter on a day off or on an off day! Peter was like Elisha who was called when his hands were firmly on the plow, just as Simon's were firmly on the net. He was fully engaged in his work, a fisherman through and through, hook, line and sinker, until Jesus called him to fish on the landward side of the beach. Like the others, he left men to find men.

His work was his life, yet he had the expectation that the Messiah was coming. The Messianic hope was in his heart, otherwise Andrew would not have run to tell a brother who wasn't interested. For Simon and Andrew, James and John, the Man on their beach was the fulfilment of Paul's message, *"the grace of God that brings salvation has appeared."*[4] *"Immediately"* they left all to walk with the One who ministered grace, not least into Simon's faults that he might make him into the kind of man who would minister to others, including us.God doesn't hide His failures. He restores them. There's something very stimulating and encouraging about God's making room in His Word to record Simon's mistakes, but it's been well said that 'the man who never made a mistake never made anything.' Simon made lots of them, but the Lord made a lot out of him, and in this we find the grace that helps us not to lose heart when we fail. Failing doesn't make us a failure!

None of these men paid any attention to the new Figure who walked on their beach at the beginning of His ministry; nor did they know that the grace of God had appeared until He spoke, and believing men stepped forward. There was a very different reaction at the end of His ministry in Gethsemane when He said, *"I am,"* and unbelieving men fell backward. Four men left their boats, their father, their family, their friends, and their inheritance to follow a Man through whom they would discover that a far greater inheritance lay ahead of them.

What did the hired servants think as sons left their father with the future of the work in the hands of servants instead of sons? They also turned their backs on the waves and billows of Galilee to follow Him until He faced the waves and billows of Golgotha. *"All Your waves and billows have gone over Me"*[5] could have been written of Him as He endured the spiritual storm of the middle cross. He also called them spiritually to engage in the different aspects of their fishing habits.

In Matthew 4:18, they were *casting* a net; in Mark 1:19, they were *mending* their nets; and in Luke 5:2, they were *washing* their nets, but these were as nothing to Luke 5:6 when their net was *breaking*. What they had been accustomed to on a daily basis found its spiritual counterpart as they walked with Him. Each was a foretaste of Peter's dependence on the Lord for the day came when, meeting Him after His resurrection, he *"cast himself into the sea."*[6] He did with himself what he had done with the nets. Later, when he wrote to the churches in Galatia,[7] his message was in harmony with Paul's appeal *"to restore"* a sinning brother.[8] The word Paul used would appeal to Peter for *katartizō* is identical to what fishermen did when *"mending"* their nets. Peter was learning that the net was no longer in his hand, but in his pen; and it must have meant a lot to him that Paul used the same analogy.

It appealed so much to him that he used it himself in 1 Peter 5:10 when longing that the God of all grace would *"perfect"* those in the assemblies – meaning that He would restore their fellowship as a fisherman repairs a broken net. They were doing for people what they had done at the end of a catch, when their nets were breaking under the strain and they had to reconnect the broken mesh. Paul and Peter are interested in the God who restores broken men. It's one feature of *"He who worked effectively in Peter ... also worked effectively in me."*

Through his work, others would experience the *bathing* (Gr. *louō*) that the

Lord grants in salvation.[9] This was their spiritual washing – a thorough cleansing, just like the nets in Luke 5:2. Peter would never forget the lesson he learned from the Lord in this chapter for he discovered that the Son of God is in control of both sides of the beach and of the boat, and he submitted himself to His control.[10] He had once been quite emphatic when he resisted the Lord's command and sailed out of His will by saying, *"Master, we have toiled all night and caught nothing."* His initial reaction was to debate with the Lord, as if to say, "Let me tell You something - we did this for a living, we know the sea, and it's pointless."

Then came the turnaround – *"nevertheless* [Gr. *de:* but] *at Your word I will let down the net"* – He introduced the *"but"* that delivered him from the selfishness of self and caused him to speak in submissiveness to the mind of the Lord, and he sailed into His will. The opposite was seen in John 6:9 when Andrew said, "There is a lad here who has five barley loaves and two small fish." If only he had stopped there, but he didn't. He added, "but what are they among so many?" He spoiled it by introducing the word *"but"* that caused him to be delivered from the mind of the Lord, to speak according to self, and sail out of His will. Isn't that what we do, too? Peter started well by saying, "Master" (Gr. *epistatēs:* commander), but didn't let Him have the mastery until after voicing his own will. But then he learned:

- **Acceptance** of the Lord's will, in spite of personal logic;
- **Awareness** of the Lord's sinlessness and his own sinfulness;
- **Assurance** of the Lord's help in catching men.

In the acknowledgement of his own sinfulness, he also recognised his personal limitation.Lessons can be learned, progress can be made, but imperfect man can't become perfect in his actions. This includes Peter. He was an apostle, but his impulsive nature led him into other contradictions. For example:

1. His Defiance

a. When the Lord Jesus was speaking to His disciples in Matthew 16 they were in the north of Israel, in the region of Caesarea Philippi, now called Banias, near the foot of Mount Hermon where a spring becomes the Banias River and one of the tributaries of the River Jordan. Significantly, He had just introduced, for the first time, the great truth of building His church (v.18); and then, also for the first time, spoke of His death and resurrection through which it would be made a reality. Peter was standing there, and we know the conversation that took place when the Lord asked, *"Who do men say that I, the Son of Man, am?"*[11]

The people evidently had thought of this and suggested John the Baptist, Elijah or Jeremiah; apparent compliments, but were they? Hardly! They had concluded that John had *"a demon"*[12]; Elijah had been called the *"troubler of Israel"*[13]; and it had been said of Jeremiah, *"This man does not seek the welfare of this people, but their harm."*[14] To make matters worse, they thought Jesus was a blasphemer.[15] Peter was in no doubt that He is *"the Christ, the Son of the living God,"* in full agreement with the I AM's eternal name.[16] The Lord was revealing the Deity of His Person, but with the Person of Deity He revealed the purpose of Deity – to be the Builder of His church, which Paul described as *"the church, which is his body."*[17]

Peter listened well, but when the Saviour changed the subject to His inevitable suffering, death and resurrection, it was too much for him. He reacted strongly and took Jesus aside – Gr. *proslambanō*, which implies he seized Him and took Him aside, as if saying, "Come over here" – and then began to rebuke Him saying, *"Far be it from You, Lord; this shall not happen to You!"*[18] It was as if Peter felt he could enlighten the Lord for this could be translated as, "God forbid it, Lord, this shall definitely not happen to You," which was directly in opposition to the divine plan, and another contradiction by Peter. He had made the mistake of saying "Master" in Luke 5:5 before counter-reasoning with the Commander's will. Now, he opposed His Lordship by combining *"Far be it"* and *"this shall never happen to You"* with *"Lord."*

By using the word *kurios* he implied that he was subject to the authority of his Controller, yet strongly resisted what He said. The Lord immediately sensed the Tempter's voice behind Peter's words and addressed him directly by saying, *"Get behind Me, Satan! You are an offense to Me, for you are not mindful of the things of God, but the things of men."* Through Peter, he attempted to sow the doubt that the way of the cross was avoidable. Yes, Peter made a mistake, but *"He who worked effectively in Peter"* would turn him around, even though other mistakes would follow.

b. In the next chapter[19] Peter, James, and John were with the Lord on the Mount of Transfiguration when Moses and Elijah appeared as the representatives of the Law and the Prophets, undoubtedly appearing to honour the much greater glory of the One who had come to fulfil them.[20] Luke says, they *"appeared in glory and spoke of His decease."*[21] They were discussing His exodus. The exodus of the children of Israel was because of the Passover lamb and well known to both men; but this time they talked about the exodus of the Lamb. Luke is the only one who tells us that the three disciples slept until *"when they were fully awake, they saw His glory and the two men who stood with Him."*[22] It wasn't when they were half-asleep, and this reminds us of the miracle of changing water into wine at the wedding in Cana of Galilee when He *"manifested His glory"* in waterpots that had been filled *"to the brim"*[23] – not half-filled – and it's still the same in our lives. It's not half-filled vessels that give Him glory, just as it wasn't the half-awake who saw His glory on the Mount.

Peter was fully awake to that glory, but it was a drowsy mind that wanted to let the Lord know what he was thinking. Once again, he began by saying, *"Master"* – still holding on to *epistatēs*, the Controller (i.e. more than Instructor, Commander), but denying its meaning. Then he added, *"it is good for us to be here"* – when he had been asleep for most of the time! To top it off, he went on to suggest, *"let us make three tabernacles, one for You, one for Moses, and one for Elijah."*[24] No wonder the voice of the Inspirer caused Luke to sum up Peter's mistake by concluding, **"not knowing [Gr. eidō: as in perception, seeing] what he said"** – that is, he had no idea. However, it would have been a greater mistake had he asked for six!

The day will come when Old Testament saints will share in His millennial glory,[25] but the Mount was the revelation of the Saviour's supreme glory, and they were to *"Hear Him!"* and see *"Jesus only."*[26] The grace of God had appeared to them on the beach as the lowly Servant calling servants. On the Mount, the grace of God appeared again, this time in glory bringing sons to glory.

This was another of Peter's mistakes, but *"He who worked effectively in Peter"* was still working. Peter was an unfinished and on-going work, and so are we. God was working in him to produce a man who was fit to write for Him, just as He is still working in us to produce men and women who are fit to work for Him. Peter's letters show how well God turned him around for, in the first he tells us that he was *"a witness of the sufferings of Christ"*[27]; and in the second he says, we *"were eyewitnesses of His majesty."*[28] He had become "fully awake" in every sense. We can be too, though our minds can switch off while we consider His Word, but it's when the mind is fully awake that it can absorb the richness of its ministry and we see the Saviour in ways that are manifestations of His glory.

2. His Defence

Peter leapt to the Lord's defence in the Garden of Gethsemane, even as the power of the *"I AM"* was unleashed and *"they drew back and fell to the ground."*[29] Imagine if He had spoken like this all the time. He could have done, but didn't. He could have unleashed the same force before Pilate when He spoke at Gabbatha, and sent him toppling from his judgment seat. He upholds *"all things by the word of His power,"*[30] and He floored these people

18

by it in Gethsemane. All too suddenly, the man who had stood in defiance now felt he should stand in defence, and in a flash his sword was drawn and off came Malchus' ear. Had Peter been a swordsman and not a fisherman, it could have been worse!

The Lord of Hosts could have called for *"more than twelve legions of angels,"*[31] so there was no need for one of twelve disciples on earth to think he was needed for such a role. Earlier, as He prayed, one angel strengthened Him in Gethsemane[32]; and there were only two who sat in the tomb where His body had lain.[33] There was no need for hosts to accompany Him in His suffering, but they will come in His glory.[34] In the Garden, Jehovah Sabaoth's voice was enough! And, once again, *"He who worked effectively in Peter"* brought him through this crisis too.

3. His Denial

The Lord anticipated Peter's denial,[35] addressing him as, *"Simon, Simon."* Why not, "Peter"? Perhaps it was to indicate that the disciple was about to enter into something that was contrary to his new name,[36] and out of character with his true spiritual walk. The Lord told him, *"Satan has asked to have you* [plural – all the disciples] ... *But I have prayed for you"* (singular – meaning Simon in particular).

The old farming process of sifting was slow and laborious, either by tossing the grain upward into the wind and causing the chaff to separate from the wheat as it fell or by holding a riddle as high as possible, shaking it and, again, letting the wind blow away the chaff as the grain fell on to the threshing floor. The devil aimed to do the opposite for he always wants the grain to blow away, leaving only the chaff behind; so the Lord was insinuating, *"Simon, Simon, Satan has asked to have you ... that he might make your life chaff ... but I have prayed for you."*

He had been a complete outsider standing at the high priest's door until

John asked the doorkeeper girl to let him in.[37] Recognised and humiliated by her, he was brought to denial number one. Moving inside to warm himself at the fire, he was brought to denial number two by *"another girl"*[38] who shared her allegation with others that he had been with Jesus. Shortly afterwards, some bystanders approached him to say that they were sure of who he was, and denial number three hit home as the rooster crowed.[39] Among them was *"one of the servants of the high priest, a relative of him whose ear Peter cut off."*[40] He had seen him in the lantern-light of Gethsemane, where the sword-wielder would have stood against all-comers, yet his predicted fall came at the word of two girls, some bystanders and a servant.

His denials were heard by all, and by the Lord who could have said, like Elisha who told Gehazi, *"Did not my heart go with you?"*[41] John tells us, *"He knew all men"* and *"what was in man"*[42] yet Peter said, *"I do not know Him."* Oh Peter, how could you say such a thing? Then we realise that in these hearts of ours there's the possibility of the same thing happening, even in the times when fear makes us hold back from witnessing. Fears, like faults, are the enemies of faith!

The devil wanted to make all their lives unfruitful, leaving no harvest for the Sower, and it's still his destructive plan for all believers; but how blessedly the Advocate prays as the adversary brutally sifts! His prayer had been *"that your faith does not fail."* Is this our prayer too, or do we focus on the fault rather than on the faith? Concentrating on our faults can result in undermining us to such a degree that we become worthless in our own eyes, like the ten spies whose perception of God's people was *"we were like grasshoppers in our own sight, and so we were in their sight."*[43] They focused on their weakness, but it wasn't their strength that failed, it was their faith. The lesson to be learned is that the enemy will take advantage by seeing us in the way we see ourselves.

But it's what we are in Christ that matters, and He is *"the author and finisher of faith."*[44] It is through Him that we received faith, for *"faith comes by hearing, and hearing by the word of God"*[45] and it's through Him that *"we walk by faith."*[46] The Lord didn't pray that Peter wouldn't make any more mistakes. No, He prayed for something much deeper: His must-prayer (Gr. *deomai*: to bind oneself or beg – from *deō*, to tie, as in Matthew 21:2; and *dei*: must) centred on the adversary's target, Peter's faith. When we pray for others in difficulty, do we pray as the Saviour prays, synchronising our burden with His?

He penetrated the immediate weakness and saw the real threat, that the Christian's wrestling is not *"against flesh and blood, but ... against spiritual hosts of wickedness in the heavenly places."*[47] In this battle, their mission is not merely to make us make mistakes, it's to cause our mistakes to have such an effect on us that we lose our faith. Our Defence is on the throne, and our victory is in the Victor!

> "We rest on Thee, our Shield and our Defender;
> We go not forth alone against the foe.
> Strong in Thy strength, safe in Thy keeping tender,
> We rest on Thee, and in Thy Name we go."
> (Edith G. Cherry)

With his faith as the object of his Master's prayer, he was pointed to better days when He said, *"and when you have returned to Me, strengthen your brethren."* Peter had lost sight of his future ministry, but the Lord hadn't. During the three days between Calvary and the resurrection, Peter nursed deep sorrow for he *"wept bitterly,"*[48] until the Lord's resurrection brought a change – *"But go, tell His disciples – and Peter."*[49] What grace! This time it was He who introduced the *"But"*, not one of His disciples, and Peter knew that he still had a place in his Saviour's will.

It was no longer Simon, but Peter! The cross had come in between, and the name given at the first was given again to reassure the troubled disciple of a restored relationship. Before the denial, the Lord *"worked effectively"* for Peter in prayer, and after His resurrection He "worked effectively" by comforting him. He worked for *"Peter, an apostle"* – the failing, mistake-ridden apostle – *"of Jesus Christ."* The grace of God had appeared to him once again, just as He does in making *"intercession for"* us[50] *"before the face of God"*[51] that we might serve within the scope of His perfect will by strengthening our brethren.

4. His Discovery

Calvary was Passover time, and Passover time was barley harvest in Israel. The resurrection, fifty days later, was wheat harvest, and Peter became the preacher in the wheat harvest of Pentecost. He was appointed and privileged to witness for his Saviour, and he would have understood if He had set him aside, but *"He who worked effectively in Peter"* kept on proving that the grace of God keeps on appearing and bringing daily salvation to him. At Pentecost, spiritually speaking, he was standing in a very different place.

At Calvary, he stood at the enemy's fire, but at Pentecost he stood up with the eleven with a new fire burning in his heart, actively representing the Lord Jesus Christ. He had promised Peter *"the keys of the kingdom"*[52] and through him a door for the Word[53] was opened in Jerusalem,[54] in Samaria[55] and to the Gentiles.[56] On that first day in Jerusalem, a wide range of people from different places heard the message,[57] and Peter saw thousands coming forward in repentance, being moved by the Holy Spirit who had fallen upon them with *"a sound from heaven, as of a rushing mighty wind."*[58]

They came forward to be baptised as soon as they had been converted. Having *"died with Christ,"* right away they *"were buried with Him through baptism,"*[59] and they were added to the first church in Jerusalem – all as the result of the Spirit of God working through Simon Peter's message. What an answer to the Lord having assured him, *"I have prayed for you"*! And now He is doing the same for us. We don't know each other's mistakes, but He does, and He doesn't write us off. He doesn't discard us, because of our defiance;

He doesn't dismiss us, because of our unwarranted defence; and He doesn't disown us, because of our unnecessary denial. The One who worked for Peter works for us also.

5. His Disappointment

Going forward in the blessing and power of Pentecost, the word of the Lord came, *"Rise, Peter; kill and eat."*[60] Three commands demanded three responses, but Peter replied, *"Not so, Lord!"* The Holy Spirit took control and, having been reluctant, as it were, to cast the net on the right side of the boat, Peter obeyed and was used by God in taking the gospel to the Gentiles. There had been a threefold rejection, but, yet again, the Lord *"worked effectively"* for Peter.

A woman once approached the late Graham Scroggie at the end of a service to ask his guidance on committing her life to Christ. He turned to Acts 10:14 and pointed out that it's inconsistent to say, as Peter did, *"Not so, Lord"*, since it means objecting to His Lordship. He explained that we can't say all three words in the same sentence and asked her to go home and underline which part she wanted to say. She went back to him later with her Bible open and the word "Lord" underlined, having decided not to say, "Not so."

What about our lives? The Man of Calvary is *"the grace of God"* that has appeared for our sakes, as well as Simon Peter's. We serve on behalf of *"the Apostle and High Priest of our confession ... Jesus."*[61] He is the Apostle who came out from God to speak to man on earth, and He is the High Priest who has gone back in to God to speak for us in heaven. We will discover later how much He meant to Peter in both spheres of His ministry, and in this he is in full agreement with the writer to the Hebrews who loved the name of Jesus so much that he used it nine times.

1. Heb.2:9: *"But we see **Jesus**, who was made a little lower than the angels."*
2. Heb.3:1: *"Therefore, holy brethren, partakers of the heavenly calling,*

consider the Apostle and high Priest of our confession, **Jesus**" (the word 'Christ' is not in the pre-sixth century Greek texts we have).

3. Heb.4:14: "*Seeing then that we have a great High Priest who has passed through the heavens, **Jesus** the Son of God.*"
4. Heb.6:20: "*where the forerunner has entered for us, even **Jesus**, having become High Priest forever.*"
5. Heb.7:22: "*by so much more **Jesus** has become a surety of a better covenant.*"
6. Heb.10:19: "*Therefore, brethren, having boldness to enter the Holiest by the blood of **Jesus**.*"
7. Heb.12:2: "*Looking unto **Jesus**, the author and finisher of our faith.*"
8. Heb.12:24: "*To **Jesus** the Mediator of the new covenant.*"
9. Heb.13:12: "*Therefore **Jesus** also, that He might sanctify the people with His own blood, suffered outside the gate.*"

He is the Man of all grace, and Peter would never again say "*Not so*" to Him. After all his ups and downs, he is ready to write his letters to the churches in these five regions of Asia – still answering his Saviour's prayer by strengthening his brethren. Many must have listened to what we read in the first verse and wondered how God ever fitted this man to write such a letter to them. And how is the same God equipping us to take up His inspired Word, including what He has written through Peter, to share the incarnate Word?

Long before Peter's day, God worked through Samson, whom we could think of as the Peter of the Old Testament. Scripture says, "*And the Spirit of the LORD began to move upon him at Mahaneh Dan between Zorah and Eshtaol.*"[62] This statement is packed with meaning and shows how God works in the lives of those He calls to shape them into something very different from their old nature. The Spirit "*began*" and the Hebrew word *chalal* tells us something of how He did it for it means to break,[63] to wound[64] and includes the thought of putting in a wedge. What a gradual and patient work by the Spirit! He may break and wound Samson, as He used the thin edge of the wedge to begin His gracious work of opening him up to His will, but it was because He wanted *"to move"* him. It means He kept tapping in his life, as if to drive home the wedge that would separate him from his old ways.

Peter knew that the men God used to impart His Word also *"were moved by the Holy Spirit,"* being *"carried along"* by His power, and we can see how the wedge was beaten into his own experience with the necessary breaking and wounding. His journey was like Samson's who seemed to swing like a pendulum between *"Zorah and Eshtaol."* This is not where Peter lived, yet spiritually he did. Zorah is linked to the thought of being leprous, and Eshtaol means to entreat or to plead. Samson swung between these two extremes, so did Peter, and sometimes so do we. The God of all grace used both men, and we will see how He used Peter as we go farther into his letter.

Undoubtedly, we see much of ourselves in him, but the One who *"worked effectively"* in him wants to work effectively in us too. He *"began"* His good work in us at salvation and will *"complete it until the day of Jesus Christ."*[65] Peter's earthly walk with the Lord began with a look[66] and almost ended with a look[67]; it began with a threefold call[68] and ended with a threefold test[69]; it began with *"Behold the Lamb of God"* and closed with *"Feed My lambs."* There's no doubt that he discovered what it meant to have 'Grace restored in his mistakes,' and so can we!

"Jehovah is our strength, and He shall be our song;
We shall o'ercome at length, although our foes be strong:
In vain doth Satan then oppose, for God is stronger than His foes."
(Samuel Barnard)

1.3 GRACE RECEIVED IN THE GOSPEL

Christian living was intensely practical for Peter. It wasn't a theory. There was something about living with the Lord and for the Lord that made him enjoy what Paul called the *"deep things of God,"*[1] and he was just as careful to show that they belong *"to the doctrine which accords with godliness."*[2] As far as he was concerned, the teaching must have hands and feet on it, with each aspect being translated into spiritual energy. There was firmness in his conviction, and we get the flavour of this, not only of what he was communicating, but of how he himself enjoyed it. It's good when others get the sense that you're ministering in the enjoyment of what you're talking about, and not just some kind of exercise that leaves them wondering. His letter shows that practical construction depends on spiritual instruction, and that construction must be built on a sound foundation.

This is evident in all five chapters and, although he was addressing believers in these five provinces, God wants us to see that what he was saying also applies to us. They were Jews who had been driven out of their homeland and were now living as foreign residents with new difficulties among Gentiles. In their unsettled state, God gave Peter His own means of comfort by assuring them of how settled they were in Christ. For example, he saw them as:

Elect

His immediate aim was to underline that we are what we are because of the sovereignty of God, just as He was an apostle "of" Jesus Christ, and not only for Him. Their election was according to divine foreknowledge, and he made no attempt to launch into a protracted theological debate. On the contrary: he was way above that, and, as far as he was concerned, he expected them to accept the twofold certainties of their call.

i) It was without question that the call of God began in the heart of God, and in the counsels of Deity in the eternal past. It had then been revealed to them through the cross-work of the Lord Jesus Christ, and their conversion caused them to know that they were chosen in Him.

ii) It was put into effect in time through the work of the Holy Spirit. Paul shared this conviction and was able to say that, *"God from the beginning chose you for salvation through sanctification by the Spirit and belief in the truth, to which He called you by our gospel, for the obtaining of the glory of our Lord Jesus Christ. Therefore, brethren, stand fast."*[3]

It's good to see that these two features are presented as facts by both men through inspiration, and they make it clear that the call is to obedience. Neither these New Testament believers, nor we, were called to salvation alone. No, the work of the Holy Spirit in setting us apart is always with a view to service that is preceded by an initial change. Saving grace wanted only one thing from us, and that was the transfer of our sin to Christ when God laid on Him the iniquity of us all.[4] There on the middle cross God fulfilled a work to His own satisfaction that allows believers to live in the full satisfaction of being in Christ. Peter opens his letter by reminding them of where they are geographically and what they are spiritually, then he begins to tell them what they have.

Like them, God has called each of us to:

- A new birth
- A new Owner
- A new nature
- A new intention
- A new direction

Within these, and many other aspects of divine revelation, there *"are some things hard to understand."* For example, the Saviour's incarnation and resurrection, and our regeneration, yet we believe them by faith, even though we still borrow scriptural statements that emphasise our mental limitations.

- Job 42:3 – *"I have uttered what I did not understand, things too wonderful for me, which I did not know."*
- Ps.139:6 – *"Such knowledge is too wonderful for me; it is high, I cannot attain it."*
- Ps.147:5 – *"Great is our Lord, and mighty in power; His understanding is infinite."*
- Isa.55:8,9 – *"For as the heavens are higher than the earth, so are My ways higher than your ways, and My thoughts than your thoughts."*

To put it mildly, we are not able for it, so it's in the limited capacity of our tiny minds that we find room for the huge recognition that God's knowledge is way beyond ours. By Isaiah's measuring scale, the contrast is light years beyond us, so it's only by faith that we trust God and grasp what He has given to us in all we *"have learned and been assured of."*[5] So we thank Him for what we do understand, and trust Him for what we cannot understand. It would be arrogant to claim that our minds can grasp His infinite wisdom. Similarly, it would be arrogance to contest it. Like the smallness of earth in the grand scale of creation, and the temporal before the eternal, we bow at the majesty of God. If, at times, Moses and David could be told they were *lo' tuwkal* – you are not able – we should allow the Holy Spirit to remind us of this as we grapple with truths that are bigger than our minds.

The wonder is, that this sovereign, electing God makes Himself known at all, and Peter tells us how He does it. The very first sentence of his letter speaks of being *"elect"*[6]; and it ends by saying, *"Grace to you."* He is so impressed by grace that he closes his letter by calling God *"the God of all grace."*[7] On the same subject, and in the same way, Paul says that God *"chose us in Him"* and adds, *"by grace you have been saved through faith."*[8] This doesn't mean that faith contributes to what God has done. It simply shows that the full hand of God's grace reaches out to the sinner, and the responding empty hand of faith reaches out to receive it.

At the same time, the faith that welcomes His grace should also welcome the accompanying truth of being elect. The grace that chose us means we are fore-chosen; the grace that calls us to be *"before Him in love"* means we are fore-loved; the grace that wills it means we are fore-willed; and the grace that *"made us accepted in the Beloved"* means we are fore-accepted.[9]

Isn't it amazing, too, that the faith by which we believe is itself a gift of grace, since it *"comes by hearing, and hearing by the word of God"*?[10] This was expressed by a fifteen-year-old boy in Burma who began his testimony by saying, "God is not a God of partiality. He saved me, a poor Indian boy, not because I wanted to be saved but because He wanted to save me; and He found me, not because I was looking for Him but because He was looking for me."

Foreknowledge

In verse 2, Peter presents God's foreknowledge in relation to the redeemed. In verse 20, he presents the same truth in relation to the Redeemer, but a clear understanding of what it means in regard to Christ will help to prevent us from misunderstanding it in regard to the Christian. Some have claimed that it implies injustice, but how can the One who is both *"just and the justifier of the one who has faith in Jesus"* be unjust? Others reduce its truth to the thought of foresight, but for this to be true with the redeemed we would

29

have to deduce that God chose the Redeemer by looking down the corridor of time to see if He would fulfil His purpose, and in the hope that He would. Thankfully, Scripture helps us to see foreknowledge in the context of how it affected Him.

- Acts 2:23 – "*Him, being delivered up by the determined purpose and foreknowledge of God, you have taken by lawless hands, and put to death.*"
- Acts 4:27,28 – "*For truly against Your holy Servant Jesus, whom You anointed, both Herod and Pontius Pilate, with the Gentiles and the people of Israel, were gathered together to do whatever Your hand and Your purpose determined before to be done.*"
- Acts 13:29 – "*Now when they had fulfilled all that was written concerning Him, they took Him down from the tree and laid Him in a tomb.*"
- Rev.13:8 – "*... the Lamb slain from the foundation of the world.*"

These verses confirm this truth in relation to the Saviour who was "*manifest in these last times for you,*" and you will note how perfectly they were fulfilled. Jesus didn't go to Calvary because men took Him there, they took Him because He was going there! Likewise, they pierced His hands and feet because the Scripture said they would. They pierced His side (Jn 19:37), because Scripture said they would (Zech.12:10). But they didn't break His legs, because Scriptures said they wouldn't, and the sovereignty of God is supreme.

The following verses confirm the same great truth of the sovereignty of God in relation to those who are saved:

- Rom.8:29-30 – "*For whom He foreknew, He also predestined to be conformed to the image of His Son.*"
- Eph.1:4,5 – "*just as he chose us in Him before the foundation of the world ... having predestined us to adoption as sons by Jesus Christ to Himself.*"
- 2 Tim.1:9 – "*God, who has saved us and called us ... according to His own purpose and grace which was given to us in Christ Jesus before time began.*"

When we put all these together, we see that God is glorified in how His foreknowledge has been fulfilled in Christ, and He is being glorified again in how His foreknowledge is being fulfilled in each Christian.

Blood

It's not uncommon for believers to describe their security in Christ by saying they are "under the blood," and they say it sincerely. However, God places such a high value on the blood of the Lord Jesus Christ that He never refers to it simply as 'the blood.' Instead, He speaks of the blood of His own, of Christ, of his cross, of Jesus, of the everlasting covenant, of Jesus Christ His Son, of the Lamb; also of His blood, His own blood, and precious blood. Yes, it's a great blessing to be among the Lord's redeemed, and the present joy of our salvation is that we have been brought into a new relationship with the Lord Jesus Christ through His blood.

In the enjoyment of this, we respond to Peter's vision that God's plan for us is *"for obedience and sprinkling of the blood of Jesus Christ."* Once again, the relationship is through the application of His blood, but this time it isn't the *"shedding of blood"* that we read of in Hebrews 9:22, it's the *"sprinkling of the blood."* It's always God's desire, and Peter's too, that the application of the blood will lead to a sincere appreciation of the blood. This was the case in Moses' day, when shedding the blood of the Passover lamb allowed its application to the doorposts and lintels, but it didn't stop there. God didn't redeem them to leave them where they were. He led them out of their bondage into His freedom, and this made them free to serve Him in a covenant, at an altar, with a book, and a tabernacle. Exodus 24:6-8 paints the picture for us. Moses:

*"took half the blood and put it in basins, and half the blood he **sprinkled on the altar**; then he took the Book of the Covenant and read it in the hearing of the people. And they said, 'All that the LORD has said we will do, and be obedient.' And Moses took the blood, **sprinkled it on the people**, and said, 'This is the*

blood of the covenant which the LORD has made with you according to all these words.'"

Hebrews 9:19-21 adds that Moses, *"**sprinkled** both **the book** itself and all the people … Then likewise he **sprinkled** with blood **the tabernacle** and all **the vessels** of the ministry."* This helps us to see how God combined the altar of God, the people of God, and the Word of God. All this indicates that the people of God (His servants) were united with the altar of God (His service) on the basis of the Word of God (His Scriptures), thus pointing and appointing their direction. Leviticus 1:5 continues the theme by saying, *"He shall kill the bull [the burnt offering] before the LORD, and the priests, Aaron's sons, shall bring the blood and **sprinkle** the blood all around on the altar."*

Now we see that the sprinkling of the blood also determined the direction of Aaron's high priestly service. His presence at the altar must be preceded by the presence of the blood. We will notice that the sequence of Peter's teaching is consistent with this Old Testament picture for he links the sprinkling of blood in v.2 with the blood for redemption in verses 18 and 19 while dealing with our salvation in chapter 1 before developing its subsequent holy and royal priestly service in chapter 2.

The Old Testament theme climaxes in Leviticus 16, which describes Aaron's entrance to the Most Holy place on the Day of Atonement. This meant going through the veil to approach the mercy seat, but in order to do this he must have another veil between him and it, so there had to be a cloud of incense and the sprinkled blood. God's instructions were plain:

*"And he shall put the incense on the fire before the LORD, that the cloud of incense may cover the mercy seat that is on the Testimony, lest he die. He shall take some of the blood of the bull and **sprinkle** it with his finger on the mercy seat on the east side; and before the mercy seat he shall **sprinkle** some of the blood with his finger seven times."*

By sprinkling it before and upon the mercy seat, Aaron intimated the direction he wanted to go. Whether standing outside at the altar or inside at the mercy seat, there must be sprinkled blood at his feet as a God-given platform for his service. In His own unique fulfilment of this, the Lord Jesus Christ answered the sevenfold perfection that was foreshadowed in Aaron's standing when *"with* [Gr. *dia*: through – not with] *His own blood He entered the Most Holy Place once for all, having obtained eternal redemption."*[11]

In these delightful ways, we see that the blood, while essentially the same, is effectively different. Shedding was for cleansing the soul in salvation and deliverance; sprinkling was for the direction of the service and obedience.

Salvation

As we look back on what God had in mind for those He redeemed through the Passover lamb, it's good to know that it's like this for us, too. Christ, our Passover, has been sacrificed for us,[12] and God hasn't redeemed us to leave us unmoved from our old place in sin, in the flesh, and in the world. He wants to lead us forward into the freedom of His New Covenant, into the blessings of the cross, His Word, and His service. Peter's approach to the great truth of salvation in the opening chapter is very interesting. In verses 3-12, he speaks of its object – our security in Christ - prospectively. In verses 18-25, he speaks of its origin – our security in Christ - retrospectively.

Each of us can look back to the moment of salvation when we claimed the promise, *"Believe on the Lord Jesus Christ, and you will be saved."*[13] In undeserved grace, our sins were forgiven and we were saved from the penalty of sin. We then began our Christian walk, and the Word of God challenged us to *"work out your own salvation with fear and trembling."*[14] It's evident that Paul isn't referring to the time when we accepted Christ as Lord and Saviour, but to the here and now of our daily witness. He's urging us to reflect what has already happened: we belong to Christ and should have the desire to shine as we show this in the world.

When he talks of becoming *"blameless and harmless,"* he doesn't mean we will be sinless, but that we won't live in such a way that we put up with defects or be content with some sort of admixture. Two things will keep others from pointing the finger: one is that we let God work, so that we do His will and pleasure; the other is that we let the Holy Spirit work, so that He keeps us from doing our own will and pleasure. In other words, this second aspect of our salvation means we need to be saved from the power and pleasure of sin. It's a daily battle, and we don't need to lose it!

Peter then tells us that we are being kept *"for salvation,"*[15] and this has to do with the third aspect, that will take place at the coming of the Lord. Then, and only then, will our bodies be delivered from the presence of sin, yet Peter says, it's *"ready to be revealed."* It's to this that Paul refers in Romans 8:23 when speaking about *"the redemption of our body,"* and again in Romans 13:11 when assuring us that *"now our salvation is nearer to us than when we first believed."* If the Lord had come earlier, it was ready. If He were to come today, it's ready. Should His coming not be for a further unknown period, it's ready. The question is, are we? Being at home with the Lord is our promised objective, and anticipating it should spur our Christian character and conduct.

As he points forward to our eternal inheritance, which is the undisputed birthright of every believer, he describes it as "incorruptible", and it's interesting how he uses this word for what God will give us, has given us, and is giving us:

- Incorruptible inheritance (1 Pet.1:4) – **Future**
- Incorruptible seed (1 Pet.1:23) – **Past**
- Incorruptible apparel (1 Pet.3:4) – **Present**

Our inheritance means so much to God that He assures us of it in various ways. It's guaranteed,[16] it has glory,[17] it's eternal[18] and Peter says it's incorruptible and undefiled.[19] Each of these has been deliberately designed to make us thankful for the shedding of the Saviour's blood, and cause us to live in the appreciation of His sprinkled blood. With this in mind, our attention is drawn to the thought that we *"are kept by the power of God through faith for salvation ready to be revealed in the last time."*[20]

The word *"kept"* means guarded in such a way that no external force can take us out of the security we have in Christ. It also means that no internal desire can cause us to leave that security. We are garrisoned, therefore nothing can break in, and no one can break out! This is the ultimate goal and expectation of our salvation. It's the end of the journey when, at last, we will no longer live by faith.

Receiving … the end of your faith (1 Pet.1:9)

This is the ultimate goal and expectation of our salvation. It's the end of the journey when, at last, we will no longer live by faith. It's one of the great changes that will take place *"in the twinkling of an eye."*[21] In that moment, we will be *"caught up … to meet the Lord in the air"*[22] we will have new bodies[23] and *"we shall be like Him, for we will see Him as He is."*[24] What a difference! In the reality of His present keeping, and in the sure hope of that future meeting, Peter says, *"you greatly rejoice."*[25] Is that true? It was for those that received his letter, for he went on to say what it would be like for them when their unseeing days were over. He says that, even in the very thought of it, *"you rejoice with joy inexpressible and full of glory."* Do we? Yes, for the up-look is bright, even if the outlook isn't!

It seems strange, at first, that verse 6 should speak about rejoicing and grieving, but they are not incompatible emotions. Was it not so for the Saviour? Did He not grieve in Gethsemane while anticipating the cross and the joy that was set before Him?[26] We rejoice in what lies before us, even though we may grieve over what is beside us. It may be that domestic or secular cares, or some aspect of our spiritual walk, are among the inescapable things that grieve. Nevertheless, God longs to ensure that their presence is for the testing of faith, and not for destroying it.

Grace

Peter loves the word "grace." We will trace it as we go through his letter, and we will see how he applies it in different contexts. As far as chapter 1 is concerned, the riches of God's grace are presented in two ways: sacrificially and eternally.

SACRIFICIAL

He knew that far-seeing prophets had *"prophesied of the grace that would come to you"*[27] and looking back it's evident that there are foreshadowings in the Old Testament of *"the sufferings of Christ and of the glories that would follow."*[28] Thus angels anticipated the demonstration of God's grace in the death of His Son. Not only so, they knew that He would not be bound by death, and prophesied of His resurrection glory. Shortsightedness is not an attribute of the Spirit of God, nor did it belong to men who were led by Him to write as they did. Examples are not in short supply.

- The cross - His sufferings (Ps.22)
- The crown - His glories (Ps.24)
- The cross - His sufferings (Isa.53:5)
- The crown - His glories (Isa.52:13; 53:11)

One of the loveliest figures of this can be found in Numbers 4:13 where we read, *"Also they shall take away the ashes from the altar, and spread a purple cloth over it."* In the very same way as David and Isaiah spoke of the coming One, so also did Moses for the ashes point to the sacrifice completed – the sufferings of Christ; and the purple cloth of His resulting splendour – the glories that would follow.

As we know, Paul wrote to Titus and said, *"For the grace that brings salvation has appeared to all men"*[29] and then he acknowledged the same sacrificial grace by adding, *"looking for the blessed hope and glorious appearing of our great God and Saviour Jesus Christ."* In saying this, he projects our thoughts forward to consider the expression of grace that is:

ETERNAL

Peter's comment on this is *"rest your hope fully upon the grace that is to be brought to you at the revelation of Jesus Christ."*[30] The word *"fully"* (Gr. *teleiōs*: perfectly) means "to the end." At the beginning, we were given *"good hope by grace"*[31] and we face the end resting in the hope of more grace. In verse 10, he spoke of *"the grace"* that was brought to us through the appearing of Christ for the suffering of death. It was in the body that God *"prepared"* for Him that He brought grace *down* to us, and now we look for *"the grace"* that will be brought to us when, in new bodies, we go *up* to meet Him. *"He will appear a second time, apart from sin, for salvation."*[32]

This is what we know as 'The Rapture' when the church will be *"caught up"*[33] at His coming. It is by faith that we *"eagerly wait for Him."* Until then, He continues to give what John describes as *"grace for grace"*[34] – ever-flowing and overflowing, like a river over its bed or waves over a beach. Yesterday's flow is replaced by today's, and today's by tomorrow's, just as today's grace replaces yesterday's in the sure hope of tomorrow's and brings renewed refreshment to the soul. James simply calls it *"more grace"*[35] and Annie Johnson Flint captures this well in her hymn:

He giveth more grace when the burdens grow greater,
He sendeth more strength when the labors increase;
To added afflictions He addeth His mercy,
To multiplied trials, His multiplied peace.

When we have exhausted our store of endurance,
When our strength has failed ere the day is half done,
When we reach the end of our hoarded resources
Our Father's full giving is only begun.

Fear not that thy need shall exceed His provision,
Our God ever yearns His resources to share;
Lean hard on the arm everlasting, availing;
The Father both thee and thy load will upbear.

His love has no limits, His grace has no measure,
His power no boundary known unto men;
For out of His infinite riches in Jesus
He giveth, and giveth, and giveth again.

As we trace the riches of God's grace in each chapter, we should never forget that all God's dealings with us began with *"mercy."*[36] The Greek word *eleos* comes from *eleeō*, meaning pity and compassion, and it was in this way that He viewed our miserable sinful condition before granting us the undeserved favour of His grace through which He saved us. It has been said that the difference between mercy and grace is that mercy keeps us from getting what we do deserve, and grace gives us what we don't deserve.

Therefore (1 Pet.1:13)

This is the *"Therefore"* of suitable spiritual activity in response to God's grace. It also is the *"Therefore"* of the unsuitability of carnal activity. It's the *"Therefore"* of commitment to the real terms of godly living, to the personal acceptance of the terms of the New Covenant. Like Aaron, we have communion with the altar in our Saviour's death on the cross; and we have communion with the ark in His resurrection and ascension to the throne.

1.4 GRACE REGARDED IN WORSHIP AND WITNESS

"But the word of the Lord endures forever. Now this is the word which by the gospel was preached to you. Therefore, laying aside all malice, all deceit, hypocrisy, envy, and all evil speaking, as newborn babes, desire the pure milk of the word, that you may grow thereby, if indeed you have tasted that the Lord is gracious. Coming to Him as to a living stone, rejected indeed by men, but chosen by God and precious, you also, as living stones, are being built up a spiritual house, a holy priesthood, to offer up spiritual sacrifices acceptable to God through Jesus Christ.

Therefore it is also contained in the Scripture, 'Behold, I lay in Zion a chief cornerstone, elect, precious, and he who believes on Him will by no means be put to shame.' Therefore, to you who believe, He is precious; but to those who are disobedient, 'The stone which the builders rejected has become the chief cornerstone', and 'A stone of stumbling and a rock of offense.' They stumble, being disobedient to the word, to which they also were appointed.

But you are a chosen generation, a royal priesthood, a holy nation, His own special people, that you may proclaim the praises of Him who called you out of darkness into His marvellous light; who once were not a people but are now the people of God, who had not obtained mercy but now have obtained mercy" (1 Pet.2:25-2:10).

* * *

Up until now, we have been looking at chapter 1, and it's good for us to see how the content of chapter 2 flows out of it. For the most part, we are indebted to those who divided the Scripture into chapters and verses,[1] but sometimes we miss the flow by not connecting what we are reading to what has gone before. When we read chapter 2, it's important not to miss its connection with chapter 1. In fact, it's the breakdown that actually helps us to notice something very special for each chapter begins by applying something on earth, and ends by lifting our minds to heaven. We can trace this as follows:

Earthward

- 1:1 *"To the pilgrims of the Dispersion"*
- 2:1 *"Laying aside all malice"*
- 3:1 *"Wives"*
- 4:1 *"Christ suffered for us"*
- 5:1 *"The elders"*

Heavenward

- 1:25 *"The word of the Lord endures forever"*
- 2:25 *"The Shepherd and Overseer of your souls"*
- 3:22 *"Jesus Christ, who has gone into heaven"*
- 4:19 *"Commit your souls ... as to a faithful Creator"*
- 5:11 *"To Him be the glory"*

If only our lives were lived in this wonderful combination of something heavenly being seen in each aspect of our earthly walk!

The Word of the LORD

As Peter moves on from his introduction, we can follow a progression that reflects what happened under Moses the mediator of the Old Covenant. One parallel is seen in chapter 1:19 in the fulfilment of the Passover lamb of Exodus 12, and in chapter 2's fulfilment of the anticipation of priestly service in Exodus 24. We also can see the death of Lord Jesus Christ being the answer to the tabernacle's altar, just as the Word answers to what was foreshadowed in the laver. The altar was the first thing that offerers met when they came in through the gateway. There was heat and light, and beyond that there was the laver constantly reflecting the flame of the altar that was mirrored outside in its copper and in the water inside. It was just as if it was on fire too.

Being side by side, they remind us of the close relationship there is between the incarnate Word and the inspired Word. And isn't it wonderful how God again exalted His Word when *"Moses commanded the Levites that bore the ark of the covenant of the LORD, saying: Take this Book of the Law, and put it beside the ark of the covenant of the LORD your God."*[2] These dear men shouldered the ark and the Law, and they teach us that those who would bear a testimony to the Lord Jesus Christ must also be carriers of His Word.

Peter has been absorbed by God's grace in chapter 1, which was brought to us firstly through the death of the Lord Jesus Christ, and will be brought again when He is revealed at His coming.[3] Having drawn out our appreciation of sacrificial and eternal grace, Peter then draws out our appreciation of the Word through which we were born again,[4] and he gives it a lofty place. As the Word of God, it bears the hallmark of His Deity; as the Word of the LORD, it declares His authority; and by living and abiding forever, it presents His eternity.

In these three characteristics it amply represents the God who gave it. This isn't surprising for, in one sense, the Word of God is more connected to heaven than it is to earth. It's for earth, but was breathed out from heaven, so we can understand why Peter wants us to know that everything we are and have is Word-based. It deserves our deepest appreciation and lifelong appropriation. God has magnified His Word above all His name,[5] it is forever settled in heaven,[6] and ought to be magnified and settled in our lives too.

Quite rightly, we make a lot of chapter two, but we would automatically make more of it if we made more of chapter one. Perhaps, we miss out by not sufficiently recognising that what we are doing for the Lord Jesus in chapter 2 is the direct result of all that we have in Him in chapter 1. It tells us about the promise of the presence of the Lord with us on earth, and includes the additional promise of our presence with Him in heaven. In a very remarkable way, what we see at the beginning and end of each chapter aptly describes what Peter does in the themes and doctrines throughout his letter. They unite heaven and earth, and that's not accidental. He wants to us see that appreciation of salvation in chapter 1 leads on to the appreciation of service in chapter 2.

Paul does the same in Ephesians and, once again, we may give more emphasis to the end of chapter 2 where we read about *"a dwelling place of God in the Spirit."* Paul uses the Greek word *katoikētērion*, which can be translated as a down-dwelling or a down-residence, and its beauty is that this down-habitation should resemble and reflect *"the church, which is His body, the fulness of Him who fills all in all."*[7] It's a high standard, but the church is the heavenly template for churches on earth.

Desire the Pure Milk of the Word

As Christians, we should have a yearning, a real soul longing, for the Word. Just as it's natural for newborn infants instinctively to crave feeding, the newborn child of God should instinctively desire being fed from the Scriptures. Peter's first reason for saying this is that our growth depends on it; so we really need to ask ourselves if we are growing. God has given the means, yet some believers suffer from a kind of spiritual malnutrition because they never develop a hunger for His Word.

Feeding is a lifestyle, and being spiritually healthy demands regularly taking time to read our Bibles. Just as it is naturally, feeding is a necessity, and we should be crying out, *"Feed me with the food that is needful for me."*[8] The real force of what Peter's advice is, is to keep on desiring the Word. It won't happen by being haphazard. If we take good care of it, the Spirit of God will take care of our growth; and, if we allow Him to take care of our growth, we will discover that reading feeds our worship.

It's all part of the kind of progress that Paul wanted to see in young Timothy, and to help him on his way Paul gave him the recipe. His first ingredient was, *"Give attention to reading."*[9] This is normally taken as public reading, but Timothy's public reading must have been the result of what he enjoyed in his private reading. There's a massive lesson in this: none of us will ever be more publicly than we are privately. This is so vital, we should say it again: none of us will ever be more publicly than we are privately. Don't ever for a minute tell yourself that you can get away with bluffing your audience. God is sovereign, and His Spirit's power accompanies those who pay attention to being real in private.

Time spent reading is at its most profitable when we *"meditate on these things."* This was Paul's fifth ingredient, after emphasising that reading enables exhortation, the understanding of doctrine, and the development of gift. Meditation has different connotations, of course. Gurus of many complexions say it means emptying your mind, but this is entirely the opposite of what God means by it. To Him, it means filling the mind. One of the words He uses in the Old Testament – in Hebrew, *siyach* – means to muse or ponder, and actually describes a shrub in Genesis 21:15. The idea is of the initial stem branching out as it grows, and this is a lovely way of seeing how an initial thought leads off into many branches of wider consideration. It can be a long process, but not arduous.

The enjoyment is captured in the other word God uses – *hagah* – which describes a lion roaring over its prey.[10] When we enjoy it like this, we will be able to tell God, *"I rejoice at Your word as one who finds great treasure"*[11] and He wants to be the first to hear of it from you.

Worship

As far as Peter is concerned, our appreciation and application of grace will bring us into what he goes on to outline regarding worship and witness, and immediately he connects our service on earth with our access to heaven. Worshippers are described as *"living stones,"* born-again believers who have already come once as individuals to Christ for salvation, and in this character we are *"being built up a spiritual house, a holy priesthood, to offer up spiritual sacrifices acceptable to God through Jesus Christ."* Once again, we are *"coming to Him,"* but this time we are coming collectively and, since the word *proserchomenoi* is plural and in the present tense, it means we are constantly coming to Him in worship.

Joy of all joys, we are coming to Him in Zion, that is into heaven. When the sons of Korah thought about coming before God, they spoke of hearts being set on the pilgrimage, and of each one appearing before God in Zion.[12] Jeremiah pointed to a future day when, in the presence of Christ their Messiah, *"They shall come and sing in the height of Zion, streaming to the goodness of the LORD."*[13] The word *"streaming"* means to flow or to sparkle, like a river shining in the sun to such a degree that the sight of the water is lost and replaced by a reflection of sheer glory. It means to be so cheerful that you glow. The thought of a flowing, glowing river is exactly what God wants to see as we gather for worship.

If the people of Israel could have such pleasure in coming to Zion on earth, how much more should we as we flow to Zion above? When we flow into His presence, heaven sees the reflection of the One with whom we have lived for the previous seven days. Radiating from our hearts is the gleam of exaltation from those who are boasting in their risen Saviour. Defying the gravity of earthly things, we flow upward as worshippers with our praises merging, and heaven rejoicing in the bright reflection of the Son. Wouldn't that be marvellous? Thrill of all thrills!

But how do we go about it? It means that we have to be prepared beforehand. David tells us how to come: *"Give to the Lord the glory due to His name; bring an offering, and come before Him. Oh, worship the LORD in the beauty of holiness."*[14] His order was *"Give ... bring ... come"*; but we reverse the order as we prepare to worship, and we come, bring, and give. This is how we should be ready to enter God's presence, but we will catch the sense of giving Him glory only if we have come and are truly ready to glory in Christ Jesus.

The writer to the Hebrews puts it this way: *"having boldness to enter the Holiest by the blood of Jesus ... let us draw near"* and *"by Him let us continually offer the sacrifice of praise to God."*[15] This is called *"the fruit of our lips,"* but why does God use such an analogy? It means He is looking for the ultimate purpose of the tree. All its energy and growth has been poured into producing fruit, and this represents the fruitfulness that should be evident in our thoughts and words as we worship Him. We don't bring twigs, and we don't bring leaves. God is waiting for the fruit of our meditation, and we should approach Him saying, *"Let the words of my mouth and the meditation of my heart be acceptable in Your sight, O LORD, my strength and my Redeemer."*[16]

A fellow-believer came to me one Lord's Day and asked, "Tell me what was different between what you were doing this morning and what I was doing this morning?" I said, "My brother, the last thing I'm here to do is to demean what you did this morning. It's not my business to downplay what you did this morning, but let me ask you one thing. Where did you go?" He said, I went to the Hall." "And what did you do when you went to the Hall?" "Well, we worshipped." He then asked me, "So what did you do?" I replied, "I went to heaven." In surprise, he said, "Come on! What do you mean?" I said, "Let's have a look at Hebrews 9 verse 12 – *"that the*

45

Lord Jesus through his own blood entered into the Most Holy Place once for all, having obtained eternal redemption." I said, "Brother, where would that be?" "Oh", he says, "that's heaven." "Well, let's look over the page at chapter 10 verse 19 – "*Therefore, brethren, having boldness to enter into the Holiest by the blood of Jesus.*" I stopped reading and asked him, "Where would that be?"Right away, he said, "Well, I never saw that before."

Peter is showing us the very same thing and, in doing so, takes us back to the cause of it all: we have tasted that the Lord is gracious. Now, we could assume that this is another precious aspect of God's grace in Peter's letter, but it's not. Instead of the word *charis* he has used the word *chrēstos*, which refers to the Lord's goodness, just as Paul did in Romans 2:4 when he asked, "*Do you despise the riches of His goodness ... not knowing that the goodness of God leads you to repentance?*" In the selfsame kindness that led us as sinners to repentance, God leads us into His presence as worshippers, to worship by the Spirit of God and glory in Christ Jesus.[17]

Later, in chapter 4:10, Peter uses the phrase *charitos Theou* to speak about the grace of God, but here he actually says "*chrēstos ho kurios,*" which means "the Lord is gracious" or "the Lord is good." He doesn't want us to miss the connection that verse 3 provides, as it reaches back into chapter 1 and forward to our worship in chapter 2. Our union with the "good Lord" is the basis of our communion, and fellowship is the basis of our worship.

What is Worship?

- It's presenting the worth of Christ to God. The Old English spelling was *worthship*, and this means we are engaged in thinking about what God thinks about Him. True *worthship* is thinking lofty thoughts of Christ.

- It's the whole being, all that we are, rejoicing in the worth of the Lord Jesus Christ. It's every part of us – body, soul and spirit – united in enthusiastic praise of the Saviour.

- It's a holy excitement in the presence of God, when our spirits are raised and we cannot rest until the mouth expresses what the heart feels. So it's definitely not flattery.[18]

- It's an attitude of homage and adoration. The word includes the thought of crouching down in His presence like a dog licking the hand of its master.

- It's having the tongue of a ready writer with thoughts flowing from the heart. But they will never flow out if they never flowed in, and they will never flow in unless we have daily communion with the Lord. How vital it is that we learn to ask, "Where do You want us to prepare?"

If only we could gather in that kind of spirit, we would not only move one another, we would move Him! Do you ever wonder if heaven has been moved by our worship? When we read Revelation chapter 5 there's a pulsating sense of worship in the presence of God as the four living creatures, the elders and the angelic host are affected in their posture by the song that has been sung. All heaven is thrilled: touched by worshippers from earth.

Do we ever wonder what they feel when it comes to the time of our drawing near and they watch the Man in the midst receiving what we place in His hands? Since they can be so moved, can they sense our mediocrity too? Do they ever say to one another, "Is that the best they can do? He never went to the cross for me, yet that's all they gave! He never died for me, yet I give more than that!" What a sad possibility that heaven isn't moved by present worship from the redeemed of earth!

What is Worship Not?

In chapter 22 of the first book of our Bible, when Abraham took Isaac to Moriah, he told his servants, *"The lad and I will go yonder and worship."* In chapter 22 of the last Book, the angel told John, *"Worship God."* The Scriptures have much to teach us about worship, and one of the things we learn is that the word "worship" is sometimes a verb, sometimes a noun, but never an adjective. This has been turned around in much of what is called worship in the present day. It's not unusual to hear of, 'Worship Leaders ... Worship Leader Training Manual ... Worship Leader Online Academy ... and Worship Team Building,' with each of them using worship as an adjective. We are not condemning the appropriate God-honouring use of music, but perhaps we should bow to the definition given by its Designer.

Witness

Alongside our access to God as a worshipping holy priesthood, we also have access to people as a witnessing royal priesthood. What a privilege it is, that we are called to live in the character of the holiness and majesty of God! It's not that we cease to be a holy priesthood when our times of collective worship are over, or that we are no longer a royal priesthood when we are not sharing the gospel. The truth is, we are worshipping as we witness and witnessing while we worship. Paul makes this clear in two ways.

Firstly, our lives are spent in spiritual worship when we present our bodies as a living sacrifice.[19] He also tells us that, *"We are to God the fragrance of Christ among those who are being saved and among those who are perishing."*[20] The illustration behind Paul's words is very meaningful. It depicts a returning army, probably with its generals at the head. In front of them were the incense swingers leading a parade of victorious soldiers, behind whom were enemy prisoners that had been taken captive. As the incense wafted its savour, it had two different effects. To the victors, it was of *"life to life"*; to the losers, it was of *"death to death."*

Whenever we read of fragrance in the Scriptures, it often has to do with the aroma that ascends to God from sacrifice, and we can see this again in 2 Corinthians 2:15–17. When Paul says *"we are a fragrance to God of Christ,"* that's worship. When he says, *"we speak in the sight of God"*, that's witness, and it's significant that the worship part is "to God" and the witness part is "from God." Together, they show that worship and witness go hand in hand.

Secondly, as we remember Him and worship together, we *"proclaim the Lord's death till He comes."*[21] It's a testimony to others, and a very meaningful witness as we worship. Although it's a proclamation to fellow-worshippers, it also is to any who hear and see what is being said and done. This widens into a proclamation of Christ's excellencies and virtues, as we share the glories of Him who calls His own *"out of darkness into His marvellous light."*

Let our prayer be that God will see Christ in what we say, and then when we go outside that others might see Christ in what we say. This is the ministry of worship that's upwards and Godward and heavenward, and it's also the ministry of witness that's outward and manward and earthward. May it be so, for His Name's sake.

1.5 GRACE REINFORCED IN TRIALS

"Beloved, I beg you as sojourners and pilgrims, abstain from fleshly lusts which war against the soul, having your conduct honourable among the Gentiles, that when they speak against you as evildoers, they may, by your good works which they observe, glorify God in the day of visitation. Therefore submit yourselves to every ordinance of man for the Lord's sake, whether to the king as supreme, or to governors, as to those who are sent by him for the punishment of evildoers and for the praise of those who do good. For this is the will of God, that by doing good you may put to silence the ignorance of foolish men— as free, yet not using liberty as a cloak for vice, but as bondservants of God.

Honour all people. Love the brotherhood. Fear God. Honour the king. Servants, be submissive to your masters with all fear, not only to the good and gentle, but also to the harsh. For this is commendable, if because of conscience toward God one endures grief, suffering wrongfully. For what credit is it if, when you are beaten for your faults, you take it patiently? But when you do good and suffer, if you take it patiently, this is commendable before God.

For to this you were called, because Christ also suffered for us, leaving us an example, that you should follow His steps: "Who committed no sin, nor was deceit found in His mouth"; who, when He was reviled, did not revile in return; when He suffered, He did not threaten, but committed Himself to Him who judges righteously; who Himself bore our sins in His own body on the tree, that we, having died to sins, might live for righteousness—by whose stripes you were healed. For you were like sheep going astray, but have now returned to the

50

Shepherd and Overseer of your souls" (1 Pet.2:11-25).

* * *

It's never a random work when God scatters. Men may scatter destructively to achieve their purpose, but God does it constructively to achieve His. There's evidence of both kinds of scattering during the days of the Acts. When Gamaliel spoke about the death of Theudas in Acts 5:36, he states that his followers were scattered and came to nothing. They came to nothing, and their scattering – *dieluthēsan* – means the whole movement dissolved. Another revolt, led by Judas of Galilee, also came to a fruitless end when he was killed and they were scattered – *dieskorpisthēsan* – like sheep scattered in disarray by a wolf. It's no accident that this is the word applied to the disciples when the Lord said, *"you will be scattered, each to his own, and will leave Me alone."*[1] On that occasion, their scattering was of the flesh and not a work of God.

In Acts 8:1, it was very different, for this scattering was His means of spreading His children into regions away from Jerusalem, and He consistently refers to this scattering as *diaspeiro.* It was as if he blew them like seed that was being sown farther afield, and this is exactly the kind of scattering that James and Peter speak about at the beginning of their letters.[2] In all these, God was working to fulfil the Lord's promise in Acts 1:8, *"you shall be My witnesses in Jerusalem, and in all Judea and Samaria, and to the ends of the earth."*

During the time when work of rebuilding the temple ceased in the days of Ezra, a promise was given through Zechariah the prophet. There had been singing and shouting when the foundation stones were laid, but he encouraged the people by assuring them that the headstone would finish the work, and that it would be brought out with shouts of *"Grace, grace to it!"*[3] Perfect grace, multiplied grace, shown in days of law. What triumph! Haggai and Zechariah were great men of God, and they encouraged the people.

Haggai did it by urging the people to work. Zechariah never mentioned the word "work." His ministry was different; he did it by pointing the people to the Man.

In chapter 1:10 and 11, He is the Man who stood among the myrtle trees, as the Angel of the LORD, and this is known as a Theophany or a Christophany, a pre-incarnate appearing of the Lord Jesus Christ.[4] In Zechariah 6:12, God urged His people to look at Him as *"the Man whose name is the BRANCH!"* In chapter 13:7, He points them to the cross through the words of God the Father speaking about God the Son, *"Awake, O sword, against My Shepherd, against the Man who is My Companion ... Strike the Shepherd and the sheep will be scattered."* Ever since Calvary, the Jew has been scattered, but a day of gathering will come and, in preparing them for millennial glory in the presence of their Messiah, they will look unto Him whom they have pierced.[5] Their days of scattering will be over.

To Peter, his readers were scattered pilgrims, and he said this literally of them because they were foreign residents in a place that wasn't home. But, even then, he was assuring them that God in His grace had uprooted and scattered them into areas where the gospel would take root and develop. This is the point he develops in chapter 2:11, but this time he calls them sojourners and pilgrims and applies it spiritually. As Christians, they are foreigners in a world that is alien to them, and they to it. As strangers, geographically, in some ways they would have to adapt, but now he is telling them that they are strangers, spiritually, and that they had not to adapt.

To encourage them, he pointed, not to something on earth in Jerusalem, but to Someone in heaven. He lifted their eyes of faith to see the risen Lord Jesus Christ, the *"living stone,"* that they might see Him as the One whom God has laid *"in Zion as the chief cornerstone."* And they could cry, *"Grace, grace"* to Him with the assurance that grace would cause them to triumph in their trials.

It's worth noting that chapter 1 begins and ends with birth, and chapter 2 begins with growth. We could say that chapter 1 is about the deliverance of the sinner, and chapter 2 is about the direction of the believer. Chapter 1 is about coming to Christ for salvation, forgiveness, and conversion; chapter 2 is about coming to Him in service, fellowship, and commitment. There are other considerations too: in chapter 1, we have the sacrifice, sufferings and submission of Christ; in chapter 2, we read of the sacrifices, the sufferings and submission of the believer. All of these need grace. In chapter 2, we discover our need of grace as worshippers and as witnesses and we need to produce the evidence of it in our walk. We need it in spiritual service toward God in the Holy Place, and we need it as servants of men in the workplace.

However, the real lesson for us to learn is that if God supplies grace sacrificially and eternally, then we should let Him apply it experientially and daily. We could even make a case for using the word 'experimentally' for it conveys the thought of something tested, as in a science lab, that proves the theory and leads us to end up with the intended conclusion. Either way, God wants us to experience His grace and He does it by proving, not only the availability, but the applicability to help us in every aspect of growth.

It would be a very strange person who was satisfied with a child that never grew. Would we not feel the same with a child of God? Do we not think there's something seriously wrong when we see a child of God who doesn't grow? God has done everything to make our growth a reality, yet sometimes we don't allow Him to make it a possibility. Let's think of three ways in which His grace enables our spiritual growth.

Through Discipleship

When we come to think of how God helps us to grow in grace, we discover that He often uses the avenue of discipleship. The Lord's parting words at the end of Matthew 28 reinforce this: *"Go therefore and make disciples of all the nations, baptizing them in* [into, RV] *the name of the Father and of the Son and of the Holy Spirit, teaching them to observe all things that I have commanded you."* By saying this, He left us in no doubt that disciples teaching disciples is an effective means of growth. But what makes a good teacher? The Lord Jesus Christ obviously meant that disciples should understand what He had commanded and be able to pass this on to others. So there's a need for teaching disciples to understand His Word, and a complementary need for learning disciples not to expect Word-less growth.

Through Fellowship

The early churches were well schooled. Paul says, *"I kept nothing back that was helpful, but proclaimed it to you, and taught you publicly and from house to house."*[6] When two of his friends, Aquila and Priscilla, heard Apollos teach, they took him privately and *"explained to him the way of God more accurately."*[7] This is a valuable service that disciples can do for each other, and it takes grace to help someone who already speaks accurately to speak more accurately. There is never a shortage of public and private opportunity, and it's in the provision of God's grace that our times of fellowship together as churches are intended to fulfil a teaching ministry.

This is the real impact of Acts 2:42 where those who were saved, baptised and added to the church in Jerusalem continued steadfastly in the apostles' teaching and fellowship, in the breaking of bread, and in the prayers. These four are inseparably blended for our good and for our growth, and it's helpful to see that God intends that we adhere to them all. It also means we have fellowship with all: we have fellowship in teaching, fellowship when we meet to break bread, and also when the assembly gathers for prayer. All of them combine as a unified means of teaching and of learning.

Another aspect of fellowship is presented in Galatians 6:6 – *"Let him who is taught the word share in all good things with him who teaches."* This takes us into the wider expressions of grace that accompany actual teaching, and helps us to recognise that there's more to teaching than explaining something. Sharing in all good things really means having fellowship through teaching by example; by acts of kindness, thoughtfulness, and generosity. These are the additional evidences of grace, which prove that teaching doesn't stand alone.

Through Headship

The headship of Christ is of great value to God, and is to us too. It also is humbling for us and honouring for Him, since His headship presents His preeminence in five ways:

- In His relationship to God (1 Cor.11:3);
- In His relationship to all principality and power (Col.2:10);
- In His relationship to the church, which is His body (Eph.5:23);
- In His relationship over all things to the church (Eph.1:22);
- In His relationship to the spiritual house in service (1 Pet.2:7).

In the Old Testament, the word for "head" is *ro'sh* and can be linked to the conspicuous head of a poppy, and there's no doubt that His place within the Trinity is demonstrated in His supremacy over all creation and created beings, His church and over the house. His headship ought to be conspicuous as it's presently being made known:

- Through every saved man and woman's submission, witnessed on earth and by angels[8];
- Through the manifold wisdom of God being made known to the principalities and powers by the church[9];
- As each local assembly fulfils its resemblance to the church, which is His body, and through living stones serving together in union and communion with the Head of the corner.[10]

Some versions translate verse 7 as *"chief cornerstone,"* but *kefalēn gōnias* is more accurately translated as "head of the corner," and we should be humbled to think that God has willed the supremacy and authority of Christ to be shown through us.

One way of showing this is in our spiritual growth for we are called to *"grow up in all things into Him who is the Head – Christ."*[11] What a glorious invitation! Brothers and sisters, we have the opportunity of growing up into Him, but this happens only as we draw nourishment down from Him. How blessed we are, that we can be fed by Him, *"from whom all the body, nourished and knit together by joints and ligaments, grows with the increase from God."*[12] We are in touch with the Head, and we reflect this eternal union as we enjoy Him as the head of the corner. As individuals, and as churches, we can thrive in Him and for Him.

Our Example

As we think about assemblies resembling His church, Peter grips our attention as he implies that we can grow in our likeness to Christ by seeing Him as our "example." Resemblance has two sides to it, of course: we can grow in the likeness of Him by absorbing character that we see in Him, but this goes hand in hand with abandoning features we have that are not in Him. He loves righteousness and hates iniquity,[13] and we need to be like that too. Some of the old Puritans used to say, "We have learned to equivocate ... Our convictions sit easily about us like an old lady's loose gown. Righteousness has lost its wholesome sternness. The other side of love is hate, but we do not love truth so ardently that we hate a lie. We are too casual. We need His sense of right and wrong, of black and white."

As our perfect example, the Lord Jesus never had anything to hide. One thing is certain: as worshippers, nothing is hidden from God. However, as witnesses, we can hide things from others. Having spoken about worship and witness, Peter suddenly changed course to speak about *"fleshly lusts which war against the soul."* Oh, this is where it can be hard to grow in grace, isn't it? So how do we let it grow? It's partly by deciding not to grow in the

56

things that satisfy the wrong kind of appetite.

Our desire for grace causes us to shun everything else, so he uses the word "abstain." He doesn't say that we should cut it down; he says we should cut it out. The last thing we should want is a walk that weakens our worship and witness. We don't have the desire of the unsaved for we belong to Christ and have crucified the flesh with its passions and desires,[14] so how we walk, and with whom we walk, and where we walk are all indications of how we treat the grace of God.

This is Commendable

In the modern world, everyone has rights. There are human rights, civil rights, social rights, workers' rights, childrens' rights, and the right to protest. Being assertive is seen as commendable, but this is a long way from 1 Peter 2's view that being submissive is commendable. In the face of justice or injustice from governments or employers, the Christian has further opportunity to grow in grace. Peter loves the word *charis* so much he used it ten times in his letter, and we find it in each of the five chapters.

However, it's more difficult to find in chapter 2 for the simple reason that none of the main versions translates the word *charis* as grace in verse 19. There's a list of variations – acceptable, approved, a credit to you, commendable, favour, gracious, thankworthy – yet Peter simply says, *"For this is grace, if because of conscience toward God one endures grief, suffering wrongfully."* In a very different way from the world, we may suffer for our rights, but we need to know what they are. There are four defining characteristics of our rights:

- In verse 13, for the Lord's sake;
- In verse 15, for the will of God;
- In verse 19, for this is grace;
- In verse 19, for conscience toward God.

If we feel that we suffer for conscience' sake, we have three litmus tests:

- ·Is my response for the Lord's sake?
- ·Is it according to the will of God?
- ·Does it demonstrate the grace of God?

If the answer to all three is, 'Yes', then we have a right – to submit. Submission is our only God-given right, but never protest. There will be times when reasoned discussion is possible, but we must never give way to aggression. There may be times when the world's 'freedom of speech' approach lures believers into offending God in their attitude to government. There's no doubt that some laws go against the Word of God and violate consciences, but this is not new. The psalmist's comment in Psalm 94:20 must have been relevant in his day, yet we can ask with him, *"Shall the throne of iniquity, which devises evil by law, have fellowship with you?"* The thought of fellowship has no appeal, but neither does the thought of fighting battles.

When lawmakers present perverse things, where sinful things are put on the statute book, as citizens of these countries we have decisions to make. How do we handle it? Do we protest? Do we get up in arms? God says we should pray and submit. It was far from easy for Christians in the days of the early churches. Brutality was commonplace, as was immorality, yet God's word through Paul was: *"Let every soul be subject to the governing authorities. For there is no authority except from God, and the authorities that exist are appointed by God. Therefore whoever resists the authority resists the ordinance of God, and those who resist will bring judgment on themselves."*[15]

"God everywhere hath sway,
And all things serve His might;
His every act pure blessing is,
His path unsullied light."
(Paul Gerhardt)

Chapter 2 of Peter's letter brings us into definite areas of trial for which God has provided the means of grace and, irrespective of what it may be, the Spirit of God is able to give comfort. It may be, as you read this, there is a burden that burns into your very being and you may not have the slightest understanding of why our great God would permit it in the first place. As you bring yourself before His sovereignty and to the safety of His Word, in that Spirit you join with others in whom the grace of God is being reinforced. Whatever your trial is, in grief or in loss, in bereavement, unemployment, or some inward struggle against sin, bring it to the Saviour and, in the sanctifying effect of His Word say, "God, in the name of the Lord Jesus Christ, by Your Spirit, please reinforce Your grace."

Even as Peter's ink was drying on the page, the Spirit of God was directing believers to the Example. In many ways, He suffered wrongfully. He lived, and died, with injustice, yet never committed sin, nor was deceit found in His mouth. This was how He reacted to all sorts of abuse: no wrong thoughts, and no wrong threats. Instead, He surrendered to God who judges righteously. After all that, *"He bore our sins in His own body on the tree, that we, having died to sins, might live for righteousness"*[16] – and not resort to sinful reactions. By seeing Him as our example, we follow His steps. And this will be *charis para Theō(i)* – grace with God.

1.6 GRACE RECIPROCATED IN MARRIAGE

"Wives, likewise, be submissive to your own husbands, that even if some do not obey the word, they, without a word, may be won by the conduct of their wives, when they observe your chaste conduct accompanied by fear. Do not let your adornment be merely outward — arranging the hair, wearing gold, or putting on fine apparel — rather let it be the hidden person of the heart, with the incorruptible beauty of a gentle and quiet spirit, which is very precious in the sight of God.

For in this manner, in former times, the holy women who trusted in God also adorned themselves, being submissive to their own husbands, as Sarah obeyed Abraham, calling him lord, whose daughters you are if you do good and are not afraid with any terror. Husbands, likewise, dwell with them with understanding, giving honour to the wife, as to the weaker vessel, and as being heirs together of the grace of life, that your prayers may not be hindered" (1 Pet.3:1-7).

* * *

At a stroke of Peter's pen, God turns inward to have a right good look at our home-life and consider how grace can be demonstrated there. Under the care and guidance of His grace, God leads us **upward** in our worship, **outward** in our walk before the world and in our work, and now he moves

inward to our homes.

At this stage, we can see what God has done for us in chapter 1 of Peter's letter has opened the door into chapter 2, and now we are about to discover that what we read in chapter 2 opens the door into chapter 3. This makes us look back on our salvation with a real sense of thankfulness that chapter 1 is ours. We live and rejoice in the grandeur of His salvation from its beginning in His eternal purpose to its end in His eternal presence. Well could we write over it, *"From everlasting to everlasting, You are God"*[1] for it begins in eternity past with a God who elects, and points us to eternity future to anticipate our predestination.

Next, Peter leads us into chapter 2 where we learn about grace that causes us to handle the delights of worship and witness, alongside the difficulties of suffering wrongfully for doing what's right. By this avenue of worship and witness, our walk in the world and at work, Peter suddenly says, *"Wives."* This means that the God who brought us into His house in chapter 2, and up to the Shepherd and Overseer of our souls, now comes down to our house in chapter 3 and, just as He welcomes us into His house, He wants us to welcome Him into ours. The One who brings us into the precinct of His dwelling place in heaven waits for us to bring Him into the precinct of our homes on earth. By doing this, we permit the One who is at home in our hearts to be the One who also is at the heart of our homes.

He has such a practical way of helping us see that our lives are not broken into compartments with differing behaviour going on in each. Far from it! They are components interlinked by the consistent theme of grace, and we are left in no doubt at all that as children of God and churches, our commitment and conduct, plus our conscientiousness at work are all dependent on us *"desiring the pure milk of the word."* It will take the enjoyment of reading the Scriptures at home to safeguard us from showing a different face at church from what others see at work. Otherwise, it will be very easy to live one way at church and then be a different kind of person elsewhere.

Home is the place where we either decide to put things right or where we drop our guard and let things slip. Preparing our homes for Him means more than preparing its rooms as we might do for a guest, it means the preparation of ourselves. This means seeing how we live, and actively engaging in our communion with Him in our homes. It's the interaction of father, mother, and children being a family who live in such a way that He is able to see things that are consistent with what we are at church. At the end of a church service, a Christian woman was approached by another who wanted to compliment her, because her husband was such a good preacher. Even as she listened to the praise that was being heaped on him, she couldn't help thinking about his abusive ways and saying to herself, "If only you knew what he's like at home."

Some of us may be single. Irrespective of that, God still wants to look in our homes. He wants to look inside the marriage home – He wants to be able to see to what extent we have grown in the grace and knowledge of our Lord. Jesus Christ as individuals, as couples, and as families. This brings us to think of grace in a way that is ...

MARITAL

The introduction of grace to our lives in salvation has laid a foundation that allows us to build a whole lifestyle that shows we belong to God. In building a Christian testimony, it's only as we follow on in our understanding and enjoyment of grace that what affects us spiritually will also affect us practically. God's outpouring of grace is for our assistance in worship. We hear the evidence of this in every worship gathering, as brethren offer their appreciation of Christ, and God sees the same evidence in sisters as they silently offer theirs. We can say, like Barnabas, that we have seen the grace of God, and are glad.[2]

Peter was a married man and his wife accompanied him in his work for the Lord.[3] She was a believer, but this didn't mean that he was freed from the challenges that belong to a marriage where one isn't a believer. In his case, both he and his wife would demonstrate to one another the adorning that belongs to *"the hidden person of the heart."* In this way, they would thoroughly enjoy that they were *"heirs together of the grace of life"* and be thankful for the wide-ranging opportunities to share it with each other.

Back in the days of horse-drawn carriages in the mid-18th century, a man sat opposite a woman who was visibly moved by what she was reading. The man asked if she would show him what it was that affected her so much, and she passed him the book. He read:

> "O to grace how great a debtor
> Daily I'm constrained to be!
> Let that grace, Lord, like a fetter,
> Bind my wandering heart to Thee.
>
> Prone to wander, Lord, I feel it,
> Prone to leave the God I love;
> Keep my heart from wandering, keep it
> Till I'm perfected above."

The man reportedly handed the book back to her with the words, "Would to God that I were in the condition now that I was when I wrote these words!" He was Robert Robinson, the author of the hymn.

Many know what it is to turn aside temporarily from the Lord at some stage in their lives, and then look back on it with deep regret. Thankfully, the Lord graciously restores the years that the locusts have eaten, even when they have been destructively nibbling away inside a marriage. For some, this has been a real source of prayerful concern regarding their partnership, their family and home life.

Wives, Likewise

Chapter 2 ends with our eyes being fixed on *"the Shepherd and Overseer"* – the Pastor and Protector – *"of your souls,"* and chapter 3 begins with *"Wives."* Some versions say, *"Likewise"* or *"In the same way."* The original says *'Homoioōs hai gunaikes'* – which means, "Similarly the wives." Peter has a fitting way of making it clear to us that the One who is the cause of our worship also is the cause of our submission.

> "Come with Thy light divine into each room to shine.
> Master, the house is Thine, search Thou and see."

He has come right inside your house, and is longing to see that everything is consistent with your service in chapter 2 and with your salvation in chapter 1. We would think it strange if someone received a letter and had forgotten the contents of pages 1 and 2 by the time page 3 was being read. In exactly the same way, Peter wants us to see that chapter 2 is the doorway into the home in chapter 3. By saying, *"Likewise,"* he helps us to focus on the submissive spirit that causes us to worship, helps the effective witness of our walk, makes us live as good citizens before the authorities, and be the kind of workers that respect employers. It is Peter's way of saying that the marriage relationship has to be exactly the same, and for the same reasons.

Two thoughts should promote a desire to submit: i) to reflect our higher relationship with the Shepherd and Overseer of our souls and ii) to maintain a good relationship with others – authorities, employers, marriage partners. It's as if God is knocking on the door of our homes to say *"Wives ... be submissive,"* but this doesn't always go down well in today's world, where feminism can resist any thought of submission. No sister should ever let it enter her mind that chauvinism and feminism have any place in God's order of divine service. No sister should ever feel that she is of secondary importance to God, for there's nothing degrading of women in His Word. There's a harmony of teaching where one complements the other, and there may not be the slightest difference between the value of what a sister gives and what comes from brethren. There are sisters who have served the Lord monumentally, and God knows all about it. He also knows your service, and it's not second-rate to your husbands, never for a moment.

Adornment

The wife who wins her husband must be winsome! But where does her winsomeness come from? Some women obviously believe it's from the appeal of outward glamour, but Peter identifies it as belonging to an inner glory. The word *kosmos* and its derivations is used one hundred and eighty-six times in the New Testament and is translated as "world" on every occasion except this one. God could hardly have given Christian women a higher or more elevated commendation. Since it normally refers to the order and beauty of His creation, to the evidence of His handiwork in the world, it's as if He says to our sisters, "I think the world of you."

Their adornment is of His making, and Peter applies it to how it becomes evident in the life of the believing wife. It's not standing in front of the mirror, but looking into the mirror of His Word. It's not the decorating of the outside, but the cultivation of the inside. It's not what she does externally for herself – an elaborate hairdo, decorating herself, or wearing the best dress in her wardrobe – but the ornamentation God produces internally that only believers can possess.

It's in a gracious way that this former rugged fisherman held out the positive beauty of the inner person that has been created in Christ. The new nature that shines in the meek and quiet spirit reflects what He is, and is like a shaft of light from Matthew 11:29 – *"I am gentle and lowly in heart."* It was the only time He ever spoke about His own heart, and He said it at a time when He invited others to unburden theirs. It was as if He were asking them to tell Him what was in their hearts that He could take, and He would tell them what is in His heart that they could take.

Husbands, Likewise

Having begun with *"Wives, likewise,"* Peter now balances his conversation by saying, *"Husbands, likewise."* There's an onus on both of them, and he wants the woman to understand that in the eyes of her husband, and of God, he's going to treat her as the weaker vessel. This means physically; not spiritually, mentally or emotionally. Husbands have to dwell with their wives *"with understanding."* This carries the thought of careful and caring investigation, and means having due consideration of her temperament, personality, outlook, strengths and weaknesses, abilities and deficiencies, and above all her spirituality. In this way, husbands will treat their wives as the Lord intends, and cause their whole family life to be exposed to His blessing.

Showing this depth of interest in each other's character is good and healthy, but it must always be accompanied by joint spiritual investigation of what God has for them as couples. There's a lovely presentation of this in Psalm 128. The husband is the expected breadwinner, and his wife is described as a fruitful vine in the innermost part of their house. To complete the picture, their children sit around the family table like olive plants, and you may wonder why?

God's description is in keeping with the rest of the teaching about olives in the Old Testament. Oil came from the olive, and from the oil came the light for the lampstand in the tabernacle, so there's a testimony round about that table that allowed Him to see the working of His Spirit. The oil was a symbol of Him, as Zechariah 4:2-6 helps us to understand, and it was this working that allowed God to see something in their house that resembled something that He saw and enjoyed in His. Let's have a look at how Peter shows how we can arrive at this kind of marital bond and what he presents as necessary in the lives of a couple who, by God's help, can help one another in the mutual enjoyment of *"the grace of life."*

The Word

Peter is still drawing on the value of chapter 2:2-3, and reasoning that a believer's first experience of the Word in the gospel will create the desire for more of it, including in marriage. It's good when couples have a readiness to share the Word with each other, for this means they are bringing the desire for the Word into their marriage. It's noticeable, however, that Peter doesn't assume that all husbands and wives are believers. This doesn't mean that he was advocating that a believer should marry an unbeliever; but rather that he was aware that the gospel had reached one, and not yet the other. He actually acknowledges that some will keep being disobedient by rejecting the Word spoken by their wives.

Without a Word

Now he foresees both kinds of marriages and advises wives, for example, to win their husbands through the appeal of their godly conduct. Her attitude and actions may allow what she shows to have more impact than what she says. She may feel as if she's walking a tightrope as she figures out when to speak and when not to speak. There may be times when words have an effect; but it's also quite likely there will be times when body language speaks more loudly than words. This doesn't mean, of course, that he can be saved "without the word," since it is the means God uses to bring every person to Christ. James makes it clear that it is *"of His own will He brought us forth by the word of truth"*[4] and Peter corroborated this in chapter 1:23 by saying we have *"been born again ... through the word of God which lives and abides forever."*

Her wisdom in this is combined with *"fear,"* which is the same word Paul used, and is translated by the New King James Version as *"that she respects her husband."*[5] Peter recognised that husbands would *"observe"* this and, to show that they'd be paying attention, he returned to the same word he used about how Gentiles would be watching and inspecting what believers did

67

and what they didn't do.[6] Failure on her part would come from not living up to what God expected from her, but, along with this, she could cause the Word of God to be blasphemed by being unwise.[7] She had married a man, probably as two unbelievers; but now, as a believer, she was trying to win him. The reality is, she was no longer the person he married – her outlook was different, her character had changed – so Peter says it may be her behaviour that will talk. If so, the lesson is clear: let it do the talking when you know that you're unlikely to win him with words.

Heirs Together of the Grace of Life

The husband and wife, the stronger and weaker, never implies inequality, and Peter's way of confirming this is to emphasise their bond of equality as co-sharers, fellow-heirs of this particular expression of grace that God has reserved for marriage. This is of real importance, since God Himself was the Designer of marriage in the Garden of Eden. The woman He *"made"* (Heb. *banah*: built) was God's ideal for the first man Adam,[8] and God brought her to Adam as a building, a body and a bride – as a foreshadowing of the Last Adam receiving *"the church, which is His body."*[9]

It's also important from the point of view of believers being united with their Saviour as *"joint heirs with Christ."*[10] The adversary will do his utmost to keep believers from communing with God. He did it in the Garden of Eden with the first couple, and he's still doing it. As individuals, we can let sin disrupt our fellowship with Him. On the other hand, we can make sure this doesn't happen. Couples should keep their eyes fixed on their spiritual inheritance and on all the blessings it allows them to share in the deepest possible way within marriage. As two whom the Lord has joined, they have the greatest and closest opportunity to enjoy the fruits of their salvation.

That Your Prayers May Not Be Hindered

As individuals, we can let sin disrupt our fellowship with Him. On the other hand, we can make sure this doesn't happen. The writer of Psalm 66:18-20 couldn't have been more straightforward when he said, *"If I regard iniquity in my heart, the Lord will not hear. But certainly God has heard me: He has attended to the voice of my prayer. Blessed be God, who has not turned away my prayer; nor His mercy from me!"* So there can be hindrances individually, and Peter indicates there can be marital hindrances. Both partners have been guided by the word *"Likewise,"* and lack of fulfilling their obligations to each other would "hinder" their prayers. Peter means that her lack of submission, his lack of understanding and care, or their joint lack of appreciation of being *"heirs together,"* would interfere or cut into their prayers being voiced by them or heard by God.

Finally, All of You

It's as if Peter is the expert fisherman in this chapter, and no one's getting off the hook! Having focused on wives and husbands, he now includes everyone: the singles as well as the married, the old as well as the young, and he has a sevenfold standard for all:

1. **Of one mind** *(Gr. homophrones: likeminded)* - harmony in assembly life depends on everyone thinking the same.
2. **Compassion** *(Gr. sumpatheis: fellow-feeling)* - having a sensitivity for each other without being selective.
3. **Love as brothers** *(Gr. philadelphoi: fond of brethren)* - having genuine affection for one another without favour or disregard.
4. **Tender-hearted** *(Gr. eusplagchnoi: full of pity)* - having sensitivity to the hurts and pains of others.
5. **Courteous** *(Gr. tapeinofrones: humble-minded)* - having a Christlike lowly mind that takes account of everyone and being willing to serve

69

all. This can be a challenge, and easily overlooked.

6. **Not returning evil** *(Gr. kakon: harm, injury)* - having no desire to retaliate or get even with wrong actions or words, remembering that insults can be as hurtful as blows. The Jews opposed Jeremiah and urged one another to *"attack him with the tongue"* (Jer.18:18). No wonder James spoke so much about it (Jas.1:26; 3:5,6,8)!

7. **Blessing** *(Gr. eulogia: speak well of)* - having the desire to say something beneficial and praiseworthy that will be encouraging and uplifting.

These seven requirements form a vital part of our spiritual relationship with one another, and they form a vital part of God's reason for calling us to Himself, and for granting many the blessing of 'marital' grace.

1.7 GRACE RECOGNISED IN HOLINESS

"But as He who called you is holy, you also be holy in all your conduct, because it is written, 'Be holy, for I am holy'" (1 Pet.1:15,16).

"But sanctify in your hearts Christ as Lord," (RV*) *"and always be ready to give a defence to everyone who asks you a reason for the hope that is in you, with meekness and fear; having a good conscience, that when they defame you as evildoers, those who revile your good conduct in Christ may be ashamed"* (1 Pet.3:15,16, NKJV).

* see marginal footnote

* * *

It's impossible to make Christ what He already is. We can't make Him holy, nor can we make Him Lord for He already is holy, and He already is Lord. In eternity past, in His time on earth, and now on the throne of heaven, His holiness and lordship are without question and always intact. So how do we sanctify Him as Lord? We cannot improve them in Him, but He can improve them in us. So what does Peter mean? The key to the question is *"in your hearts"*; He resides there, but does He preside? How do we know, and how can others tell? This is the experiential enthronement of our Saviour, not only as Purchaser but also as Proprietor of our lives. He is Lord, which means He is the Master; but if we say *"He is my Lord,"* this means the Master has the mastery. We can think of this in three ways:

- It affects Him - through having constant communion with Him;
- It affects us - through His constant claims on the whole person;
- It affects others – through communicating Christ to personal contacts.

In each of those three areas of sanctification, the accent is on our being set apart in Him and for Him. In 1 Peter 3:15, the emphasis is on His being set apart in us. Peter's ten-point checklist is right here:

- Am I sufficiently growing in the Word? (1 Pet.2:2)
- Am I a thankful worshipper? (1 Pet.2:4,5)
- Am I an active witness? (1 Pet.2:9,10)
- Am I careful in my walk? (1 Pet.2:11,12)
- Am I submissive to worldly authorities? (1 Pet.2:13-17)
- Am I submissive at work? (1 Pet.2:18-20)
- Am I a submissive wife or husband? (1 Pet.3:1-6)
- Am I a blessing to others in the church? (1 Pet.3:8,9)
- Am I always ready to defend my hope? (1 Pet.3:15)
- Am I living with a clear conscience? (1 Pet.3:16)

How blessed we are that the crucified *"Lord of glory"*[1] and the exalted Lord who has been *"received up in glory"*[2] should want to be set apart in holiness in our hearts! Right at the outset, we acknowledge our unworthiness even to think or speak about something so lofty as the holiness of God. It's a very high privilege that He would allow our very limited minds to consider what He intrinsically is by nature, since He knows what we instinctively are in ours.

It's not only that His conduct is holy, He is holy; and it's not simply because there's an absence of sin in Him. When Pilate interrogated the Lord Jesus Christ, He wasn't proved holy because Pilate found no fault in Him; rather Pilate found no fault in Him because He is holy. As we delight in the privilege of stepping inside the precinct of the holiness of God, it towers above us causing us to sense our own sinfulness. It's not that the absence of sinfulness in Him makes Him holy, it's that the presence of infinite holiness makes Him sinless. It wasn't only when He was on earth that He did no sin: the eternal truth is that *"in Him there is no sin."*[3] There is never a moment when He stepped out of *"being in the form of God."*[4] He is never less than eternally holy for He is eternally God!

James tells us that when we enter into a transaction that confirms our sinfulness, it's because the temptation conceives with the lust in our nature and produces sin.[5] This was not the case with the Saviour. In His unique holiness, there is nothing in Him with which lust can conceive. There is a complete absence of anything in His nature that would allow temptation to become an inward thought, and therefore no possibility of a sinful outward action being produced. Some have said that He could have sinned, but didn't. The truth is that in absolute holiness He didn't sin, because He couldn't. He is the Holy One, Son of the holy God, and the Holy Spirit is called the Spirit of holiness.[6]

It's not that holiness is a characteristic of Their joint-nature, just as light and love are not simply features of Their Being. It's what They are, and what They share. They are contrary to our human nature, yet They choose to share some of Their attributes through saving grace. This allows us to receive imputed holiness by which we can become holy in lifestyle, but They are not receivers of holiness, They are its sole Givers, but we possess none of it until we know His salvation.

The way Peter presents this in his letter is wonderfully consistent with what we have in the first reference to His holiness in the book of Exodus. After the Passover had taken place. God gave them a way out of Egypt by the blood of the lamb, and then a way through the Red Sea. In response, Moses and the people sang in triumph of the God who is *"glorious in holiness."*[7] When we go forward into Exodus 28, we read how God took them closer to Himself through a high priest with garments and a holy crown on his head that was engraved with the words *"Holiness to Jehovah."*[8]

What they had acknowledged on the day of their deliverance God wanted them to acknowledge every day when, at last, they encamped around His dwelling place. What a huge step forward! Instead of being in bondage in the presence of the enemy, they had a man who expressed their freedom in the presence of God. When we move forward again, we find the third mention of God's holiness in 1 Chronicles 16:29 when His people were invited to *"worship the LORD in the beauty of holiness!"*

These are the first three references to holiness in our Bible and we can see how God was travelling and leading His people. He began with the redeemed; then showed that there was a man in His presence for them; and then He caused them to approach and worship Him in the beauty of holy array. This is exactly the order we see in 1 Peter 1 and 2. God begins with the work of the Redeemer and the Passover Lamb in chapter 1; He continues with the work of Christ the High Priest in chapter 2; and the rest of the letter continues with a theme that begins with the worship of the people of God in the presence of God through the Man who represents us there.

Isn't it amazing how consistent God is? He has an order in the Old Testament that foreshadows His order in the New Testament. His people were well blessed through Moses, yet we have much more in Christ. In His gracious desire to deliver His redeemed through Christ, God triply blesses us by allowing us to enter into His holiness. He brings us into the holiness of the Person, into the holiness of His purpose, and into the holiness of His Holy Place to worship Him.

Sanctification

When we come to the New Testament, the triumphs of our salvation are laid out for us in Acts 26:18 – *"to open their eyes, in order to turn them from darkness to light, and from the power of Satan to God, that they may receive forgiveness of sins and an inheritance among those who are sanctified by faith in Me."* This is the beginning of God's great work of sanctification in the believer right from the moment of salvation.

Sometimes our Bibles will tell us in a marginal note that being sanctified means being set apart; but it means much more. It's very easy to set someone or something apart, but this doesn't necessarily mean that they have been set apart in holiness. The word Paul used was *hagiazō*, which means "made holy," and it has to do with the character or condition in which we are set apart by God. The word sanctified belongs to the thought of holiness, so he's really saying we have been set apart in holiness for God.

This is how God begins, and Hebrews 10:8-10 takes us back to Calvary to show us that the mainstream of His holiness has been channelled through the work of the Saviour. It was there He fulfilled the will of God, and *"By that will we have been sanctified through the offering of the body of Jesus Christ once for all."* Out of Calvary's darkness, light has flooded our souls; and out of Calvary's sinfulness, holiness has been given to us through the cleansing power of His precious blood. No wonder the writer calls it *"So great a salvation"*![9]

Paul tells us, in 1 Thessalonians 2:13, that we have come into the blessing of salvation *"through sanctification by the Spirit"* – that was His part; *"and belief in the truth"* – that was our part. Even in the very nature of our calling, God has made it clear that it is high, and holy, and heavenly.[10] What is God trying to tell us? Well, He wants us to know that our high calling refers to our station in Christ. We are seated with Him in the heavenly places.[11] As far as our eternal welfare is concerned, He has covered us in His holiness, and this leaves the believer completely untouchable by the destructive power of the adversary. You are out of his reach, as far as your eternal welfare is concerned. He cannot snatch you out of your Saviour's hand.[12] Our station is secure, but we have a standard to maintain, and there are two parts to it. Peter leaves us in no doubt that the station we have obtained in salvation has a standard that must be maintained and attained in our service.

He also moves on to show us that the calling, which is holy in its character, is also holy in its purpose. When God says, *"Be holy for I am holy,"* He combines His eternal name with His eternal character in the phrase *egō hagios eimi.* He is the holy I AM! This makes us partakers of the divine nature, but doesn't, of course, make us equal with Him. There's something in us that responds to the high calling, something in us that responds to the holiness of that calling, and something in us that responds to fulfilling the purpose of our heavenly calling. It's by fulfilling this that we experience the privilege and pleasure of the priestly service that Hebrews and 1 Peter speak about.

Sadly, religion has its counterfeit holiness, with its so-called holy places and holy men, yet there's nothing of the holiness of God in them - for unregenerate men can never be holy. History shows that some of the Caesars, including Julius Caesar and Augustus, had coins with an inscription that defied Deity. They claimed the title Pontifex Maximus, which in Latin means the greatest high priest. In the fifth century, it became a title of Popes and does to the present day. When Pope Benedict was active, he had a new set of doors made for the Vatican with his name and title inscribed across its four panels. It's a bold statement of Roman Catholic belief, which also claims the title of Holy Father and His Holiness. In the Upper Room, the Lord Jesus addressed God in prayer as "Holy Father," and He is the only One who rightly bears the Name. Similarly, the Lord Jesus Christ is the only great High Priest, yet Pontifex Maximus, the greatest high priest, claims to be two levels higher!

In marked contrast to all this, Peter introduces the personal holiness of believers in chapter 1, then he speaks about a holy priesthood and a holy nation in chapter 2 before urging us to set Christ apart in holiness in our hearts in chapter 3. How significant it is that the 'Holy I AM' calls us individually to live in His holy character, collectively to live in the holy atmosphere of assembly service, and then emphasises that we must live in the purity and authority of the holiness and lordship of His Person. Service is very important, but having the right environment for spiritual service

76

makes it more important. We should notice how appropriate this is. He is asking us to give an answer to everyone who asks a reason for the hope that is in us, that we do it with meekness and fear.

It's not simply a matter of giving an answer. The character of the answerer is what matters. Without this, the answer will never be right. Well, it could be the right thing, but said in the wrong way. It needs to be a Christlike answer. In fact, in the last chapter, we saw it was possible for a wife to win her husband through silence that allows Christian character to speak; for there are times when conduct has a louder voice. So we need to take both chapters: one, to learn what to say in the right place; and, secondly, to learn what not to say in another place. We just need to see these two opportunities as ways in which the holiness of God can speak through each one of us.

This will enable us to fulfil two things: i) the silent witness of our manner of life (1 Pet.3:1) and ii) the verbal witness that's done in meekness and in fear (1 Pet.3:15). The Lord is *"the Faithful and True Witness,"*[13] whether silent or speaking, and we take character from Him.

> "Lord, speak to me, that I may speak
> In living echoes of Thy tone;
> As Thou hast sought, so let me seek
> Thine erring children, lost and lone."
> *(Frances R. Havergal)*

Holiness is the best preparation for enabling us to walk with God and fulfilling the kind of ministry that Peter is outlining to us. Paul wholeheartedly agrees, and his message to Timothy is as vital for us: *"Therefore if anyone cleanses himself from the latter, he will be a vessel for honour, sanctified and useful for the Master, prepared for every good work."*[14] This means leaving things behind, and going after the things that are before, so there's an essential combination: *"depart from iniquity"*[15] and *"Pursue peace with all people, and holiness, without which no man will see the Lord."*[16] Forsake sinfulness, and follow holiness. What a goal! What an ambition, to have the holiness of God before us always and to be thinking about the possibility of our lives reflecting the very nature of our God.

We have been emphasising how everything in chapter two and onwards goes back to desiring the pure milk of the Word, and it's vital that we do this in the matter of knowing when to speak and when not to speak. Solomon's advice was that there's *"a time to keep silence, and a time to speak."*[17] This is what Peter is saying, too, but now he's asking us to take on board that holiness must be harnessed to the Word.

It's beneficial to follow his reasoning: in chapter 1, *"Be holy, for I am holy"*; in chapter 2, *"desire the pure milk of the word."* You see, it's not enough to use the Word without the spiritual back-up of the holiness of God. Speaking the Word without holiness being our motivation will make the Word powerless through us. It's important to come to our Bible and recognise it as the Holy Word of God, written by men who spoke from Him as they were moved by the Holy Spirit. When we recognise the holiness from which the inspired Word has come, we have a responsibility to pass it on in a similar way. It has to be communicated in holiness through the sanctified vessel.

So we go back through everything we have been thinking about and we discover the need to ask, once again, are we growing in the Word? We can add to this by asking if our desire for holiness is causing us to grow in the Word? And is our desire for the Word causing us to grow in holiness? Both should happen, shouldn't they? The Word will help us to grow in holiness, but the initial desire for the Word will come from your enjoyment of the holiness of God. The One who has spoken to us, in the first place, wants to speak through us, so that others might hear and see Him.

Partakers

Ever since Eden's Fall, God has desired fellowship with men and women on earth, and the chequered journey from Genesis to Malachi reveals the ups and downs of maintaining it. These were long years, during which the unchanging God was served, challenged and tested, by changeable individuals and a very unreliable people. There was failure among leaders, prophets, priests, kings, and tribes, yet the omniscient God who knows the end from the beginning never failed them. He held true to His promise that He would lead them into the land as victors over opposing nations, and His reliable assurance was based on this: *"God has spoken in His holiness."*[18]

When an unfaithful people forsook His law, He remained faithful. When they failed to show love to Him, His lovingkindness remained, and His whole promise was securely wrapped in this, *"Once I have sworn by My holiness."*[19] Holiness makes it impossible for God to lie or mislead, and His faithfulness is eternally rooted in His unchanging holiness.

Even at the place of the altar's intended close communion, the God-given mandate of *"Holiness to the LORD"* on the high priest's golden crown was no guarantee against inappropriate or unacceptable sacrifice in the days of Malachi.[20] It was the place where proper sacrifice permitted those who offered to eat of the sacrifices as partakers of the altar,[21] yet they lost the joy of sharing in holy things. This is how the Old Testament closes, on a note that holds a salutary warning, lest we should fail in the same way and lose our joy in holy things. God was patiently waiting for the opportunity to be given to us through the coming of His Son.

At last, the perfect Servant, the perfect Sacrifice, the perfect Saviour, and through Him perfect salvation! The gospel of Christ has come, and all things are ours *"according to the glorious gospel of the blessed* [happy] *God."*[22] With the gospel of Christ comes God's *"promise in Christ,"* and of this promise we have been made *"partakers."*[23] And what fellowship it is! The wealth

79

of this verse increases when it is translated (as in the Revised Version) as, *"the Gentiles are fellow-heirs, and fellow-members of the body, and fellow-partakers of the promise in Christ Jesus through the gospel."* It's a threefold fellowship that links us, outwardly, with believers throughout the world; with the closest inseparable bond, inwardly, that we are in Christ; and have joint-fellowship in this glorious promise that points us, upwardly, to Him.

Paul uses three words – *sungkleeronoma ... sussēma ... summetocha* – and each one is an adjective to describe what Gentiles have, as well as believing Jews, in Christ. All three words begin with the prefix *sun*, which means union, togetherness and companionship, and Paul definitely enjoyed what God asked him to share. It was as if his heart was so full that no one word could capture the full extent of the blessing, and so his final word is rather special. On its own, the word *metochos* means a sharer or a partner. Adding the little word *sun* expands the thought of union and togetherness, and it allows the whole word to be something like "sharing-sharers" or "fellow-fellowshippers." We catch the sense of his enjoyment as he describes the gospel as "the unsearchable riches of Christ" in verse 8.

In Philippians, we are partakers of grace; in Hebrews, partakers of Christ and partakers of His holiness; and in Peter's second letter, we are partakers of the divine nature.[24] Our fellowship, participation and sharing knows no bounds. God's grace, holiness and nature are for sharing, and although we are brought into them through the gospel, we grow in them by being on-going partakers. Peter indicates there are two sides to this: on the one hand, it's by taking and trusting God's promises; and on the other, it's because we have escaped the corruption that is in the world.

The pleasures of sin have gone; the pleasure of holiness has come. Our nature has changed. The old things have gone; what is new has come.[25] We think differently, we speak differently, and we act differently, for we are presenting our bodies as living sacrifices that are holy,[26] and this holiness, in contrast to the sub-standard offerings in Malachi's day, makes us acceptable in our service for the Lord. God sees Himself in Christ, and He wants to see Christ in us, for only then will His grace be recognised in holiness.

> "Where no stain of sin can enter, nor the gold be dim;
> In that holiness unsullied, I shall walk with Him;
> Meet companion for the Master, from Him, for Him made;
> Glory of God's grace for ever, there in me displayed."
> *(Mrs Bevan)*

There's quite a bit of parallelism in Peter's letter. He has done it with the word *"likewise"* in verses 1 and 7, and again by contrasting *"evildoers"* and *"good"* in verse 16, just as he did in verses 12 and 14 of the previous chapter. Another pairing is in verses 14 and 18 – *"if you should suffer"* and *"Christ also suffered"*; what an honour for these to be combined!

- Those who believe suffering on behalf of Christ;
- Christ suffering on behalf of those who believe.

Put to Death ... But Made Alive

The next couplet is not so easily explained. Bible scholars give different interpretations, and we understand why this is the case. Verse 18 says that Christ was put to death in the flesh but made alive in or by the Spirit. Translators also have difficulty, because the Greek language doesn't show if *spirit* should have a capital 'S' or be in the lower case. This has led to some being of the mind that He was made alive by the Holy Spirit, while others take the view that it was by His Own inner spirit.

Irrespective of viewpoint, all agree that He was *"put to death in the flesh"* by the work of men, but was *"made alive in the spirit"* by the work of God. Having said that, there are a couple of points worth considering. This doesn't refer to His bodily resurrection, for He went while His body was in the tomb,

81

during which time His own spirit was alive. His spirit never died with His body on the cross, and He had committed it into the safekeeping of His Father's hands.[27]

He Went and Preached to the Spirits in Prison

Peter used the word *"preached"* four times in this letter. In 1 Peter 1:12, 25 and 1 Peter 4:6 he used the Greek word *euangelizō*, which means "evangelise," and it's only in 1 Peter 3:19 that *kerussō* is used. It simply means to herald a public proclamation, and by not using *euangelizō* he ruled out any thought of the Lord preaching the gospel to the lost, which would have made it the gospel of the second chance. By changing to *kērussō*, he indicated in vv.18-19 that He went there to make a triumphant statement of His victory on the cross. His victorious spirit made a victorious announcement to vanquished spirits.

Baptism ... the Answer of a Good Conscience

When Philip helped the Ethiopian eunuch to understand Isaiah 53:7-8, he preached to him in such a way that he saw his need to believe in Christ and then demonstrate his obedience by being baptised. Peter's message on the Day of Pentecost had the same effect. *Those who "accepted his message were baptised"*[28]; so, just as with the Ethiopian, they understood the close connection between salvation and baptism. There was no long time gap between receiving and following. Conversion and commitment went hand in hand, as indicated in the implied sequence of death, burial and resurrection.

It's very much in keeping with the Lord's sufferings, as we read in chapters 2:21 and 3:18 that He said of them, *"I have a baptism to be baptised with."*[29] How well He knew that His deep suffering on the cross, particularly during the three hours of darkness, would be a complete immersion as God *"made Him who knew no sin to be sin for us."*[30] Like the ark being buffeted as it took the full force of the deluge, the Saviour was uniquely qualified to say to His

Father, *"All Your waves and billows have gone over Me"*[31] and *"Your wrath lies heavy upon Me, and You have afflicted Me with all Your waves."* God held nothing back. For this reason, Paul was able to write, *"He who did not spare His own Son"*[32] meaning that God did not treat Him leniently.

Through the Resurrection of Jesus Christ

It's worth noting the specific relationship between Noah's ark and the Lord's resurrection. When the deluge was over, and God's work of deliverance and judgment finished, Genesis 8:4 says, *"Then the ark rested in the seventh month, the seventeenth day of the month."* This is significant. The seventh month in Genesis became the first month in Exodus 12:2 when God introduced the Passover. The lamb was slain on the 14th day, which foreshadowed the day of the Lord's crucifixion, and therefore, three days later, the 17th pointed forward to His resurrection.

Not the Removal of the Filth of the Flesh

Cleansing of sin is provided only through the precious blood of our Lord Jesus Christ. It alone is the price of propitiation,[33] which satisfies a holy God and appeases His wrath while, at the same time, it *"cleanses us from all sin."*[34] So baptism is *"not the removal of the filth of the flesh."* Peter says it is *"the answer* [Gr. *eperōtēma*: the pledge, the inquiry] *of a good conscience."* Baptism asks questions, and then finds the answer in the genuine work that has been done in believers' hearts, which qualifies them to be baptised. It asks, like the Ethiopian, *"What hinders me from being baptised?"* Conscience and the heart replies, "Nothing!" The Lord went through a baptism of judgment that we might follow Him in a baptism of blessing. Can we, in all *"good conscience,"* say "No"? Instead, we say "Yes," because *"the love of Christ compels us,"*[35] and because it's a step in sanctifying Christ as Lord in our hearts.

83

Angels and Authorities and Powers Having Been Made Subject to Him

The chapter begins with submissive wives, and it ends with submissive angels. Such is the triumph of the cross that sinful human beings and all sinless angelic beings bow before the supremacy of the resurrected Saviour,[36] and those fallen angels who heard the Victor herald His conquest on the cross bow in submissive defeat.

> "Yonder throne for Him erected, now becomes the Victor's seat,
> Lo, the Man on earth rejected, angels worship at His feet!
> Day and night they cry before Him, 'Holy, holy, holy Lord,'
> All the powers of heaven adore Him, all obey His sovereign word."
> (T. Kelly)

1.8 GRACE REVEALED IN SPIRITUAL GIFTS

"As each one has received a gift, minister it to one another, as good stewards of the manifold grace of God. If anyone speaks, let him speak as the oracles of God. If anyone ministers, let him do it as with the ability which God supplies, that in all things God may be glorified through Jesus Christ, to whom belong the glory and the dominion forever and ever. Amen" (1 Pet.4:10,11).

* * *

Like a jewel in its setting, Peter embeds three sentences that radiate thoughts of the glory of God and of His being glorified, and it's noticeable what lies on either side. On the one hand, he draws our attention to the sufferings of Christ and, on the other, to the sufferings of the Christian. It's as if he wants to remind us of the cost and of the consequences of spiritual gifts. They are traceable to the lowly mind of the suffering Saviour, and it should be evident in all our service that we arm ourselves with the same mind. Our will must be His will, just as His will was God's will[1]; and our use of spiritual gifts must show a mindset that bears His lowliness.

It was through what He fulfilled in that lowly mind that His glory followed, and it was out of that glory that He *"gave gifts to men."*[2] Through the glorified Christ, He set the members in the body according to His pleasure,[3] and it's also for his pleasure that we want to glorify Him through the gifts. So, just as the gifts flow from His sufferings and glory, we serve with them knowing that, even if suffering is ours, the glory will always flow back to Him.

Peter's references to the Lord's sufferings are significant from this point of view, that he uses two different words to describe them. In 1 Peter 1:11, he considers the hardship and pain of His afflictions, and we recognise right away that our word "pathos" lies at the heart of the Greek word *pathēma*. This word never left Peter, and we find it again in 1 Peter 5:1 where he says that he was *"a witness of the sufferings of Christ."* In both verses, he indicates the severity of the Saviour's sufferings by using the word in its plural form, *pathēmata*. Between these two verses, Peter follows the theme of the sufferings of Christ, but in chapters 2, 3 and 4, the word he uses is *paschō*.

Both words combine to tell of the physical and spiritual sufferings He endured: the first, includes the brutality from the hands of men; the second, focuses on the deeper suffering endured from the hand of God when *"He made Him who knew no sin to be sin for us,"*[4] our sin-bearer and sin offering. In 1 Peter 2:21, He suffered to be our Example; in 1 Peter 3:18, He is the Just dying for the unjust; and in 1 Peter 4:1, He is the Servant who pleased His God.[5] Peter speaks very tenderly about the sufferings of his Saviour, and he does it in a way that was very personal to him. There's no doubt that he would wish his readers, in his days and ours, to think as tenderly and personally as he did.

Now that he is speaking to us about the blessing of spiritual gifts, he makes it clear that unless we have an appreciation of His sufferings – His hardship and pain, and feel the passion of Christ – then these things will register rather low on our scale. They were much higher on Peter's, and they will have to be high on ours, too, as we try to fulfill our worship, our witness, our walk, and as wives before their husbands. So this is the setting within which he wants us to think about the manifestation of the grace of God that we could call …

86

PENTECOSTAL

We were thinking in chapter 1 of grace that's eternal and sacrificial; then we thought of grace that is experimental in chapter 2, by which we prove our experience in the Word of God. It's only through this kind of scriptural experience that we prove that God's Word actually works in our lives. Chapter 3 applies grace to the marital bond; and chapter 4 goes on to speak about *"manifold grace,"* which we trace to the Day of Pentecost when the initial distribution of the gifts took place in the coming of the Holy Spirit.

Manifold Grace

The marvel is that God has never missed out a single person who ever came to Christ, all of them without exception being sharers in the diversity of spiritual gifts. It's this variety that Peter says is *"manifold."* It is multi-faceted and variegated, one complementing the other as mutual expressions of grace. In every New Testament reference to spiritual gifts, God provides for *"each one,"* so it's impossible to miss the point. Paul says it in Romans, Corinthians and Ephesians, and Peter does the same.[6]

When he heard what Paul had written, he must have rejoiced in knowing that the Spirit of God had told him exactly the same thing, that each of us is gifted. This means that each one of us has a ministry, and it's up to us to make sure that we carry 1 Peter 2:2 with us. Peter encourages us that we should *"desire the pure milk of the word,"* knowing that it feeds our worship in chapter 2, fills our walk in chapter 3, and fuels the witness of our gifts in chapter 4. The truth is we can't worship without it, we can't walk without it, and we can't witness without it.

No gift can function without the Word, so it's vital that we avoid a low-burn lifestyle by spending time in it. If we gather the fuel, God will provide the fire! If He has called you to teach, expound the Word. If you are a preacher, preach the Word. If you are an encourager, use the Word. If you are among the helps, support others with the Word. Whatever He asks you to do, do it. *"Take heed to the ministry which you have received in the Lord, that you may fulfil it,"*[7] but never attempt it without immersing yourself in the Word. We need to learn the secret of bowing before God and asking Him, *"Please, God, help me to know my role from Your Word."* As He feeds you with it, ask for His help in passing it on and, as He does this, gradually He will confirm your gift.

Good Stewards

Assembly life is the place He has given for our gifts to be exercised. Look around the disciples in your church and two things should come to mind: you are surrounded by that amount of gift, and each of you has to acknowledge that you have received a gift and *"minister it to one another, as good stewards of the manifold grace of God."* This combination is presented in each chapter that deals with spiritual gifts:

- Romans 12: To each one (v.3) – members of one another (v.5);
- 1 Corinthians 12: To each one (v.7) – the same care for one another (v.25, NASB);
- Ephesians 4: To each one (v.7) – bearing with one another (v.2);
- 1 Peter 4: As each one (v.10) – minister it to one another (v.10).

By doing this, Paul says each one of us will be *"for the profit of all,"*[8] so we should be able to help in the recognition of gift – but how often have we been aware of this happening? Think of the Saviour's ministry. When He spoke to someone, did they profit? When He touched someone, did they profit? In His reaching out, whether speaking or serving, did others profit? For many, the answer was "Yes." It should be like this for us, too; but those who speak, Peter says, let (them) speak *"as utterances from God"* (NKJV margin). And those who serve, let them *"do it as with the ability that God supplies."* It's not the person's ability, but God's, and He is the only One who can supply it, which means He alone choreographs the working of the gifts.

Each church has to consider the Giver rather than the gifted, since He is the source and supplier. We fulfil our ministry and get fulfilment from it only when we are in tune with the triune God. This is made very clear in 1 Corinthians 12. There are diversities of gifts, but the same Spirit. There are differences of ministries, but the same Lord. And there are diversities of activities, but it is the same God who works all in all. There are differences in the gifts, ministries and activities, but they own the same Spirit, Lord, and God.

The gifts (Gr. *charismata*) are expressions of variegated grace; the ministries (Gr. *diakoniōn*) present various ways of serving; and activities (Gr. *energē-matōn*). No matter which aspect of spiritual gifts we possess, we own them with thankfulness to the Giver, and we take the lowly place as speakers, servants and stewards. This will ensure that our relationship with God and one another is right, and that our stewardship from God and toward one another is right, too.

Opportunity and responsibility go together, just as how we serve must always be coupled to where we serve. The local assembly is the initial sphere of service, and should be the place where individual responsibility finds encouragement from the church's collective responsibility, and from its leaders. Stewardship puts everyone on the same footing, for it means we all share in the caring management and overall function of the gifts to the glory of God and the assembly's good.

The inference is, of course, that we can be poor stewards. Manifold grace can be abused, just as grace can be. Paul knew well that some took advantage of God's free grace by thinking that, if grace allows you to be forgiven for sin, then the more you sin the more grace you will get. That's why he asked, in Romans 6:1, *"Shall we continue in sin that grace may abound?"* and immediately answered, *"Certainly not! How shall we who died to sin live any longer in it?"* Peter wants to safeguard us from the possible abuse of God's manifold grace, either by our gifts malfunctioning or not functioning at all.

Paul is a superb example of how we can be good stewards. In 1 Corinthians 4:1, he wanted others to see him as a servant of Christ, and he used a very unusual illustration. His choice of word was *hupēretēs*, to let them know that he was like an under-oarsmen way down low in the galley that probably had three tiers of oarsmen with him in the bottom level. In that lowly frame of mind, he added, *"and steward[s] of the mysteries of God."* That would make anyone row well, wouldn't it? What an exalted place for a lowly man!

Sometimes, if we are being honest with ourselves, we struggle in our rowing. There was a time when Jesus saw His disciples *"toiling in rowing,"*[9] as He watched over them from His mountain place of prayer in the fourth watch of the night. Somewhere between three and six o'clock in the morning, in the last watch before dawn, they saw Him coming. It's such a graphic picture of us, isn't it? It's just before the dawning of the morning of that great and glorious day, and maybe we are toiling as we row.

"Oft we tread the path before us, with a weary, burdened heart;
Oft we toil amid the shadows, and our fields are far apart;
But the Saviour's "Come, ye blessed" all our labour will repay,
When we gather in the morning, where the mists have rolled away."
(Annie Herbert)

Unlike the disciples, Paul's lowly mind was on higher things, but this didn't make him high-minded. Listen to him, as he appeals to us from his lowly way of thinking: *"I say, through the grace given to me, to everyone who is among you, not to think of himself more highly than he ought to think, but to think soberly, as God has dealt to each one a measure of faith."*[10] There's always a danger that being gifted makes us think in ways we shouldn't. Our minds can shoot off into areas where we shouldn't be, and we assume that somehow or other the gifts reflect well on the individual who might be gifted. But it's all about the Giver, not the gift, and not the gifted. We must speak and serve as good stewards!

Neither Male Nor Female

When we are thinking of the distribution of spiritual gifts, it's important that we take in the implications of what Paul wrote in Galatians 3:28 – *"There is neither Jew nor Greek, there is neither slave nor free, there is neither male nor female; for you are all one in Christ Jesus."* Culture, class and gender are completely overcome, so we know right away that the redeemed among Jews are as equally gifted as Gentiles. Born-again slaves are equally blessed as their free counterparts, and no distinction exists between males and females in the distribution of the gifts. All these natural differences are removed in the church, which is the body of Christ, and all believers are members of one another.[11]

In all this equality, it's just as likely that a sister will be a teacher, as a brother; it's just as likely that she will be an evangelist, as a brother; and pastoral tendencies will be just as evident in some sisters, as they are in some brethren. The same applies throughout the range of the gifts: her gift may be identical, but a difference will be seen in her sphere of service. This doesn't imply inequality or inferiority, simply that God has determined that her role is different. He has arranged that women should *"learn in silence with all submission,"* so they receive the same teaching as their brethren, even though they are not permitted to teach publicly in the church.[12] However, other opportunities are open to them, so that they can fulfil a speaking or written ministry, including one of teaching or encouraging.

In fact, older women are expected to be *"teachers of good things"*[13] (Gr. *Kalodidaskalos*) so this is one example of a God-given sphere, and there are others such as youth work and camps, and in missionary work. Some sisters have shown teaching ability in their letters to those who are going through difficult times, and their spiritual perception is well known. There are many ways of teaching, witnessing and encouraging, and God will always make sure that those He feeds are never without outlets for their gifts.

After listening to a message about spiritual gifts, a dear old sister was heard saying, "You're not trying to tell us that sisters are gifted, are you?" Yes, sisters, you are gifted. Your way of presenting His Word may be different, but doesn't this also happen among your brethren? Not all of them teach in the same way. They all teach from the same Book, many are gifted in Bible Class situations; others are able writers, but don't have a freedom in public preaching or teaching; and still others are called to share in a platform ministry. The vital thing is that brothers and sisters are led by the Spirit of God to share the Word of God with fellow-believers, relatives, friends and neighbours.

Romans 16 is a wonderful example of sisters' gift. Right from its opening verse, we are introduced to Phoebe, who evidently was as bright as her name implies, and her brightness shone as a sister, a servant and as a supporter of many, including Paul. Then we meet Priscilla and Aquila, a wife and husband, renowned as Paul's fellow-workers and as teachers who helped to equip Apollos in *"the way of God more accurately."*[14] A whole list follows, including Tryphena and Tryphosa who, even though their names mean Dainty and Delicate, wore themselves out in the Lord. Each generation has its sisters who are of great practical help in many ways, but all should know that God has called and gifted you for a spiritual role among His people.

Foot ... Hand ... Ear ... Eye

If ever there was any difficulty about identifying gift in an assembly, Paul helps us in 1 Corinthians 12 to accept that they ought to be recognisable. By illustrating the connections of the human body, he shows the interaction of spiritual gifts in the local assembly, as its character reflects the church, which is the body of Christ.[15] None is isolated from the other, and none is invited to think of itself as being of lesser value. For instance, the foot should never say it's of lesser value than a hand, nor should the ear ever say it's inferior to the eye. We are not graded in a way that makes anyone more important or less important. All that matters is that an aspect of Christ is being fulfilled in you.

Paul's reasoning seems to be that, just as the members are recognisable in the physical body – we know what a foot looks like, what a hand looks like, and what they do – therefore we should know what a teacher looks like. We should know what an evangelist sounds like and we should know who fills the role of a helper or one of administrations by what they do in the service of God.

Just as He Pleased

God's pleasure should be our highest motivation, our greatest obligation, and our deepest satisfaction. His choice of us, and purpose in us, is *"according to the good pleasure of His will."*[16] That is how our spiritual journey began, and it will end at the coming of the Lord when He gives each of us a body *"as He pleases."*[17] As for the present, Paul says that our setting *"in the body"* is *"just as He pleased"*[18] so we need to see what His objective is in the spiritual gifts.

This should prompt each one of us to ask some serious questions. Should my own body be for His pleasure? Should my assembly, as a small reflection of the church, which is His body, be for His pleasure? Yes, but can we know how? Again, the answer is "Yes." In the context of Romans 12, can I fulfil my gift and not fulfill verses 1 and 2? Or can I fulfill these verses and not fulfill my gift? Now the obvious answer is "No." There's real value in seeing why gifts are included in chapter 12, and not in one of the other chapters, for they are integral to the holiness and acceptability of presenting our bodes as a living sacrifice. God's pleasure rests on you and your service being laid on the altar as a sacrifice to Him, and in you fulfilling the first two verses by fulfilling the next five.

It's similar in 1 Corinthians 12. Can I serve my Lord and Master in an assembly without fulfilling my place in the church, which is His body? Is it possible that an assembly can profit without us fulfilling our gifts? In this chapter, God leaves us in no doubt that His saints profit through the ministry of the gifts and, for this reason, it's vital that a combination of gifts provides what each brother and sister doesn't possess. Our bodies are wonderful examples of the interdependent unity in the church, which is His body, and God purposefully transfers this image to the local assembly and says of its character, *"Now you are the body of Christ."*[19]

More questions arise when we look into Ephesians chapter 4. Verse 12 alerts us to the fact that our gifts are *"for the equipping of the saints for the work of ministry, for the edifying of the body of Christ."* There are evangelists, pastors and teachers, and other gifts besides, but the real test of our ministry is in knowing how it is equipping the saints. How is our ministry helping to build up the church, which is the body of Christ? We say to all our brothers and sisters that if your ministry helps the work of someone else, and their input helps you, then our mutual care for each other brings us to what Peter has written. His aim is *"that in all things God may be glorified."* Is it possible fully to do this without the God-honouring service of the gifts? On a personal level, we ask, "Can I really glorify God without fulfilling my gift?" Well, we can glorify God in our prayer lives; we can glorify Him by desiring to be Christ-like, and by growing in the grace and knowledge of our Lord Jesus Christ (2 Pet.3:18). All this will glorify God, but Peter encourages us to make sure we also glorify Him in the use of our gift.

A Man's Gift

Before rounding off this chapter, it may be worthwhile looking at an often-quoted verse from the Old Testament book of Proverbs, which says, *"A man's gift makes room for him, and brings him before great men."*[20] Some have used this to suggest that a brother's spiritual gift will overcome his timidity and bring him to the foreground of spiritual service. God certainly will enable those whom He calls, but this is not what Solomon had in mind. He was thinking about a bribe, some would call it a backhander, which causes some to turn a blind eye to an offence and makes the offender accepted.

Spiritual gifts belong to the New Testament teaching of the church, which is the body of Christ, and, of course, nothing of this was known in Solomon's day. So, whenever you hear this particular verse cited in the matter of spiritual gifts, you know it really doesn't apply. Even so, there's plenty to encourage you in the New Testament of your Bible, and God is waiting for you, even if it's only to fill a little space and Christ being glorified.

> "Father, where shall I work today?
> And my love flowed warm and free
> And he pointed me out a tiny spot
> And he said, "Tend that for Me."
>
> I answered quickly, "Oh no, not that!
> Why, no one would ever see
> However well the work was done,
> Not that little place for me."
>
> The word he spoke, it was not stern,
> He answered me tenderly:
> "Ah, little one, search that heart of thine,
> Are you working for them or for Me?
> Nazareth was just a little place, so was Galilee."
> *(Meade MacGuire)*

1.9 GRACE REFLECTED IN LEADERSHIP

"The elders who are among you I exhort, I who am a fellow elder and a witness of the sufferings of Christ, and also a partaker of the glory that will be revealed: shepherd the flock of God which is among you, serving as overseers, not by compulsion but willingly, not for dishonest gain but eagerly; nor as being lords over those entrusted to you, but being examples to the flock; and when the Chief Shepherd appears, you will receive the crown of glory that does not fade away.

Likewise you younger people, submit yourselves to your elders. Yes, all of you be submissive to one another, and be clothed with humility, for 'God resists the proud, but gives grace to the humble.' Therefore humble yourselves under the mighty hand of God, that He may exalt you in due time, casting all your care upon Him, for He cares for you" (1 Pet.5:1-7).

* * *

To Peter, grace is a kaleidoscope. It has been conveniently packaged into a one-size-fits-all GRACE acrostic – God's Riches At Christ's Expense – which suits our modern liking for soundbites, but it doesn't quite capture Peter's thinking. His own word, *"manifold,"* is colourful in itself, yet it describes only one aspect of God's riches regarding spiritual gifts. To him, their spectrum of usefulness in service is like a range of heavenly iridescent colour, like aurora borealis or aurora australis, yet much more. He sees the nature of God, resplendent in Christ, in each chapter with all their colours blending: it's eternal, sacrificial, experimental, marital, Pentecostal, and now a new colour comes into the mix, for it is pastoral.

Left to ourselves, we might struggle to equate or define leadership with grace, but how graciously Peter does it for us! In its earlier expressions, in chapter 1 it's evidently for everyone who owns God's salvation; then it's for all who engage in spiritual service, brothers and sisters alike. Moving into chapter 3, it's for wives and husbands, as a beautiful reflection of *"Husbands, love your wives, just as Christ also loved the church and gave Himself for her."*[1] But, even here, it is extended to *"all of you"* in its wide-ranging aspects of care. The beauty of chapter 4's array of gift is that no one is missed out. Without exception, every believer is included. Then we step into chapter 5, and there seems to be a sudden change, but is there?

PASTORAL GRACE

There's no doubt whatsoever that Peter is speaking to a group within a much larger group – *"the elders who are among you"* – so it's not everyone who is called to share in the work of overseers among the gatherings of the Lord's people, yet all are called to relate to them in their work. We are called to be supportive of them, to a sense of a common understanding and mutual appreciation. It's with a deep sense of God and His will that, just as they fulfil their responsibilities as overseers, so also does the flock. So, as we think about pastoral grace, we want to see it from both sides. We are looking at brethren who are called by God to be overseers and to the rest of us who are called within the range of assembly service to acknowledge that their responsibility to Him and the flock needs to be reflected in our responsibility to Him and to them.

Some versions begin 1 Peter 5:1 by saying, *"Therefore"* or *"So,"* which links it directly to what has been said before and translates *presbuterous oun* as *"Elders therefore."* As we read the end of chapter 4, we may wonder why Peter didn't introduce his message to the elders at the beginning of chapter 3, when he had just referred to the Lord Jesus Christ as *"the Shepherd and*

Overseer of your souls." He must have expected these dear brethren to trace his reasoning farther back than the thought of Christians suffering in 1 Peter 4:19 to the sufferings of Christ in 1 Peter 2:21-25.

We were thinking of how Peter has gone very carefully from the grace that was required in the man to the grace that was restored in his mistakes, and these remind us of our own need for remedial grace. Overseers are not exempt from being under the umbrella of requiring grace, or of needing times of restoring and uplifting grace. They must never lose their sense of all the aspects of grace that have come through the gospel, because we can't lose these and keep our understanding of the sheep. Missing out in our relationship with the Shepherd and Overseer of our souls will guarantee that we miss out in our relationship with His flock.

Elders are among the flock. In some ways it's true that they are over the sheep[2] but time after time the apostles, both Paul and Peter, use the word *"among."*[3] When Peter thought about overseers in all five regions, he was pointing out to the assemblies that these men know what you are going through. They are in it with you. They are among you, not at a distance from you. The Shepherd must never be far from his sheep. In much of a shepherd's work on a farm, practically speaking, he's within hand's reach of his sheep. If this is true in the physical realm, it's equally true in the spiritual. If we don't live in a close relationship with the sheep there will be greater difficulty in assisting them in their times of need.

'Among the flock' means being in touch. These men faced the same circumstances. Their struggles were the same, for they also lived as foreign residents in a country that wasn't theirs. They'd been dispersed throughout this region and as total strangers they were spiritual pilgrims who had to make the best of it. God had put them there and in His sovereignty had a reason for doing so: He would be glorified, even on the basis of this one condition, that pastoral grace would be appreciated among the elders and among the flock.

Peter then changed the imagery by saying, *"Shepherd the flock which is among you,"* so there was a real sense of intermingling and mutual belonging. The shepherd doesn't feel like a stranger among the sheep, and the sheep don't feel like strangers among their overseers. These people were connected, in the goodness of God; they belonged to one another. The Greek language puts it differently for it speaks about 'the among you flock' – *to en humin poimnion* – and this emphasises they are mutually placed, not only to be with one another, but there for one another. The flock was to be comfortable in the shepherds' company to show that:

- God ministers to us through you;
- We sense the hand of God in your touch;
- We hear the voice of God in your speech;
- We see the example of the Lord Jesus Christ in your manner.

Everything in the shepherds' conduct was sheep-related. At home on the farm, we can walk through a field and the sheep will scatter, but they will automatically come to the shepherd when he walks through. It's simple – they know who the Shepherd is. They know his voice and can sense his movements. Their eyes are rectangular, and have such good peripheral vision they can see behind them without turning their heads. They also have good memories and recognise those who care for them. Spiritually speaking, these are the kind of eyes spiritual shepherds need. It's not something we are born with, but by the grace of God and the help of the Spirit of God spiritual sight can be formed until it not only has sight, but an ability for insight. This is tremendously important in the heart and work of an overseer.

I Exhort

Peter's view of the flock is commendable for he says, *"I exhort."* What a lovely approach! As an apostle, he had been through three years of ministry with the Saviour walking at his side. He had gone through the difficulties of

Calvary and had been wonderfully used as the preacher at Pentecost. Now, as he writes, he has the authority of a man who has been called of God. He is Christlike in his appreciation of eternal and sacrificial grace, and has the authority to speak to them about their worship and witness, because he is a well-formed worshipper and fearless witness.

He also speaks with the authority of a married man whose wife accompanied him in the Lord's work,[4] and well equipped with spiritual gifts. By the time he addressed the elders in chapter 5, they would be in no doubt that he spoke with authority on each aspect of Christian service. Now he is the well-rounded overseer, shaped for the purpose and authorised by God to write to them. In other words, he lived his own letter. So what would he say, and how would he say it?

He could have said, *"I command you in the name of the Lord"* or *"I demand as an apostle with apostolic authority,"* but he didn't. He could have ordered them, but he spoke in pastoral grace, *"I exhort,"* and the word he used means he was coming alongside to call them. Even by the way he spoke, he drew near to work beside them. It's as if he were saying, "I want to draw near to you, and I want my ministry to have an effect on you. I want you to sense the voice of God in what I'm saying."

How tragic it would have been if God had not been heard! Oh, if this doesn't happen in our ministry there's something seriously missing, but there was nothing missing in Peter's. Along with his word of encouragement, there was his attitude of fellow-involvement: *"I who am a fellow elder."* This was the bondservant speaking. He could have said, *"I exhort you, I who am an apostle of Jesus Christ,"* and who would have questioned it? By divine inspiration, God spoke through His servant as a fellow shepherd, a fellow overseer, a fellow elder. He wasn't above them, nor were they beneath him. He was beside them as an equal. No tiers, only tears!

If you went to a market on a day when sheep were being sold, the men that lean on the ring bidding have only one thing in their minds. They are not talking about a host of other things, they are thinking about sheep. Meet shepherds at their work or in their homes, and it's highly likely they will be talking about sheep. What about us? When as elders we go into each other's company, does the conversation automatically turn to sheep; and sheep, in your homes does the conversation automatically turn to shepherds? That's the way it should be – not in a critical sense, but constructively with the voice of appreciation being heard.

Shepherd the Flock

When God was speaking through Peter about shepherding the flock, he used a word that simply means 'to feed'; so the verse could easily say, "Feed the flock of God." It's an interchangeable word. The Shepherd is expected to feed, he's a feeder; and the flock is entitled to be fed. When we walk and work among the saints of God as shepherds our priority is to feed.

The only time sheep will come to a stranger in a field is when they hear the familiar sound of a bag of feed or smell the attraction of a bale. In one way, it's very easy to feed sheep – you just need to go into the field, scatter some feed and they'll come. It may be different in wintertime. There are times when deep snow means it's a long way down to uncover any grass, and it would be pointless to throw cake or hay into the snow. A space must be cleared where you can spread some feeding, so it's not simply a matter of making it available, it has to be accessible.

That's the work of the overseer, too. He must make the teaching of God's Word accessible as well as available. It has to be something that's enjoyable; not something they have to search for, but something that has been searched out for them. The shepherd has to provide in a way that means the sheep can't miss it, and it has to be the number one priority that he doesn't leave the field without knowing his sheep have been fed. There's a whole range of ministry that is reflected in shepherding and if you were following a shepherd on a farm you would soon discover lots of spiritual parallels. In many ways, we would see things being done that ought to have counterparts in your church.

The New King James version of the Bible quotes Peter as speaking to men who are *"serving as overseers,"* which is clearer than the Revised Version's *"exercising the oversight."* The word *"oversight"* is easily misunderstood and misapplied. Many use it to describe an overseers' meeting or a company of overseers, but the word Peter used – *episkopountes* – isn't an adjective or a noun. It's a verb, so oversight is something that overseers do and applies to overseers overseeing, and to when these particular men are doing what they are. This is similar to what we have in Psalm 23. We are accustomed to saying, *"The LORD is my Shepherd,"* yet the Hebrew word *ra'ah* is a verb and means "The LORD shepherds me." Other examples of this are found in Ezekiel 34 where the same word for shepherd is a verb six times in verse 2 and throughout the chapter.

It seems unlikely that Peter could write about this without thinking of the Lord's conversation with him after His resurrection when He spoke about feeding and tending His sheep. The words can mean very different things for feeding is something that can be done when sheep are together, whereas there are other aspects of shepherding that can't be done collectively.

Tending sheep can include shearing, dipping, dosing, paring sore feet, or helping one that has fallen on to its back. Each of these must be done individually. It's very evident in shearing - as soon as you take the fleece from a sheep, you will likely see it leap in the air. It will normally hoist itself as if it were on springs at the delight at being released from the weight it's been carrying around. That's one effect a shepherd can have by doing one job – but there are other things too.

In a similar way, the flock of God can be fed when the assembly is together and more widely at District conferences and the like, but it's very unlikely that tending will be achieved without personal interaction with the shepherd. There are times when sheep have to be medicated. But there's no point in medicating one and assuming that others will benefit. In our work with one another, the pastoral evidence of grace is the spiritual good that shepherds provide for each one. As assistants of the great Shepherd who has gone above, we need to know what medication each sheep needs. We need to ask, "What is there about its behaviour that I need to understand?" If we don't understand the way of a sheep we will never understand how to medicate it, and that's one of the great ministries of shepherding in the spiritual atmosphere of an assembly.

There are times when a sheep has to be turned upside down and its feet examined because something, such as dried mud or a small stone, has compacted between the cleats of its feet. The sheep will limp around and its walk may be so badly affected it will not lie down. As it moves around, it needs the eye of the shepherd to spot it and deal with its feet, for only then will it walk normally and be able to rest. There's a day coming when God will gather the lame[5] and, by His great shepherding, He will bring Israel back to Himself. He will show them the Man of Calvary, their limping days will be over, and they will walk with Him at last.[6]

Sometimes a sheep may fall over on its back and not be able to right itself, especially if its fleece is heavy. The only way to help is to stand the sheep up between your legs and stay there until it recovers. Leaving it too soon to stand on its own can mean it will tumble over again, due to poor blood circulation in its legs. Christians can go through stages of limping too, and we can be in real danger of losing them if we don't attend to their walk at the proper time or spend enough time with them.

There are times in our Christian lives when all these shepherding skills are needed in a spiritual sense: the shepherds need to be aware of the opportunity, and the sheep also need to be aware that they can depend on the shepherd providing that ministry.

It was David who said, *"He makes me to lie down in green pastures."*[7] Sheep are not dogs. You can't tell one to sit, and it's impossible to make one lie down. You have to be able to look at sheep and know what will 'cause' them to lie down. This is what David meant. Provide the right conditions and they will lie down. It's one of the wonders of shepherding that the sheep know themselves when to lie down but the shepherd has a lot to do with it.

First of all, he has to make sure they're fed and well-watered. Sheep won't lie down if they are still hungry or thirsty; nor will they lie down if there's something wrong with their feet; and thirdly, they won't lie down if there's a predator in the field. The sound or sighting of a fox in a field will keep sheep from lying down. They will circle their lambs, protecting them as best as they can. If they have twins, they can cope, but if she has triplets then one of them is almost guaranteed to go, because she can't protect all three.

Overseers are not superhuman, neither are their sheep, and sometimes they get stretched in how they are to look after this one and that one. The danger is that while looking after one they may just miss the attack that is taking place on another. It's a difficulty that shepherds, both natural and spiritual, have to admit. The opportunity of being everywhere at once is just not possible.

Likewise, You Younger

Peter deals so patiently with these dear men that are doing the shepherding work, and then he urges younger men to submit to them – now there are those who take this to mean he was addressing younger overseers and, if that's what you think of the portion, let me be the last to take it away from you. However, it seems equally likely that he was broadening his appeal and application, just as he did in chapter 3 with *"wives ... husbands ... all of you."* It seems to be by the same widening of his reasoning that a further aspect of submission is presented in chapter 5 – *"The elders ... Likewise you younger ... all of you"* – as widening circles. The elders are like moulds – Gr. *tupos*: types or patterns – for others to emulate. As elders, in more ways than one, he calls for them to be respected, and for everyone in the churches to embrace the opportunity to wear the servant's apron of submission and humility.

In this way, everyone would know that they are important to the shepherds, and the shepherds would know that they are important to the sheep. Peter must have thought about the Lord Jesus Christ giving this example to His disciples in the Upper Room when He laid aside his garments, just as he had laid aside His glory. And now he says *"be clothed with humility"* – be like the Saviour, humble yourselves under the mighty hand of God. He wore the towel for our sakes, and now we hear Peter's appeal to wear the apron for His sake!

The Chief Shepherd

Peter would never forget the day when the Good Shepherd came to his beach looking for fishermen,[8] and he left his nets to follow Him. Following wasn't always his strongpoint, and he knew that he had let Him down, but then the Great Shepherd[9] appeared in resurrection and spoke to him about the matter of leadership.[10] In marvellous grace he was then enabled to preach in Jerusalem in response to the coming of the Holy Spirit, and how able he was! Quoting freely from Joel's prophecy and from David's psalms, he spoke as a man of God who was immersed in the Word of God and filled by the Spirit of God to speak about the Christ of God.[11] At the end of his message, he watched as droves of sheep came forward at the sound of their Shepherd's voice, and they followed Him into the first church planting that ever took place.

The Lord introduced himself as the good Shepherd[12] – the dying One; the writer to the Hebrews introduced Him as the great Shepherd – the risen One; but it was Peter the leader who introduced Him as the Chief Shepherd

– the coming One. As we wait for His coming, what a blessing it would be, and what assemblies we would be, if every sheep and every lamb knew that the hand of a shepherd had touched it, ministered to it, assisted it whether in its walk or in its feeding as a demonstration of the pastoral grace of God.

1.10 GRACE REGAINED IN BIBLICAL TRUTHS

"But may the God of all grace, who called us to His eternal glory by Christ Jesus, after you have suffered a while, perfect, establish, strengthen, and settle you. To Him be the glory and the dominion forever and ever. Amen. By Silvanus, our faithful brother as I consider him, I have written to you briefly, exhorting and testifying that this is the true grace of God in which you stand" (1 Pet.5:10-12).

* * *

God has His own way of showing that He is the source and the supplier. There are different times when He reveals Himself as the "God of," and then says that something is "of God."

Reference	Source	Supplier	Reference
Ex.5:1	God of Israel	Israel of God	Gal.6:16
Deut.32:4	God of truth	Truth of God	Rom.1:25
1 Sam.2:3	God of knowledge	Knowledge of God	Prov.2:5
Ps.29:3	God of glory	Glory of God	Ps.19:1
Ps.59:17	God of mercy	Mercy of God	Ps.52:8
Ps.68:20	God of salvation	Salvation is of the Lord	Jon.2:9
Rom.15:33	God of peace	Peace of God	Phil.4:7
2 Cor.1:3	God of all comfort	Comfort of God	2 Cor.1:4
2 Cor.13:11	God of love	Love is of God	1 Jn 4:7

As he came to the end of his letter, Peter knew that grace had been well presented, like the recurring movement of a musical overture that comes to the fore, only to recede before rising again to a more rousing finale. But he knew that he wasn't the composer, and that the variations had come from a greater mind than his own. It was in this certainty that he bound them together in unison to ascribe glory to their source in *"the God of all grace"* and to exalt Him as the sharer of *"the true grace of God."* So the character of God comes out in what He does and the glories of His Being are shared with us in such a way that He is glorified in those who own His grace.

Having traced its varied applications in all he has written, it's as if Peter wanted to gather the whole message under one canopy before closing. He had been given the honour of being one of God's penmen, but he knew that while he was the communicator of God's grace, he was not its mediator. This belongs to the One who called him from his boat to cast a greater net for Him, and he knew that all its facets would cause us, like Paul, to speak of it as *"the grace of our Lord Jesus Christ."*[1]

When Paul was closing his second letter to Corinth, in his benediction – *"the grace of the Lord Jesus Christ, and the love of God, and the communion of the Holy Spirit"*[2] – he was thinking about the grace of the One who:

- Gave Himself for us (Gal.2:20);
- Saved us (Eph.2:8);
- Brought us to God (Heb.2:10; 1 Pet.3:18);
- Pleads for us before God (Rom.8:34; 1 Jn 2:1);
- Receives and perfects our worship (1 Pet.2:5);
- Is coming for us (1 Cor.15:50,51).

The letter to the Hebrews speaks about the Holy Spirit being *"the Spirit of grace,"*[3] so He also fulfils an intermediary role. Just as we are indebted to the Saviour for bringing us to God through His redeeming and reconciling work on the cross, we owe deep gratitude to the Spirit of grace for bringing us to Christ. It is in grace that He:

- Convict us of sin, and of righteousness, and of judgment;
- Guides us into all truth;
- Reveals the beauties of Christ to us (Jn 16:8,13,14);
- Intercedes for us in prayer (Rom.8:27);
- Leads us in our daily walk (Gal.6:16);
- Leads us in worship and prayer (Phil.3:3; Eph.6:18).

All three Persons put us hand in hand with each other, so that we might enjoy fellowship with Them. It doesn't mean that the Son's saving work caused God's grace to be given to us; it's the other way around: the grace of God the Father caused the saving work of the Lord Jesus to bring His salvation. We look at Him, as John did in chapter 1 of his gospel, and we see Him as *"full of grace."* He is what God is, and the grace of the triune, co-equal God is behind the wealth of grace through which we are saved and kept. Together, They are *"the God of all grace."*

There's no shortage of references to grace in the world. Many speak of "the grace of god", but it's of a god with a small 'g.' It was no different in Peter's day. Idols were everywhere, yet they were incapable of imparting grace, and it's still the same. They have mouths that can't speak, so there are no words of grace; they have eyes that can't see, so there's no look of grace; they have hands that can't handle, so there's no touch of grace; they have feet that can't walk, so there's no companionship of grace.[4] Grace has no source outside of the Father, Son and Holy Spirit, and where there is no source there can be no sharing. It cannot be found elsewhere apart from Them; They are the co-equal source and, having exactly the same nature, They are co-equal sharers.

DOCTRINAL GRACE

But Peter wants to take us farther. He wants us to see that, since grace resides in the God of all grace as one united Person, He shares it through one united purpose in *"the true grace of God."* It's the summation of all he has been writing. It's not that we take refuge in His eternal and sacrificial grace in chapter 1 and decide to go no farther. There's more, much more. Like Paul in Galatians 3, where He who supplies the Spirit expects us to begin and continue by the Spirit,[5] with Peter we begin and continue by grace. Before God in worship, before men in witness in the world and in the workplace, before our families in the home, before the assembly in the discharge of spiritual gifts, and before the flock in leadership, grace abounds.

Going into chapter 1 is like entering an archway that has the inscription, *"The God of all grace,"* and, having seen all its aspects, we emerge from the other side to read its corresponding statement: *"This is the true grace of God."* Peter has been led by the Spirit of God to gather up all that has been highlighted in a way that was, as he calls it, *di oligōn* – through a little while. It hasn't been a major treatise on each aspect of teaching, yet he was in no doubt that they should give believers a greater sense of God. In the accumulation of grace, in the aggregate of teaching, we should discover, not only that grace is revealed, but a greater revelation of God. This brings us to the question: having paused briefly at each stage, have we been brought closer to Him?

Each aspect of teaching unveils His character, and this in itself should give us affection for and appreciation of doctrine. Sometimes, words such as theology and doctrine are treated as the poor relations of our Christian walk, but Peter's mind is that we need to see them as God sees them. They are His 'doctrinal grace'; the presentation and explanation of His kindness to us in Christ. Even in their suffering, the truths of God's grace were to be the strength in which they would actively take their stand.

"Leave to His sovereign sway to choose and to command;
So shalt thou, wondering, own that way, how wise, how strong His hand.
Far, far above thy thought, His counsel shall appear,
When fully He the work hath wrought that caused thy needless fear."
(Paul Gerhardt)

Perfect, Establish, Strengthen and Settle

It's probably true that the fisherman can be taken away from fishing, but that fishing can't be taken away from the fisherman. Peter knew all about the work of perfecting. In fact, it would be an everyday practice in Galilee. When the Lord moved on from calling him and Andrew, they were at His side when He called James and John who were busy mending their nets. They'd been out fishing and the nets had broken, so they were going through the careful work of tying the loose ends together to make the fishing net intact again. The fisherman's future depends on this; the Greeks called it *katartizō*, and it's the very word Peter has drawn from his own background and used for *"perfect."*

111

Like fishing nets, damage can be done to the network of Christian character and conduct, so that they become less effective. The work of repair and restoration is just as vital in Christian life, and Peter lets us know that the God of all grace is ready to mend the mesh that the stresses of life have tested beyond breaking point. In a very different line of work, a doctor would have used the same word for resetting a bone, and this also helps us to see the hand of God at work when someone has been hurt. When things go wrong, He will put them right. Whenever you feel the hurt of things that are hard to understand, He will help to reset the situation. Some nets are harder to mend than others, some bones are so fractured it's almost impossible to reset them, and sometime Christians find it difficult to let the Lord restore them by His grace.

He also will establish you. We are not always as spiritually stable as we should be through our own lack of steadfastness. Times set apart for reading and study of God's Word become less until they disappear altogether, times of prayer go, and our whole sense of having a stable relationship with the Lord is lost. It's a self-inflicted wound, but sometimes others can stumble you. The adversary knows how to use this. Paul asked the Galatians, *"You were running well. Who hindered you?"*[6] He also knows how to keep you from getting over it. Scripture says, *"A brother offended is harder to win than a strong city"* (Prov.18:19), and this is very true, but it's equally true that being unforgiving will stop the stabilising process.

The God of all grace is able to establish you. His grace can cure all instability and solidify your relationship with Him, and He can rebuild when needed, but He has to establish us first. He wants to take what He has given you in salvation and build on it in such a way that the former instability will have gone and He is able to do something through you to His glory.

He also wants to strengthen, to empower you by removing whatever weakness has limited your progress, and replace it with divine strength. Each of us knows the things that cripple spiritual progress, and perhaps

112

mediocrity is among the most likely causes. Did you ever think that this could be the biggest danger in churches, too? We can be content with the ordinary when we have a God of unlimited ability who is able to build, develop and expand through us if only we would allow Him.

Another is being content to drift along in the shallows without ever going deeper, happy with an average middle-of-the-road sort of commitment. Daniel's words are as true today as they always were: *"the people who know their God shall be strong, and carry out great exploits."*[7] There's a tendency in our lives for something to creep in and obstruct the perfecting work that God wants to fulfil, something that prevents whatever He wants to build in us. He is able to reach others and touch them through us, yet mediocrity and the possibility of just drifting along will remove the opportunity of the Spirit of God ministering to others in such a way that He not only strengthens you but helps others to be strengthened through you.

Finally, God wants to settle you. You may look back on times when you felt really unsettled, as if the foundation of your Christian life had been shaken. Being settled is the opposite of being unstable, and God wants to replace that unsettled feeling. You will remember that when dear old Jacob was dying, he gathered his twelve boys at his bedside and had something very personal to say to each of them. Here was an old father speaking to his boys for the last time. One thing is certain, none of them would ever forget what was said to him. Starting with the eldest, he said, *"Reuben, you are ... unstable as water."*[8]

If you had been standing at that bedside, can you think of what he would have said to you? God knows that all of us need to be stabilised by a foundation, and that spiritual service is impossible without one. Even the portable structure of the tabernacle had one in the form of its "sockets." They were called *'eden*, which can also mean "foundation."[9] They are related to *'adōn* (lord), and *Adonāi*, such as in Psalm 8:1 – *"O LORD, our Lord [Yahweh 'Adonēnū] how excellent is Your name in all the earth!"* So the tabernacle stood in sockets that announced His lordship. Later, the temple had its foundations of *"large stones, costly stones, and hewn stones,"*[10] so that God's dwelling place on earth might reflect what He has done in heaven.

Of it, He says, *"Behold, I lay in Zion a stone for a foundation, a tried stone, a precious corner stone, a sure foundation."* He was speaking of His exalted Son, and risen Victor of the cross: well proven, infinitely precious, and eternally sure. His own description of Christ is that He is a *"sure foundation,"* which in Hebrew is *musād mussād.* In Psalm 45:2, He is seen as *yāph---eyāphiythā,* "fair fair" or "beautiful beautiful," and both duplications mean He is beyond description. As Son, and Stone, He is greater, costlier and more tested than any other, and it's only on Him that God can *"perfect, establish, strengthen, and settle you."*

It's for this reason that one aspect of His true grace is to lay a sure foundation for our lives of service, and to make it possible the Son became identified with His Father making Him perfect. For our sakes He experienced *katartizō* when God "prepared" a body for Him. He was prepared for suffering, and it was this that allowed *"the grace of God"* to appear.[11] In the experience of believers, God perfects them through suffering. The wonderful truth is that Christ's perfect network of attributes is made known to us through the teaching of Scripture, and it's this that allowed John to write, *"He who abides in the doctrine of Christ has both the Father and the Son."*[12] It takes the truth that is in Jesus [13] to let us know Him and enjoy everything that belongs to the true grace of God.

Perfected

There is something else to enjoy. The one whom God made perfect for suffering also knew what it was to be *"made perfect"* (RV) through suffering.[14] Unlike Aaron, who became high priest and offered many sacrifices for others and himself, Jesus offered one sacrifice for sins forever[15] – for others, and not Himself – and was *"perfected."*[16]

The thought, this time, is very different. Instead of *katartizō*, the word is now *teleiōtheis*, which means He became the completer of His Father's will. As finisher of the work that had been given Him to do, He entered into the gain of His cross as the author, the cause, of eternal salvation. He also became equipped as High Priest, having been *"perfected forever."*[17]

So, He is the means of our salvation; we have been *"perfected forever"* and set apart in holiness.[18] He also is the means of our service. He came as the perfect Man and, having fulfilled His Father's will as sin-bearer, went Home as the perfected Man. As for believers, He has brought us into His Father's will, and we are going Home perfected forever.

As we listen to these closing verses of Peter's letter, what is our response as he says, *"May the God of all Grace, who called us to His eternal glory in Christ Jesus ... perfect ... you."*? Will you let him perfect you? Do you know of areas in your life where He needs to perfect you? Could you actually sit down and identify what He sees that others may not see? They might think you are doing fine, but we know there are times when, under the eyesight of God, something is being seen that only He and we know about. He wants to perfect us, that in our maturing He may see integrity, quality and stability and the removal of frailty, impurity, mediocrity and instability.

Will we let Him remove them?

Of course, He may ask to walk through each of Peter's five chapters with you and ask you to read it as He were at your side. To settle you, He may want to spend some time with you, just to have a talk about each one.

Will you let Him:

- Restore to you the joy of His salvation in chapter 1?
- Refresh your worship and witness in chapter 2?
- Renew your marriage and revive your desire for holiness in chapter 3?

- Reignite the flame of usefulness in your gift in chapter 4?
- Recover your zeal to lead or be led in chapter 5?

The God of all grace is asking you to take your stand and, as you pause with Him chapter by chapter, He will give you the grace to keep standing in the true grace of God till Jesus comes.

> "Shall we, dare we disappoint Him? Brethren, let us rise!
> He who died for us is watching from the skies."
> *(Alice J. Janvrin)*

1.11 GRACE RE-EMPHASISED IN PAUL'S LETTERS

"For you know the grace of our Lord Jesus Christ, that though He was rich, yet for your sakes He became poor, that you through His poverty might become rich" (2 Cor.8:9).

* * *

Do you ever look at a verse in your Bible and ask it a question? For instance, why is God saying this right here when the same verse would seem so apt in many other places? Could it not have been appropriately slotted into Peter's letter alongside one of his many references to grace? Let's imagine we had been absorbing what he said about God's 'eternal grace' in chapter 1, and thinking of what this meant to the Saviour in His condescension. Would we have been surprised if he then went on to say, *"For you know the grace of our Lord Jesus Christ, that though He was rich, yet for your sakes He became poor, that you through His poverty might become rich"*?

Had we been thinking of 'sacrificial grace' and the value of the Lord Jesus Christ offering Himself to God for His satisfaction as well as ours, would Paul's words not have been a very fitting addition? When the Holy Spirit led us and put our hands into the hands of Christ to know Him as our Saviour, right at that moment God could have said, *"You know the grace of our Lord Jesus Christ."*

The same question could be asked as we read on and apply it to thoughts of experimental grace that causes us to worship God and witness to others. Would it not have relevance to us as we experience 'marital grace' in our home lives? Then He enriches us again through the variegated grace of spiritual gifts, and we seek to fill the place for which He has fitted us. At that point too, He says, "You know." The whole way through to what we have considered of 'pastoral grace' and 'doctrinal grace,' would it have felt out of place if these words about the Lord's enriching grace were attached?

No, at any one of these points we probably would feel the impact of the Spirit of God as He whispers, "You know ... you know." Peter's letter is so Christ-centred, but these words don't belong here; God has set them in 2 Corinthians 8:9, so we have to decide why they are there and not in 1 Peter with all the accumulated reference to the wonders of God's grace.

Paul tells us why it's here. It's because the Macedonians were an outstanding example of giving and he was giving the church in Corinth a lesson on generosity based on the dear ones in the churches in Berea, Philippi and Thessalonica. He was using them as a model, but wanted to raise Corinth's sights even higher to the greatest Giver of all by saying, *"For you know the grace of our Lord Jesus Christ, that though He was rich, yet for your sakes He became poor, that you through His poverty might become rich."* It was said in the context of selfless surrender that was for the good of others, and there is no greater example of this than the Saviour Himself. There are many who give of themselves, but only One who gave Himself! He went out bearing the cross for Himself, knowing that it would bear Him, and that on it He would bear our sins in His own body. It's also true that there have been many gracious men and women, but only He is "Grace."

When God says, *"You know the grace of our Lord Jesus Christ,"* He expects us to breathe in the value of what He has breathed out. These are His words about His Son who is "The grace" – co-equal with the God of all grace of 1 Peter 5:10. As co-equal, He also is co-eternal, and this is included in the words *"though He was rich."* The word "was" sounds very ordinary, but God is so exact He uses two different words to convey what He means. One means "always was," and the other means "became." The Son of God is eternally rich, but became temporarily poor. The difference is set out in John 1. In verses 1, 2 and 4, the word "was" is the same six times. It is *ēn*, which belongs to the word *eimi*. When we read of the Lord being the "I AM", the words are *egō eimi*, which means He eternally was, is, and will be. He is the eternal Word, the eternal light, and the eternal life.

The striking thing about John is that he knew when to use this word, and he knew when not to use it. However, when he said, *"without Him nothing was made that was made,"* he used a different word. This time he twice uses *egeneto*, which means it became or it happened. So there's a hugely important distinction between the two words. God is very careful in His use of words and He never leaves His writers with loose grammar.

His Poverty

If you are already thinking that Paul used the first word, you are absolutely right. By saying, *"He was rich,"* he meant eternally rich, the riches of the eternal I AM. But He became poor, not simply in a financial way, but in His whole lifestyle that brought the limitations of hunger, thirst, tiredness and weakness. And He did this *"for your sakes."* His poverty in becoming our substitute has brought us the riches of His substitutionary work. How humbling it is that this purpose was in the counsels of Deity even before creation, and overwhelming to think that the place of substitution was marked out as it was being created. As Abraham and Isaac made their way to Moriah, the Maker watched and knew they were bound for the place where He would give His life as a ransom for many.[1] Yes, God will provide the lamb,[2] and He did it at Calvary in the Lamb slain from the foundation of the world.[3]

Brothers and sisters, you know the grace of our Lord Jesus Christ. He gave

Himself sacrificially, substitutionally and sovereignly in the sovereignty of God. Does that not move you? Does it not make you bow at your Saviour's feet to thank Him for thinking you were worth it? He is not only wealthy, He is worthy, yet through His poverty He took your unworthiness to transform you. God designed you and took that old clay jar, broke you at your Saviour's feet, and turned you into a vessel of mercy prepared beforehand for glory.[4] For your sake He became poor.

El Shaddai the Mighty One was crucified in weakness. God the eternal was confined in six hours of absolute agony and misery, God the all-knowing wondering why the Father had forsaken Him; yet knowing, at the same time, it was that He might never forsake us. He laid aside His glory that He might bring us to glory. These are contrasts that He built into his life for our sakes. He became poor, but how do you define the poverty of Christ? The Lord used the same word about Lazarus: *"a certain beggar,"*[5] which means He became beggarly poor. But did he mean financially? Was it only by asking the spies to show Him a penny[6] that He demonstrated His poverty? No, the poverty of Christ has nothing to do with being financial, or our riches in Him would be financial. This is no prosperity gospel, other than that he makes your soul prosper not your pocket.

Is there not something far richer about the Lord Jesus to be experienced than financial? Is the answer not that, just as His poverty was identified with His humanity partaking of our humanity, so our riches belong to being linked with the riches of his divinity? We are partakers of the divine nature.[7] He became a partaker of flesh and blood,[8] and was made in the likeness of sinful flesh.[9] He had the resemblance, but was never an identical. He partook of our humanity, but not our depravity. The ingredient of sin was missing, yet it was in becoming Man that He became poor.

Our Riches

In the north of Burma, it's common to see eggs in the collection box, cabbages and bananas laid on the floor beside it, and rice poured into a separate basket. This is how they fulfil 1 Corinthians 16:2 – *"On the first day of the week let each one of you lay something aside, storing up as he may prosper."* They know how to give, as the Macedonians did, and we could borrow Paul's words to describe them: *"sorrowful, yet always rejoicing; as poor, yet making many rich; as having nothing, and yet possessing all things."* Do we ever wonder if we might be in danger of possessing all things materially, yet having nothing spiritually?

Once again, we hear the words, *"He became poor, that you through His poverty might become rich."* He never had to become rich, but He did have to become poor. We are just the opposite. We didn't have to become poor, but we did need to become rich. He saw us in our poverty and gave up His riches to sacrifice Himself to bring us to God and into His riches. But what are they?

-The riches of His goodness speak of what He does. He leads sinners to repentance. In His goodness, He brings us out of the poverty of sin, its guilt and sorrow, into the riches of His forgiveness, peace and hope. Even repentance itself is a blessing for, even though it is the result of godly sorrow, it brings us into the joy of salvation and never brings regret.[10]

-The riches of His grace speak of what He gives. He causes us to discover the good pleasure of His will by which He grants redemption through his blood with the forgiveness of sins to all who are chosen in Christ before the foundation of the world, that we should be holy and without blemish before Him in love.[11]

-The riches of His glory speak of who He is. He shares the splendour of His own Being with our redeemed beings through the inner power of His Spirit and presence of Christ. Isn't that just like God? What grace to say He would grant you according to the riches of His glory, so that we might know what it is to be moved by His might and power through His Spirit in the inner man!

Having already known the riches of His goodness that prepare us for salvation, and the riches of His grace that provide us with salvation, God continues to share the riches of His glory so that He might be prominent in us after salvation. Only through the riches of His own glory can we enjoy the blessing of sharing His attributes – His might, His love, and every aspect of His likeness.[12]

The author G.F. Dempster is known to have said, "In all Christians, Christ is present; in some Christians, He is prominent; but in very few Christians, Christ is preeminent. God's purpose is that *"in all things He may have the preeminence,"*[13] and those who long for the riches of His glory and to be *"filled with all the fulness of God"* share His desire. We bring ourselves to Him like small containers before a much larger vessel. It's *of* His fulness we have all received,[14] not *all* His fulness! The Immeasurable is filling the measurable:

- According to the good pleasure of His will;
- According to the riches of His grace;
- According to the riches of His glory.[15]

The Infinite is filling the finite. We have no lack for He gives abundant life, abundant grace, abundant joy, abundant mercy, and to have the Holy Spirit abundantly.[16]

The wonder of God manifested in the flesh is that He is perfect in body, soul and spirit. Well might we say of Him, as Job said of God, *"He is unique, and who can make Him change? And whatever His soul desires, that He does."*[17] He is completely at one with Himself, so that His character and conduct are one, His intentions and actions are one. He is unchangeable. He stands alone.

No matter how godly we may become this will never be said of us, yet we need the riches of His glory before our behaviour can match our beliefs. One way of seeing this is in how we deal with one another. Paul pleaded with the disagreeable Corinthians *"by the meekness and gentleness of Christ,"*[18] and the Manhood of Christ was being reflected in him.

When he wrote to the churches in Galatia, he urged them to act in the same way toward any who had been caught off guard and had sinned. Somewhere, someone may have been waiting to be restored – and, here again, Paul uses the fisherman's word that Peter used, *katartizō*, mend the broken net. No fisherman would let untrained hands near his damaged net, and it's better that no untrained hands ever attempt to "restore" those who have slipped up and lapsed into sin. This is why Paul's three conditions are so vital:

You who are spiritual – the great need is for mature servants of God who are Spirit-filled and Spirit-led. They will be Word-based, and prayerfully caring in their approach.

Restore – they must not be heavy-handed or ham-fisted. No net will be improved by clumsy handling; neither will any damaged child of God. Being well-meaning or well-intentioned isn't enough. We need to be, as Joshua and Caleb said under different circumstances, *"well able to overcome."*[19]

A spirit of gentleness – the Lord was masterly at this, and was the essence of being *"well able to overcome."* He is meek and lowly in heart,[20] and He knew how to speak a word in season to him who is weary.[21] The way He won us is the way we have to win others, with soft words tenderly spoken.[22] What a lesson for us! How easy to trip ourselves up just by a wrong word and impulsive reactions. We can be impatient, even when trying not to, but we will never hear impatient words from Him.

If only our tongues didn't work as fast as our minds! A thought gets sparked and immediately it ignites the tongue that's a flame of fire[23] and out it goes, too quickly to be caught and brought back. It's gone, and that flame may do burning damage in someone's mind that they might never forget. But how do we get a spirit of gentleness? It comes from the riches of His glory, as we let the nature of Christ speak through us. Galatians 6 opens with the need for "a spirit" that is right for the job, and it ends with the only way to get it: *"Brethren, the grace of the Lord Jesus Christ be with your spirit."*

So the end of the chapter answers its opening. It tells us how God meets our need before we can meet the other person's need. Those who enjoy fellowship with God are best prepared to help someone's restoration to fellowship with Him. How does such a brother or sister feel welcome unless there's a spirit of meekness being shown? But how can it be shown unless we have been in the presence of God and He has shown it to us? If He has, then both parties will see the grace of the Lord Jesus Christ in each other. What a fitting time to hear the echo of Paul's words, *"You know ..."*!

As we gather up something of Paul's appreciation of God's grace, we hear his comments on other aspects of God's character. The foolishness of God is wiser than men, and the weakness of God is stronger than men.[24] Well might he say these things, for he also wrote that *"the message of the cross is foolishness to those who are perishing, but to us who are being saved it is the power of God."*[25] He also wrote, *"He was crucified in weakness, yet He lives by the power of God."*[26] Finally, we read these outstanding words again, *"You know the grace of our Lord Jesus Christ, that though He was rich, yet for your sakes He became poor, that you through His poverty might become rich,"* and it's as if we hear the apostle reply, 'And the poverty of Christ is richer than men!' With thankful hearts, we also reply, "We know!"

THE GOD OF SMALL THINGS

Psalm 24:1; Micah 5:2; Mark 3:9; 1 Corinthians 1:27-29

Of all the galaxies that fill
The limitless expanse of space,
God chose this little place called Earth
And here revealed the matchless worth
Of One so full of truth and grace.

Of all the towns in Israel spread,
Whose fame was never held in doubt,
He chose Ephrathah's House of Bread
To birth the One whose coming forth
Was known by Him from going out.

Of all the ships that plied the coast
And braved the Galilean Sea,
He chose a little boat as host
To wait on Him, to bear the cost,
And serve its Guest compliantly.

So, instantly it left the fleet
Of other ships of high degree,
That it might bow beneath His feet
And, like disciples, steadfastly
Be yielded to His Captaincy.

How can we glory – of this world,
And lowlier far than Galilee?
He calls us, foolish, weak and base,
Unknown and nothing, yet by grace
He lifts us up to fill the place

Of wisdom, strength, and known by Him.
No longer least, no longer lost,
For in His cross He paid the cost,
That in His presence now we boast
And praise His Name eternally.

FOOTNOTES

1.1 GRACE REQUIRED IN AN UNGRACIOUS MAN

(1) Mk.1:16,17 (2) Heb.11:8 (3) 1 Cor.2:8 (4) Gen.12:1; Acts 7:2 (5) Jn 8:56 (6) Gal.2:11 (7) Gal.2:12 (8) Gal.2:13 (9) Gal.2:11 (10) 2 Pet.3:15,16 (11) Phil.3:5 (12) Acts 4:13 (13) Jn 1:41,42 (14) Lk.2:25 (15) 1 Cor.11:19; 2 Cor.11:26; Gal.2:4; 1 Jn 4:1; Jas.1:26; Jude v.4 (16) 2 Pet.3:16 (17) 2 Tim.3:16 ESV (18) Rev.3:1 (19) Lev.10:20 (20) 2 Sam.23:2 (21) Ps.139:4 (22) Col.4:6 (23) Ps.106:33 (24) Job 13:7

1.2 GRACE RESTORED IN HIS MISTAKES

(1) 2 Cor.5:20 (2) Matt.2:13-23 (3) Matt.4:18-19 (4) Tit.2:11 (5) Ps.42:7 (6) Jn 21:7 RV, KJV (7) 1 Pet.1:1 (8) Gal.6:1 (9) Jn 13:10 (10) Jn 21:6 (11) Matt.16:13-16 (12) Lk.7:33 (13) 1 Kin.18:17 (14) Jer.38:4 (15) Matt.9:3 (16) Ex.3:14 (17) Eph.1:22-23 (18) Matt.16:21-23 (19) Matt.17:4 (20) Matt.5:17; Lk.24:44 (21) Lk.9:30-31 (22) Lk.9:32 (23) Jn 2:7,11 (24) Lk.9:33 (25) Lk.9:26 (26) Matt.17:5,8 (27) 1 Pet.5:1 (28) 2 Pet.1:16 (29) Jn 18:6 (30) Heb.1:3 (31) Matt.26:53 (32) Lk.22:43 (33) Jn 20:12 (34) Matt.16:27 (35) Lk.22:31-32 (36) Jn 1:42 (37) Jn 18:16 (38) Matt.26:71 (39) Matt.26:73,74 (40) Jn 18:26 (41) 2 Kin.5:26 NASB (42) Jn 2:24-25 (43) Num.13:33 (44) Heb.12:2 (45) Rom.10:17 (46) 2 Cor.5:7 (47) Eph.6:12 (48) Lk.22:62 (49) Mk.16:7 (50) Heb.7:25 (51) Heb.9:24 RV (52) Matt.16:19 (53) Col.4:3 (54) Acts 2 (55) Acts 8:14 (56) Acts 10; 14:27; 15:7 (57) Acts 2:5-11 (58) Acts 2:2,6 (59) Rom.6:1-8 (60) Acts 10:13

(61) Heb.3:1 (62) Judg.13:25 (63) Ps.89,31,34 (64) Ps.109.22 (65) Phil.1:6 (66) Jn 1:42 (67) Lk.22:61 (68) Jn 1; Matt.4; Lk.5 (69) Jn 21:15-17

1.3 GRACE RECEIVED IN THE GOSPEL

(1) 1 Cor.2:10 (2) 1 Tim.6:3 (3) 2 Thess.2:13-15 (4) Isa.53:6 (5) 2 Tim.3:14 (6) 1 Pet.1:1,2 (7) 1 Pet.5:10 (8) Eph.1:4;2:8 (9) Eph.1:4-6 (10) Rom.10:17 (11) Heb.9:12 (12) 1 Cor.5:7 (13) Acts 16:31 (14) Phil.2:12-15 (15) 1 Pet.1:5 (16) Eph.1:14 (17) Eph.1:18 (18) Heb.9:15 (19) 1 Pet.1:4 (20) 1 Pet.1:5 (21) 1 Cor.15:52 (22) 1 Thess.4:17 (23) Phil.3:20,21 (24) 1 Jn 3:2 (25) 1 Pet.1:8 NASB (26) Heb.12:2 (27) 1 Pet.1:10 (28) Lk.24:26; 1 Pet.1:11 (29) Tit.2:11,13 (30) 1 Pet.1:13 (31) 2 Thess.2:16 (32) Heb.9:28 (33) 1 Thess.4:16-17 (34) Jn 1:16 (35) Jas.4:6 (36) 1 Pet.1:3

1.4 GRACE REGARDED IN WORSHIP AND WITNESS

(1) The divisions in most versions of the Bible were introduced by Stephen Langton, Archbishop of Canterbury (1207-28), and Robert Estienne added verses in 1551. (2) Deut.31:26 (3) 1 Pet.1:10,13 (4) 1 Pet.1:23 (5) Ps.138:2 (6) Ps.119:89 (7) Eph.1:22,23 (8) Prov.30:8 ESV (9) 1 Tim.4:13-16 (10) Isa.31:4 (11) Ps.119:162 (12) Ps.84:5,7 (13) Jer.31:12 (14) 1 Chron.16:29 (15) Heb.10:19-22; Heb.13:15 (16) Ps.19:14 (17) Phil.3:3 (18) Ps.5:9; Ps.78:36; Mk.7:6 (19) Rom.12:1 (20) 2 Cor.2:15 (21) 1 Cor.11:26

1.5 GRACE REINFORCED IN TRIALS

(1) Jn 16:32 (2) Jas.1:1; 1 Pet.1:1 (3) Zech.4:7 (4) See Gen.18:1,2; Ex.3:2; Judg.6:11-24 (5) Zech.12:10 RVM (6) Acts 20:20 (7) Acts 18:25,26 (8) 1 Cor.11:10 (9) Eph.3:10 (10) 1 Cor.12:27; 1 Pet.2:6,7 (11) Eph.4:15 (12) Col.2:19 (13) Heb.1:9 (14) Gal.5:24 (15) Rom.13:1,2 (16) 1 Pet.2:24

1.6 GRACE RECIPROCATED IN MARRIAGE

(1) Ps.90:2 (2) Acts 11:23 (3) 1 Cor.9:5 (4) Jas.1:18 (5) Eph.5:33 (6) 1 Pet.2:12 (7) Tit.2:5 (8) 1 Cor.15:45 (9) Eph.1:22,23 (10) Rom.8:17

1.7 GRACE RECOGNISED IN HOLINESS

(1) 1 Cor.2:8 (2) 1 Tim.3:16 (3) 1 Jn 3:5 (4) Phil.2:6 (5) Jas.1:15 (6) Rom.1:4; Josh.24:19; Lk.1:35 (7) Ex.15:11 (8) Ex.28:36, see also Isa.23:18 ASV (9) Heb.2:3 (10) Phil.3:14 KJV; 2 Tim.1:9; Heb.3:1 (11) Eph.2:6 (12) Jn 10:28,29 (13) Rev.3:14 (14) 2 Tim.2:21 (15) 2 Tim.2:19 (16) Heb.12:14 (17) Ecc.3:7 (18) Ps.60:6 (19) Ps.89:35 (20) Mal.1:7-14 (21) 1 Cor.10:18 (22) 1 Tim.1:11 (23) Eph.3:6 (24) Phil.1:7; Heb.3:14; 12:10; 2 Pet.1:4 (25) 2 Cor.5:17 (26) Rom.12:1 (27) Lk.23:46 (28) Acts 2:41 (29) Lk.12:50 (30) 2 Cor.5:21 (31) Ps.42:7; 88:7 (32) Rom.8:32 (33) Rom.3:25 (34) 1 Jn 1:7 (35) 2 Cor.5:14 (36) Eph.3:10,11

1.8 GRACE REVEALED IN SPIRITUAL GIFTS

(1) 1 Pet.4:1,2 (2) Eph.4:8 (3) 1 Cor.12:18 (4) 2 Cor.5:21 (5) Isa.53:10,11 (6) Rom.12:3; 1 Cor.12:11; Eph.4:7; 1 Pet.4:10 (7) Col.4:17 (8) 1 Cor.12:7 (9) Mk.6:48 KJV (10) Rom.12:3 (11) Rom.12:5 (12) 1 Tim.2:11,12 (13) Tit.2:3 (14) Acts 18:24-25 (15) Eph.1:22,23 (16) Eph.1:4,5 (17) 1 Cor.15:38 (18) 1 Cor.12:18 (19) 1 Cor.12:27 (20) Prov.18:16

1.9 GRACE REFLECTED IN LEADERSHIP

(1) Eph.5:2 (2) 1 Thess.5:12; Heb.13:7,17, 24 (3) Acts 20:28; 1 Thess.5:12 (4) 1 Cor.9:5 (5) Mic.4:6 NIV (6) Zech.12:10 (7) Ps.23:2 (8) Matt.4:18-22 (9) Heb.13:20 (10) Jn 21:15-17 (11) Acts 2 (12) Jn 10:11,14

1.10 GRACE REGAINED IN BIBLICAL TRUTHS

(1) 2 Cor.8:9 (2) 2 Cor.13:14 (3) Heb.10:29 (4) Ps.115:5-7 (5) Gal.3:3-5 (6) Gal.5:7 ESV (7) Dan.11:32 (8) Gen.49:3,4 (9) Job 38:6 (10) 1 Kin.5:17 (11) Tit.2:11 (12) 2 Jn 9 (13) Eph.4:21 (14) Heb.5:8,9 (15) Heb.7:27; 10:12 (16) Heb.5:9 (17) Heb.7:28 (18) Heb.10:14

1.11 GRACE RE-EMPHASISED IN PAUL'S LETTERS

(1) Matt.20:28 (2) Gen.22:8 (3) Rev.13:8 (4) Rom.9:23 (5) Lk.16:20 (6) Lk.20:24 (7) 2 Pet.1:4 (8) Heb.2:14 (9) Rom.8:3 (10) Rom.2:4; 2 Cor.7:10 (11) Eph.1:4-7 (12) Eph.3:16-19 (13) Col.1:18 (14) Jn 1:16 (15) Eph.1:5,7; 3:16 (16) Jn 10:10; Rom.5:17; 2 Cor.8:2; 1 Pet.1:3; Tit.3:6 (17) Job 23:13 (18) 2 Cor.10:1 (19) Num.13:30 (20) Matt.11:29 (21) Isa.50:4 (22) Prov.15:1 (23) Jas.3:6 (24) 1 Cor.1:25 (25) 1 Cor.1:18 (26) 2 Cor.13:4

II

The Apostle Jude's Tripod - A Survey Of The Man, Method and Message of the New Testament's Forgotten Book

The apostle Jude's little letter can easily be read within five minutes, yet it spans eternity past and future, history and prophecy, blessing and judgment, past revelation and fresh revelation, things known and not known, heaven's glory and hell's grief. And, like all Scripture, it has a God-given relevance for us in the present day.

2.1 INTRODUCTION

As you pick up this study of Jude's letter, the first thing you will discover is that it is one of God's little books, and that He has much to say to us through it. We have no idea how long it took to write, but it can easily be read within five minutes. Even so, it spans eternity past and future, history and prophecy, blessing and judgement, past revelation and fresh revelation, things known and not known, heaven's glory and hell's grief. Like all Scripture, Jude's brief contribution confirms that even the shortest messages such as Obadiah, Philemon, two of John's letters, and now his own, have a God-given relevance for us in the present day. They are equally inspired as larger books, and equally relevant for:

- reproof – showing when we are off track;
- correction – helping us to get back on track;
- instruction – enabling us to keep on track.

Halfway through the Book of the Revelation, we will find God's final "little book," and it's interesting that He calls it a *biblaridion*, which literally means 'a little book', diminutive of *biblos* (from which we get our word Bible). Significantly, it had been opened, so that its message from God and its consequences would be revealed, and we expect a similar sense of purpose as we explore Jude's message from God and the Holy Spirit opens it for us. It bears the hallmark of being part of the divine Word, and we can safely enjoy it as being 'a little Bible.'

Jude, the Author

In attempting to decide which Jude was called by God and enabled by the Holy Spirit to write this short letter, we can do no more than appeal to Scripture for clarification. Each of them drew his name from the Hebrew name *Jehudah*, which means celebrated or praise, yet it has been translated into English as Judah, Judas, and Jude.

- Two are mentioned as Judah in the Old Testament genealogies recorded in Matthew 1:2, also Luke 3:30 and 33;
- Another two were disciples of Jesus: one was *"the son* of James," though the King James Version calls him *"the brother* of James" (Lk.6:16). In both cases, the words in italics don't form part of the original text, which means this particular Judas was simply "of James";
- One was a "brother" of Jesus in Matthew 13:55 and Mark 6:3;
- One was Judas of Galilee, mentioned in Acts 5:37 with details of his mission and death;
- One lived in Damascus, and Ananias visited him after Saul's conversion (Acts 9:11);
- One also was known as Barsabas in Acts 15:22.

Of all these, only two are possibilities: Judas the apostle in Luke 6:16 and Jude the Lord's brother, but the likelihood of the former being the son of James makes the latter more likely.

The First Recipients

Unlike most other New Testament letters, Jude gives no indication regarding where his was received. It may be that the churches in Judea, including Jerusalem, were reeling from the effects of false teachers, and so his balanced approach was one of reassuring the faithful and recovering the fallen, while rebuking the falsifiers.

His Approach

A careful reading of the letter's twenty-five verses will show the possibility of identifying an orderly and very inter-connected outline, which addresses the problem and affirms a pattern of renewal and rebuilding.

1. Salutation - On the basis of 'Who?'
2. Salvation - On the basis of 'Why?'
3. Contention - On the basis of 'How?'
4. Condemnation - On the basis of 'What?'
5. Revelation - On the basis of 'When?'
6. Benediction - On the basis of 'Where?'

We trust you will be blessed, as the Spirit of God leads us step-by-step through each section of this very important letter. It's only small, but our God is the God of small things.

GOD'S INFANT, BOY, AND MAN

Omnipotence was well-concealed within His Infanthood,
Yet, even then, in Infant form He was th'incarnate God
Whose tiny frame in secrecy was wrapped and shaped by Him,
With every attribute combined within His tiny form.

Omniscience was thinly veiled when as a Boy He shared
With Temple-teachers of the Law and found them unprepared;
For what He asked, and things revealed, surpassed their range of thought,
And showed th'unlimited wealth of truth this unknown Boy had brought.

But infancy and boyhood were forerunners of the Man
Who came to show the power and thought of God's eternal plan.
Through Him – in wisdom, righteousness, and in His holiness
Redemption's Man was made a curse for those He'd save and bless.

(A. McIlree)

2.2 SALUTATION: ON THE BASIS OF 'WHO?'

"Jude, a bondservant of Jesus Christ, and brother of James, to those who are called, sanctified by God the Father, and preserved in Jesus Christ: Mercy, peace, and love be multiplied to you" (Jude vv.1,2).

* * *

Jude's letter might be short in its length, but it's definitely not short of teaching. He begins with a salutation and ends with a benediction, and it's enlightening to see how the close complements the opening. There is no clear way of knowing who his readers were, but they were under severe fire from false teachers who aimed to undermine them as believers. Isn't it strange that assembly life can be helped by those who are mining and hindered by those who are undermining? The sad thing is, that even the essential character of God and the gospel of God were under attack, and Jude wanted to write to them about things that belonged to what he called *"our common salvation."* He didn't mean that it was ordinary or mediocre. No, he was concerned about them not having real fellowship in the gospel, and not sharing it with each other as they should.

Can you imagine an assembly losing its way in the gospel? As we will find out from our study, their opposition was as serious, and as fundamental, as challenging the Lord's sovereignty and authority. No wonder Jude was concerned! He had learned the hard way: growing up as an unbeliever in the same home in Nazareth as the Saviour before trusting in Him after His death and resurrection;[1] but the good thing is, he learned. At least, when he was an unbeliever, he knew he was an unbeliever, not like the men he speaks about in his letter who pretended to be believers and *"crept in unnoticed"* to upset those who believed. We may not have had too much trouble like that over the years, but we still need to check the temperature and pulse of assemblies to see if we really are living in the safety and enjoyment of *"our common salvation."*

His Background

Some Christians face fiercest opposition inside their own homes, but who would have thought it would be like that for Christ? When He said, *"If they persecuted Me, they will also persecute you,"*[2] who would have imagined that "they" could ever apply to family members? However, unlikely as that may have seemed, it became crystal clear that He had the home in mind when He said, *"a man's enemies will be those of his own household."*[3] His words were a quotation from Micah 7:6 where the word "household" (Heb. *bayith*) can be translated as "house" or "family," as we find it three times in 1 Chronicles 13:14 – *"The ark of God remained with the family of Obed-Edom in his house three months. And the Lord blessed the house of Obed-Edom and all that he had."* How remarkable it is that saying it *"remained"* infers it was settled, as if wedded to that home for it normally belonged in the Most Holy Place of the Tabernacle – the symbol of Christ in glory. That's where it truly was at home, yet God gave honour and blessing by causing it to be revered by Obed-Edom and his family in their home.

If only the Lord Jesus Christ had been as welcomed in His earthly home, but the Son of God never sensed the acceptance that was given to the ark of God. His true home is on the throne of God where He *"ascended far above all the heavens,"*[4] yet He exchanged it and descended to live under the same roof of unbelieving brothers and sisters who didn't show Him the same reverence as their parents. Far from it!

Little is said of His childhood years, other than His visit to the temple as a twelve-year-old.[5] Perhaps, the contrast comes into sharper focus if we borrow Asaph's words in Psalm 50:20-21 – *"You sit and speak against your brother; you slander* [Heb. *dophiy*: push] *your own mother's son. These things you have done, and I kept silent; you thought that I was altogether like you; but I will rebuke you, and set them in order before your eyes."* Their hostile words were intended to have the same effect as those who urged one another to *"smite"*[6] Jeremiah with the tongue. How wrong they were in thinking of the One who came *"in the likeness of men"*[7] that this meant He was *"altogether like"* what they were. Nothing could have been farther from the truth. He never shared their critical spirit, their selfishness or their abusive way of thinking. Scripture says, *"who, when He was reviled, did not revile in return; when He suffered, He did not threaten,"*[8] and that included His home-life.

As co-equal with His Father in character, He kept silent just as God did in Asaph's Psalm. But He not only condemned their actions, He noted their attitude as they assumed the right to despise His Word (v.16), His own (v.20), and Himself (v.21). He kept silent as they voiced belittling thoughts of Him, yet He could see that they were as settled in their irreverence as Obed-Edom's family were in their reverence. He made this very point by saying, *"You sit,"* which is exactly the same in Hebrew as when the ark *"remained"* with Obed-Edom. They were settled in their scorn and abuse, just as many others would be during the later years of His homelessness when He had *"nowhere to lay His head."*[9]

G.K. Chesterton spoke about "the place where God was homeless and all men are at home,"[10] yet the Lord had come to help them see that *"every good gift and every perfect gift is from above,"*[11] even if His own brothers fanned the well-known question, *"Can anything good come out of Nazareth?"*[12] No matter how many had looked askance at Nazareth's reputation, it was the place where the *"Lord of glory"*[13] who *"made himself of no reputation"*[14] chose to spend His pre-ministry years. It was one thing for Solomon to ask the question, *"Will God indeed dwell on the earth? Behold, heaven and the heaven of heavens cannot contain You. How much less this temple which I have built!"*[15] If the Temple seemed too little, what then about God manifested in the flesh dwelling in despised Nazareth? Joseph and Mary's humble home was the first household in Israel that, spiritually speaking, was too small for the Lamb,[16] yet Jude would grow up in it and discover that this God had great purposes for him.

His Foreground

There is inescapable evidence, and no room for doubt, that a great work of God was done in the hearts of Mary and Joseph's four sons – James, Joses, Simon, and Judas – during the forty days between Calvary and being included in the one hundred and twenty who gathered in Acts 1:14-15 to wait for the coming of the Holy Spirit. How and when the change took place, we don't know, but change they most certainly did. Perhaps, somewhere in the darkness of Calvary's cross, they felt their own darkness; perhaps, during the earthquake, they also were shaken; and perhaps, when the tombs were opened, they began to sense their own spiritual awakening. What we do know is that the Lord Jesus Christ was seen after His resurrection *"by Cephas, then by the twelve. After that He was seen by over five hundred brethren at once"* and *"After that He was seen by James, then by all the apostles."*[17] The exalted Christ had come into their lives in a wonderful fulfilment of the ark's covenant blessing.

The opening words of his letter put this at the forefront of his relationship with his Lord and Saviour, and come to us as a sincere acknowledgement of two births: one, spiritual, that allowed him to be *"a bondservant of Jesus Christ"*; the other, natural, that allowed him to be a brother of James. We should note how carefully he identified himself and realise that he did it by the leading of the Holy Spirit, just as John did when graciously distinguishing that another Judas was *"not Iscariot."*[18] Jude, the writer, was none other than one of Jesus' brothers, all of whom were unbelievers during the Lord's time on earth. No doubt, he could look back on these unbelieving days when all four taunted Jesus by saying, *"Depart from here and go into Judea, that Your disciples also may see the works that You are doing. For no one does anything in secret while he himself seeks to be known openly. If You do these things, show Yourself to the world."*[19]

Their comments were made in the hollowness of unbelief, and with the intended mockery that He should perform before a larger audience. Jesus knew that it would not be long until He was shown to the world in a very different way from what they meant, for His crucifixion would take place at the Passover of the following year. God's timing is always exact, as Acts 1:7 points out by referring to *"times or seasons"* which in Greek – *chronous ē kairous* – means indefinite periods of time or definite moments in time. Jesus knew this, but His brothers didn't; yet they decided to voice their advice. How right Paul was when he emphasised that Deity needed no advisors in eternity – *"For who has known the mind of the Lord? Or who has become His counsellor?"*[20] – yet His brothers offered theirs.

However, the cross so effectively had come in between and, rejoicing in his blood-bought forgiveness, Jude took his place as a bondservant. There was no familiarity in his opening remark. He could easily have said, "Jude, a brother of Jesus Christ and bondservant with James," but, like James in his letter, he owned the Lordship of the One they formerly spoke against and their transformation as servants of the King. James called Him *"our Lord Jesus Christ, the Lord of glory"*[21] – or, more accurately by removing the words in italics, "our Lord Jesus Christ of the glory." By saying this, James was not only convinced of the glory of the place from which his Saviour had come, and to which He had returned, he was thinking of the glory of the Person and of how that glory should radiate through "the faith" that we hold. It was this that Jude made his aim by describing his servanthood with the Greek word *doulos*. He could have used other words, each with its own characteristics. For instance:

141

- *diakonos*: a deacon, a menial helper (Lk.22:27; Matt.23:11; 1 Tim.3:8);
- *hupēretēs*: an under-oarsman in the lowest tier of rowers where he would feel the sweat and the spit from those who rowed in the upper tiers (Jn 18:36; Acts 26:16; 1 Cor. 4:1);
- *leitourgos*: a Temple minister or worshipper. Hebrews 1:7 refers to angels who minister (*leitourgeō*) Godward, and in v.14 as they minister (*diakoneō*) manward. Hebrews 8:2 refers to the Lord as the Minister (*leitourgos*) of the sanctuary; and Acts 13:2 describes certain brethren as they ministered (*leitourgeō*) to the Lord.

Each of these is a fitting description of a servant of God, but the Spirit of God attached the word *doulos* to Jude to speak of one who is tied to the task like a slave and not loosed without his master's permission. This is illustrated in Matthew 21:2 by the donkey and colt that were *"tied"* (Gr. *deō*, the root of *doulos* – Dr Strong) and loosed by their owner who showed subjection to the Lordship of Christ when told, *"The Lord has need of them."* And the unbroken colt showed its submission by allowing the Lord to ride on it. The word *doulos* also is linked to the word *dei* from which we get our word *"must,"* and we see the Lord Jesus Christ as the exemplary *doulos* when He said, *"The Son of Man **must** suffer many things"*[22] and *"I **must** work the works of Him who sent Me."*[23]

Another interesting use of the word is associated with essential or **"must-prayer"**. This time, the word is *deomai* – to beg or plead with binding prayer, and we find examples of this:

- **In the Lord** – *"But I have prayed for you ..."* (Lk.22:32);
- **In the early church** - *"And when they had prayed, the place ... was shaken"* (Acts 4:31);
- **In the apostle Paul** – *"As though God were pleading through us, we implore you"* (2 Cor.5:20).

We should pause here to ask ourselves how often we are conscious of striving with this degree of necessity and intensity in prayer, not only in our personal prayer lives but in church Prayer Meetings. Each of us will recall times in both when we sensed and felt the evidence of deeply burdened prayer, and it may be we recall them with a sense of the unusual – a 'once-in-a-blue-moon' experience! Crises of one sort or another have the tremendous ability to drive us to prayer with greater urgency and dependence, and we plead for those much-needed answers that will glorify God and bring relief to our spirits. But isn't it true that our 'normal' prayer times can be made up of what the late Guy Jarvie, missionary to Burma and India, called "hospital prayers"? Prayer lists, prayer boards, prayer guides all have their place for they cover many 'prayer-points' that are important, but when last were you shaken as a Christian, and how long is it since your church's Prayer Meeting *"was shaken"*?

The first step that the early Jerusalem church took was in what was described as *deēthentōn* – binding, must-prayer – and the whole church prayed with an intensity that came from being *tied* to the need for prayer (Acts 4:31). They were discovering that continuing steadfastly[24] didn't simply mean regularly or routinely, but actively and unitedly casting their burdens on the LORD or, as it can be translated, casting *"what He has given,"*[25] and waiting for Him to sustain them. If only we could be moved as they were! It was a God-given disturbance, a Spirit-led stirring. Greeks called it a *salos* from *saleuō*, which includes the thought of "waves."[26] Oh for prayer times that are out of the ordinary and make the right sort of waves! For those in the Jerusalem church, it meant three vital needs being fulfilled:

· They were filled with the Holy Spirit;
· They spoke the word of God with boldness;
· They were united in one heart and one soul.

The inescapable lesson is, that those who are tied to the Lord as *doulos*-servants will be tied to Him in *doulos* prayer. Others were - are we?

Bondservant *(doulos)* seen in:
- The Lord– Phil.2:7;
- The early churches – Jn 15:15; Rom.6:19; 1 Pet.2:16;
- Paul – Rom.1:1; 2 Cor.4:5; Gal.1:10.

Must *(dei)* seen in:
- The Lord – Acts 17:3; 1 Cor.15:25;
- The early churches – Acts 4:12; 5:29; Heb.11:6;
- Paul – Acts 9:6.

For Jude, being a bondservant *(doulos)* was the spiritual result of recognising Jesus Christ as Lord *(Kurios)*, and we will see later how he applied this reasoning to his condemnation of false teachers who couldn't be servants since they didn't know the Lord.

His Tripods

As we go through Jude's short letter it will become very noticeable that, like a surveyor, he sets up a series of tripods, eighteen in total (see APPENDIX 1), as he navigates the rugged contours of the gathering he had in mind. He was about to address the ups and downs of their Christian experience knowing full well that, while they were in this world, but not of it,[27] there were evil men among them who were in the church, but not of it. With this in mind, he drew their attention to the first triplet through which he commended the believers and condemned the unbelievers.

Like all Scripture, his little letter may seem to take the proportions of a dagger rather than a sword, yet it was breathed out by God to let His flock know how lofty their place was in Christ, and to let the ungodly know how low a place they occupied without Him. According to the New King James Version, the three spiritual blessings were addressed to those who were *"called, sanctified ... and preserved,"* but this should read, as in most other translations, *"called, beloved ... and kept."*

Called

If anything should settle the believer's faith, and unsettle the unbeliever's faithlessness, it's the God-given assurance that all His children have been called. Paul believed this, Peter was equally convinced, and Jude held the same conviction. Rooted in the heart of God, and settled in electing grace, every believer's spiritual journey begins with a much-needed response to the call of God. The voice of the LORD is powerful[28] and, by the power of the living word of truth,[29] He penetrates the hearts of those who are weak[30] and dead,[31] enlightens those who were in darkness and turns them from being children of wrath to children of light.[32]

Jude knew that God's call is not a futile, empty sound. By using the word *klētos*, he assured them that it was an invitation and an appointment, and this was why Paul urged every believer to "see" their calling in 1 Corinthians 1:26. In fact, he wanted this so much that he wrote the word *blepete* in such a way that it meant they should keep looking at it. On top of this, Jude wrote this word for *"called"* as an adjective and plural, exactly the same as in Romans 1:7, and we may wonder why. Unlike its two neighbouring words, beloved and kept, which are verbs, it describes the plural nature of God's call, which is high and holy and heavenly.[33] We can well understand how these believers who heard Jude's first triplet would rejoice in their gain, and wonder how the unbelieving could not feel convicted about their loss.

Beloved

How wonderful to be at the centre of the love of God! With Jude's background, he valued being loved by Him and the word *agapao* is intentionally used to emphasise the depth of divine affection that lies, firstly, at the heart of God's call, and then at the heart of His keeping power. Paul made a different point in 1 Corinthians 1:2 when he wrote about believers being *"sanctified in Christ Jesus, called saints."* Once again, *"called"* describes those who are holy, and *"sanctified"* (Gr. *hagiazo*) refers to the permanence of His

145

preservation.

Kept

With the call of God sending our appreciation back to a past and eternal sovereign choice, Jude then directs his readers and us to an eternal future. This doesn't mean that he overlooked their present struggles, but rather that the reality of what they were going through should be viewed in the light of the past reality of their calling and the future reality of being eternally secure. In the meantime, even when it is difficult for us to keep our eyes fixed on our calling, the One who called is guarding, watching, and keeping His eye on us, which is the meaning of the word *tēreō*.

With this in mind, the Christian faces every trial and sees them through the promises of God in which He says, *"I will guide you with My eye* [upon you, ESV]*"*[34] and that *"the eyes of the LORD are in every place, keeping watch."*[35] In the comfort of these, and in the midst of all sorts of opposition, we also take heart from knowing that *"there is no creature hidden from His sight, but all things are naked and open to the eyes of Him to whom we must give account."*[36] The dear folks who listened to Jude's opening sentence wouldn't fail to see that his first tripod was central to what he was saying to them on either side of it. On the one hand, the bondservant knew His Master well and had the right spiritual credentials to share this threefold assurance. On the other, they would see that it stood related to their present need, and so he opened up the scope of his second tripod.

Mercy, peace, and love

It's wonderful to know that our salvation brought the heart of God into our hearts and that, in His grace, He also shared His mercy, made peace and showed love through the cross. By grace, we have received what we didn't deserve, and in mercy He kept us from receiving what we did deserve. In effect, Jude was saying to them that whatever spiritual blessing came to them would be confirmed by whatever spiritual blessings came through them. In other words, mercy received would make them merciful; peace received would make them peaceable; and love received would make them loving. Even so, they would have to work at it together if they were to overcome the ravages of the onslaught they were enduring.

Yes, God is merciful on the basis of His righteousness, and our showing of mercy must be consistent with the basis of His righteousness. This will keep us from margins of tolerance and intolerance that call for unrighteousness; for example, with current departures from His Word to accommodate challenges made by modern standards of morality and immorality. Likewise, peace is not at all costs, but with honour. God, and the gospel of God, must be honoured and never compromised by mercy, peace and love that are not consistent with what He has already shown. This means that whatever is received through genuine repentance cannot be shown toward those whose sins cause no repentance. Only what is multiplied to us should be multiplied through us!

The Scriptures are a two-edged sword that need to be handled wisely, and it will become evident how righteously Jude applied it during the course of his letter, to those who were faithful, to those who had fallen, and to those who were false. In encouraging *"those who have obtained like precious faith with us by the righteousness of our God and Saviour Jesus Christ,"*[37] Paul would have comforted Jude's readers by saying that their trials were *"manifest evidence of the righteous judgement of God, that you may be counted worthy of the kingdom of God, for which you also suffer."*[38] At the same time, he would tell false teachers that, *"in accordance with your hardness and your impenitent heart you are treasuring up for yourself wrath in the day of wrath and revelation of the righteous judgement of God."*[39] It's the same sword from the same God used in the same righteousness, but with two distinct messages, and this is exactly what we will find as we let Jude continue to speak.

IN CONTRAST

Wise, even in His foolishness,
And strong the weakness of His hand;
An endless deep His shallowness;
So vast, the tiniest things He planned.

Robust, yet veiled in gentleness,
And very God while truly Man;
He measures, yet is measureless,
With light years dwarfed within His span.

The Highest, in His lowliness;
Still Holy, though made sin for us,
And heaven's Best in emptiness
Dies with earth's worst upon a cross.

Engulfed in darkness is the Light,
And Love encounters hatred's power.
Heaven's Life expires within earth's night:
The Eternal One endures 'the hour'.

The Victim is the Victor now,
The One who died forever lives.
We gave our wickedness to Him:
His gentleness to us He gives.

(A. McIlree)

2.3 SALVATION: ON THE BASIS OF 'WHY?'

"Beloved, while I was very diligent to write to you concerning our common salvation" (Jude v.3).

"We give thanks to God always for you all, making mention of you in our prayers, remembering without ceasing your work of faith, labour of love, and patience of hope in our Lord Jesus Christ in the sight of our God and Father, knowing, beloved brethren, your election by God. For our gospel did not come to you in word only, but also in power, and in the Holy Spirit and in much assurance, as you know what kind of men we were among you for your sake.

And you became followers of us and of the Lord, having received the word in much affliction, with joy of the Holy Spirit, so that you became examples to all in Macedonia and Achaia who believe. But as we have been approved by God to be entrusted with the gospel, even so we speak, not as pleasing men, but God who tests our hearts" (1 Thess.1:2-7; 2:4).

* * *

Jude's salutation was exactly what this gathering of troubled believers needed to hear. It was sincere and heart-warming, and worded in such a way that they were reassured about their standing with God. At the same time, it reinforced them in their struggle for it drew the real battle lines.

They were up against ungodly men who knew nothing about being *"called, beloved, and preserved"* so it was impossible for *"mercy, peace, and love"* to be multiplied, since they had never received them through salvation.

As for the believers, having just learned that they were *"beloved"* by God, Jude immediately described them as his *"beloved"* ones and, to make sure they knew how much he meant it, he made it one of his tripods as verses 3, 17 and 20 clearly show. God knows, and so did Jude, that affection is the best ground for cultivating spiritual fellowship and for building spiritual stewardship. So they knew that urging them to *"contend ... remember"* and to *"keep building"* all flowed from loving encouragement and not mere man-management.

The churches had been infiltrated, and Jude was burdened. The ink of his salutation would hardly be dry on the page when he went on to let them know that he was *"very diligent to write ... concerning our common salvation,"* which means he was so earnest about it that he couldn't do it quickly enough. The New King James Version says that he wanted to write *"concerning"* this, while others simply say "of" or "about." Jude's actual word was *peri*, which literally means he wanted to go "all over" or "all around" the matter. Had he gone ahead, he may have produced something as long as Paul's letter to the Romans to define what they should enjoy in their *"common salvation,"* but his letter was never written. Instead, he became one of the men God moved to write what He wanted to say, and one page was enough.

Our Common Salvation

As far as Jude was concerned, he didn't change course by dropping his initial burden to focus on *"the faith."* On the contrary, he shows that what belongs to one belongs to the other and, by his own admission, they needed to hear something that would strengthen them in *"our common salvation."* Whatever he had intended to write must have been connected to glorifying the gospel of God, its content and convictions, by drawing their attention to

His nature and attributes; the nature of the message and its doctrines. His delightful phrase, *koinēs hēmon sotērias*, means "our shared deliverance and safety," and emphasises the thought of having fellowship in our salvation, in our knowledge of God as Creator and Redeemer, and in our understanding of the gospel.

This means having communion that is based solely on the conviction truths of the gospel, and fellowship in communicating what is based on the content of the gospel. What a springboard this is into our understanding and enjoyment of all that we have in Christ! It's also a safeguard against neglecting what God has given us in salvation by focusing on truth relating to what He gives us in service. So the things that are "necessary" include the necessity of checking that what we share is truly "common" and held in the assurance of Christ-centred fellowship. How lovely it is that verse 3 flows so spontaneously from verses 1 and 2, with no possibility of being divorced from them. This means that our calling, being beloved, and preserved, along with God's mercy, peace and love are attached and never detached from *"contending earnestly."* Brothers and sisters, we are wonderfully blessed!

It all goes hand in hand and affects:

- Fellowship in the gospel (Phil.1:5) - **COMMUNION;**
- Furtherance of the gospel (Phil.1:12) - **COMMITMENT;**
- The faith of the gospel (Phil.1:27) - **CONVICTION.**

It also affects:

- Fellowship in the gospel (Phil.1:5) - **PARTNERSHIP IN PREACHING;**
- The sharing of your faith may become effective (Phlm.5,6) - **PARTNER-SHIP IN FAITH.**

As believers, we do this by seeking to understand what God believes and by Spirit-led reasoning, while others deviate from it by delusion, distortion, and deceit. This protects us from the sort of tolerance Paul feared possible in Corinth: *"If he who comes preaches another Jesus whom we have not preached, or if you receive a different spirit which you have not received, or a different gospel which you have not accepted—you may well put up with it!"*[1] What a frightening departure from the truth!

- A different messenger - not a true servant;
- A different Jesus - not the true Saviour;
- A different spirit - not the true Spirit;
- A different gospel - not the true message.

The New Testament speaks of a day when *"the man of sin – the lawless one,"*[2] also called Antichrist,[3] will come, and two distinct warnings are given. The first is by Paul, that *"the mystery of lawlessness is already at work"*; and the second by John, regarding *"the spirit of the Antichrist, which you have heard was coming, and is now already in the world."* How true this was in their day, and Jude's letter was prompted by the same problem. Although far from the day of the Antichrist, the churches were under attack by men who were anti-Christ in both spirit and substance, yet they were shielded by two aspects of divine protection. Paul refers to these as, *"what is restraining"* and *"He who now restrains."*[4]

It's helpful to note that his first phrase, *to katechon,* is neuter, and the second, *ho katechōn,* is masculine. We would suggest that the latter is the Holy Spirit Himself, and the former consists of living members of the church, which is the body of Christ. As the salt of the earth, they have a restraining effect until the whole church is caught up to heaven at the coming of the Lord. The Spirit and His work can resist and overcome the spirit and work of those who are false teachers, and their end will be *"among those who perish, because they did not receive the love of the truth, that they might be saved."*[5] The great dividing line couldn't be clearer: truth is in Jesus. Those who are *"in Christ Jesus"* possess Him and *"the word of the truth,"* and the lost did not receive Him or *"the love of the truth."*

- Truth is in Jesus (Eph.4:21) - **THE SAVIOUR;**
- The word of the truth (Col.1:5) - **THE SAVED;**
- ·Disapproved concerning the faith (2 Tim.3:8) - **THE LOST.**

Having set us free, God leaves us free to preach the doctrines of God and the doctrines of grace, and nothing else. True freedom belongs to being anchored in the doctrines of *"the gospel of God ... of Christ ... of His Son."*[6] He has brought us into *"the glorious liberty of the children of God"*[7] and asks us to *"stand fast"* in it. It's the standing fast of a fixed position that resists any temptation to *"be entangled again with a yoke of bondage."*[8] It's the standing fast of a fixed understanding that doesn't stand for one point of view today and a different opinion tomorrow. He has said, *"I am the LORD, I do not change,"*[9] and we know that *"Jesus Christ is the same yesterday, today, and forever,"*[10] so the terms of the gospel can't change.

This is what makes *"sound doctrine"*[11] and *"sound words"*[12] sound, and they can never become unsound. They also shape sound preaching and sound preachers, yet it's well known that some say things, not only unadvisedly, but even *"speak wickedly for God, and talk deceitfully for Him."*[13] When the Lord Jesus Christ said, *"I am the light of the world,"* and later said of others, *"You are the light of the world,"* He did two remarkable things: He showed that our humanity would be elevated to proclaim the focus of Deity, and He conferred on His witnesses the greatest responsibility that had ever been granted to servants of God. In these two phrases He elevated our humanity and our responsibility, and in a lovely way humbled Himself by conveying such a mission from the infinite scope of His hands to the limited scope of ours. Isaiah's graphic picture of Him who *"measured the waters in the hollow of His hand, measured heaven with a span"*[14] emphasises the sheer impossibility of our hands ever being equal to His.

How well He knew that our hands, so incapable of tracking the dimensions of the galaxies, are equally incapable of tracing and gripping the doctrines of the gospel, yet He has called us to handle the only message that is capable of bringing men and women to experience the eternal dimensions of the *"new creation."* The honour was equally expressed when Paul took Isaiah's words – *"How beautiful ... are the feet of Him"*[15] – and, by the Spirit, said to us *"How beautiful are the feet of them."*[16]

The Kind of Preaching – the Content of the Message

1 Thessalonians 1:2-6 and 2:4 give a wonderful summary, for these verses cover the sower, the seed and the soil. Firstly, we are introduced to the trio who served together in the gospel of God, Paul, Silvanus and Timothy, whose satisfaction is summed up in their thanking, mentioning, remembering and knowing, which shows how conscious they were that the purpose of the gospel rests entirely on the sovereignty of God. As they thought of their brothers and sisters, they assured them that they were thankful, and able to mention and remember them before God in prayer, because they were convinced by the evidence of a work of Christ in their lives that they were among God's elect. How wonderful it is that those who are convinced they have known a work of grace also cause others to see the evidence in them that God had elected them.

So, firstly, Paul was in no doubt that the *purpose* of the gospel rests entirely on the sovereignty of God. Secondly, he was absolutely sure that the *produce* of the gospel came from the good soil of believing hearts whose commitment to the Lord Jesus was driven by the mainspring of faith, love and hope. Thirdly, we are presented with the all-important aspect of God's *pleasure* in the gospel, so we are left in no doubt that the purpose of this glorious message is that it was designed to produce and to please.

The faithful sower can be faithful to the soil only if he is faithful to the seed. Perhaps, there are times when lack of production results not from trying to sow in the wrong soil, but from attempting to sow with the wrong seed. Germination depends on putting the right seed into the right soil, so each sower should stand between two works of God when we take the gospel of God to sinners of the world. Tampering with the seed suggests that the sower knows better than the Saviour, and that the servant knows better than the Master. If we depend more on the inspiration of this seed there will be greater expectation of germination in the soil! This was the great thrill of those in Thessalonica, and it can be updated into our experience as we go with the gospel of God, to point sinners by the Spirit of God to the cross of the Christ of God.

This unites two correlated important features, the first of which is the kind of preaching and the content of the message. As we bow under the colossal thought of an electing God of all grace, it puts us into an arena where our recognition of Him allows us to approach sinners confident that the God of heaven has a plan in view, and we are only a small part of it. But it's in this smallness that we trust His greatness and pray, as others have, "Lord, lead us to the elect." What a confidence. Election is not a shackle to the gospel; it's a spur. It nerves us for the gospel that we know the Saviour has sheep still to be gathered in, and we are among the messengers who handle such a glorious message.

When Paul said, *"our gospel did not come to you in word only,"*[17] this should ring an alarm bell in our hearts for it raises the possibility of preaching to men and women in an ineffective manner, because it's in word only. If the apostle Paul knew the need to safeguard his ministry from such a pit, then, God helping us, we will endeavour to do the same. He was so concerned about this that he didn't only drive his message home to the church in Thessalonica; he did it twice to the Corinthians, and said it again to all the churches of Galatia. It wasn't in the wisdom of words, nor was it with persuasive words. It didn't depend on his intellect, on his ability or on the vehicle of his mentality to make the message convincing. His fear was that, if that's the basis of the gospel, then the cross of Christ could *"be made of no effect."*[18] He feared the presentation of an ineffective Calvary, not because of Christ, but because of the kind of preaching. Can you imagine gospel preaching that leaves the cross having no effect on some listeners?

155

Paul could! Fearful, isn't it?

Listen closely to the burdened apostle: *"Do I now persuade men or God? Or do I speak to please men? For if I still pleased men, I would not be a bondservant of Christ."*[19] This is the high price of inadequate content in the gospel: it fails to keep the preacher true to the Christ of the cross, and it fails to make the hearer true to the cross of Christ. If we fail in these, He will use another messenger. Is it the favour of men we are seeking to win or of God? Or is it men we are seeking to please, rather than Him? People-pleasing and playing to the gallery are roommates of what Job called *"speaking unrighteously for God."*[20]

Sadly, there's no shortage of this in today's range of preachers and preaching. God has put into our hands a message we should prize so fully that we will never be satisfied by sharing less than He has given. This doesn't conflict with Paul's comment about becoming *"all things to all men"*[21] for he had no intention of conflicting with the will of God or the doctrine of the Lord. He was sensitive to customs and circumstances, but he never became a weathervane pointing in all directions or pointing people in directions they'd later discover didn't comply with God's Word.

Methods can undermine the message, therefore we need to follow Paul's approach. Having spoken of the *purpose, produce and pleasure* of God in the gospel, he now speaks of its *power*. Only Spirit-led preaching is *"in power"* – with spiritual energy and impact; *"in the Holy Spirit"* for He knows the Saviour best, He knows the sinner best, He knows and speaks the message best. Only through Him is it *"in much assurance."* Only by His help do we have preaching with knowledge and conviction, and response that shows conviction and assurance. We must retain the grandeur of the message and never dilute it - for misrepresenting God is a disservice to Him and to the sinner.

This can be done quite easily, and perhaps with a desire to simplify the message, but it's a road that is fraught with danger. In an effort to make the message acceptable, some stray from being scriptural. For instance, some teach it is possible to fall away and be lost after salvation; others suggest that new converts can accept Jesus as Saviour, and, at a later stage, make Him Lord; and it has become popular for many to attempt leading souls to Christ by means of what is known as 'The sinner's prayer.' These beliefs and practices are biblically and evangelically unsound, and they conflict with the ministry of the Holy Spirit whose work it is to guide into all truth through conviction of sin and genuine repentance.

For faith to have substance, we need to present a message with substance. Even adherents of eastern religions can detect lack of substance in an 'easy-believism' gospel. This was the testimony of a Hindu man in South India who, after hearing weak presentations of the gospel, had never heard there's a glory to it, and concluded it was 'too simple.' No one ever told him about the glories of the Christ, yet they were trying to share the gospel. Scriptures like Acts 17:2-4 shows that the wealth of God's provision in sound gospel content lay at the foundation of the work in Thessalonica. It was the serious matter of reasoning ... explaining ... demonstrating ... and persuading. They didn't share it with a kind of eye-dropper approach, they immersed people in the gospel. Ignorant people whose lives were immersed in idolatry were treated to the glorious gospel of the happy God, because the preachers wanted His happiness to become theirs.

These are the four strong tracks of the gospel, which can never be replaced by anything less. The essentials of the gospel were at the core of the message. This was a carefully reasoned message that allowed something from the heart of his God to move Paul's heart and reach the heart of the sinner. Other portions, such as his letter to the Romans, include reasoning on regeneration, redemption, justification, glorification, and much more, so while the gospel may be simple in one way, it's never simplistic. As far as Paul was concerned, even crucifixion was a doctrine, and not only an action. Only two verses before speaking to Galatians about a crucified Christ being

157

clearly portrayed or placarded before them[22], he said, *"I have been crucified with Christ."*

Such was his expectation that the truths of the gospel would become living realities to those who believe. His mission was placarding Christ, not placating people! Having been won to Christ, he wanted others also to say, *"I have been crucified with Christ; it is no longer I who live, but Christ lives in me, and the life which I now live in the flesh I live by faith in the Son of God who loved me and gave Himself for me."*[23]

"If any man speak" (1 Pet.4:11, KJV). Oh, we know that preaching is not always done publicly; sometimes, it's personal witness by one to another, but the same truths apply, and the same principles apply. The message whose content is carefully presented in public preaching should be identical to what is considered in private conversation. Challenging sinners and confronting sin are central to the gospel, and unless we challenge sin we cannot help sinners to find the Saviour. Like Paul, we have the opportunity to confront man's ungodliness by presenting Christ, *"the mystery of godliness."*[24] We know – don't we? – there can be no knowledge of salvation without knowing they are lost; no possibility of forgiveness without conviction, no rescue without repentance; no possibility of peace without being troubled, no pardon without guilt; no following the Saviour without forsaking sin; and no certainty of heaven without being faced with hell.

Sensitively, we can fulfil the kind of uncompromising preaching of which it was said that the preacher "shook people over hell." That's not insensitivity, is it? It's the burden of a man's heart that makes him sit with someone to face the unthinkable, so that friends we know should never fail to hear about hell because we didn't love them enough to tell them. It may be someone in our family, a relative; it may be a friend, someone in your neighbourhood or at work - can we not love them enough to speak to them about the Saviour? If it means warning them about hell, let us do it in the love of Christ.

We sometimes have opportunities in various settings to speak to men and women about their souls. Whether it's in public preaching or in private conversation, our aims are twofold: to make them feel comfortable in whatever setting it is, but that they will never feel comfortable with God until He makes them feel uncomfortable. We also want them to feel accepted wherever we meet them, but that they will never know acceptance with God until they know they are unacceptable without Christ as their Saviour. We are presenting a Person, not selling a product, therefore inviting lives that are ruined by ambition or addiction to "Try Jesus" is another gospel. Jesus Christ is for trusting, not trying. When we speak to them about their need, it's to bring them away from the mentality of trying. Their days of trying are over. It's now the decisive moment of trust.

He is not on trial, and we must emphasise the essentials and not be content with cosy homilies and anecdotal chats. Sinners come in their emptiness, nothingness, and hopelessness to discover that the cross is their only hope for eternity. The message is held out to each one, and it's the word of the message that will cause them to turn from darkness to light, and from the power of Satan to God. We won't see it happen, but at that moment they will be delivered from the power of darkness and conveyed into the kingdom of the Son of His love.[25]

The Kind of Preacher – the Character of the Messenger

Paul knew how essential it was that his message was true *"for the gospel's sake,"*[26] but it also was vital that the Thessalonians knew *"What kind of men"* had preached to them *"for your sake."* [17] They knew what kind of message was preached, and they also knew the kind of messengers who preached it. They had heard men preach an appealing message, *"as though God were pleading through"* them,[27] and gospel preachers can do no more. Sadly, they can do a lot less, for not all realise that the currency of the gospel has been stamped on two sides of the one coin: and they remain, *"for the gospel's sake"* and *"for your sake."* It takes both for the heart of God to plead through the heart of His preacher, and for His glory in the message to be complemented by His glory in the messenger. It's important that we know the kind of messengers God sends. They are:

Approved

This is divine approval in their God-given acceptability. It shows what God thinks of them, but this will lead to a discerned acceptability among their hearers. The Lord Jesus Christ showed that God the Father had set His seal on Him[28]: a seal of affection, approval and authority, and His messengers must reflect something of this too.

Entrusted

This is divine trust in their God-given fidelity. This shows what God does through them in their faithfulness to His Name and Word, and because He sees them as trustworthy. They are like the woman's broken flask of spikenard – Gr. *pistikos* – it was genuine, and its fragrance filled the home. This is what the gospel preachers should do: they bring the fragrance of Christ with the faithful Word, and they do it through brokenness. One aspect of this applies to what we could call 'priestly preaching.' 1 Peter 2:9 (RV) calls for those who know Christ as Priest to show *"forth the excellencies of Him who called you out of darkness into his marvellous light"* - not only the marvellous light of knowing the Saviour of the sinner, but the Lord of the follower.

As ambassadors of Christ, our commission is to bring others to know Him, so that they can discover Him as their Priest too. Does this give us the liberty to share our royal priesthood witness with other believers? If so, they would have similar freedom to share in the holy priesthood's worship in verse 5, but, since verse 5 doesn't permit an open table, verse 9 doesn't condone an open platform.

Tested

This is divine pleasure in their God-given authority. He sees them as twice tested, before Him and others, and this is good for there's nothing more powerful in the hands of God than a consistent messenger with a consistent message. Paul and Silas are great examples for any preacher. They were free *"from error"* – there was no deception or fallacy; they were free from *"uncleanness"* – there was no hidden immorality; and they were free from guile – there was no slick trickery or gimmickry that they used as some sort of bait to entertain or entrap.

Jesus has commanded, *"Go therefore and make disciples of all the nations, baptising them"* into (RV) *"the name of the Father and of the Son and of the Holy Spirit, teaching them to observe all things that I have commanded you; and lo, I am with you always, even to the end of the age."*[29] This is His mandate. When we preach, we own it as our mandate, and when sinners respond, it should become their mandate. It's the baton of divine transferral. It's being serious about the great commission: emphasising the call to obedience to those who hear the gospel, so that they will see that believing is an act of obedience. When He said, *"I have given them Your word,"* what did He mean?

Was He referring to the Old Testament, from Genesis to Malachi, or was He not rather speaking about the revelation of His will that should energise their service with a transforming message? He was giving marching orders to witnesses of a gospel that demands obligation as well as reconciliation, and calling us to take His commission seriously by emphasising obedience in our preaching. The kind of gospel we preach will determine the kind of disciples we make! We must never become incomplete messengers with an incomplete message. That's not in our contract. Diluting the message always leads to diminishing the Saviour and deceiving the sinner.

Our highest aim in preaching is that it satisfies divine pleasure, and this means we should know what God feels about our kind of preaching and what it does to His heart. His pleasure in the gospel is at stake. Another danger lies in encouraging the unsaved to worship before they have yielded to Christ's ownership and discipleship. We must never invite unsaved sinners to do what God hasn't asked or fitted them to do. The preacher's greatest honour is to bring sinners to the blood of Jesus: to its shedding; and to its sprinkling.

SHEDDING

- Cleansing the sinner;
- Acceptance;
- Atonement;
- Union;
- Redemption.

SPRINKLING

- Claiming the saint;
- Obedience;
- Government;
- Communion;
- Obligation.

What a calling! Every blood-bought sinner is *"elect according to the foreknowledge of God the Father, in sanctification of the Spirit, for obedience and sprinkling of the blood of Jesus Christ."*[30] God's desire is that the knowledge of the preacher becomes the knowledge of the newly saved sinner, that the preacher's conviction will become their conviction, for this great reason, that they might be able to anticipate the *"for"* of their election.

Matthew and Mark both share the same telling message about the Lord in Gethsemane – *"He went a little farther"*[31] – but there's a valuable difference. To Matthew, He is the King; to Mark, He is the Servant. It was just *"a little farther,"* humanly speaking for the lowly Servant, but a whole lot farther for the King of kings. Mark begins his gospel record by telling us that Jesus went *"a little farther"*[32] to call James and John and, near its end, of how He went *"a little farther"* to call on God. Perhaps it's time for His messengers to go a little farther, too, so that we will be closer to men, and closer to God.

In Acts 2:41 and 42, receiving the gospel was the first of seven spiritual experiences. If we lose the value of that number one lamp on the lampstand of divine testimony, it will be like removing one of the seven pillars of wisdom's house.[33] It will be like an army that has lost its sense of recruitment, like a school that has lost the need for enrolment, so also churches need to win souls - otherwise they will cease to exist.

In days when Christ is blasphemed and His Name taken in vain, when it's politically correct to ridicule Christianity, our world needs to hear a gospel that exalts the Saviour and excites the sinner, but they won't hear it without messengers who will explain the message. Do we know Him well enough or is there too much spiritual poverty? Are our hearts full enough or are we too often empty? Are our lives pure enough or are they affected by impurity?

In darkening days, our world needs to hear a brighter gospel, and the anticipation of the Saviour's return urges us to be among those who give it its proper place. We should preach as we have never preached before, reach as we have never reached before, and shine as we have never shone before. If we do, many will get a glimpse of His glory through the preaching and the preacher before the church goes home at the Rapture and the light of the world goes out. In one way, we have to take the message down to the people, but our highest honour is in bringing the people up to the message! Let's lift them up *"in power, in the Holy Spirit, and in much assurance"*[17] to see new horizons in the faith of the gospel, in the truth of the gospel, and in the hope of the gospel.[34]

Each new height reveals another
Far outshining every other,
And farther realms to conquer when it's gained.
On to higher peaks and pleasant,
Not content with just the present,
Ever upward and to heights not yet attained.
(Marjorie Lewis-Lloyd)

* * *

THE GLORIOUS GOSPEL

Its fundamental doctrines gleam afar;
Eternal in the heavens is their source;
Each penetrates our darkness like the star
That sets the boatman's sextant and his course.

Its monumental witness towers above
All earthly concepts, helping us to find
Deep thoughts of God, and evidence of love,
In nobler thoughts shaped in His noblest mind.

Invisible, yet by His works made known,
This all-creating God is clearly seen;
His hidden things are manifestly shown,
Revealed in time His everlasting plan.

Our non-judgemental God has made us free
From sin's dark presence, penalty and pow'r.
And now electing grace calls us to be
Conformed to His Son's image hour by hour.

Since death has lost its lordship over Him,
And having died to death He dies no more;
So, under grace, we live as dead to sin:
Its lordship gone from those whose sins He bore.

(A. McIlree)

2.4 CONTENTION: ON THE BASIS OF 'HOW'?

"... contend earnestly for the faith which was once for all delivered to the saints" (Jude v.3).

* * *

No competitor in a race would ever be allowed to begin one-eighth of the overall distance ahead of the starting line, and neither should any expositor. We would hardly imagine an Olympics' swimmer entering the pool over six metres ahead of other participants, yet it's not uncommon for some teachers to dive into Jude's twenty-five verses at verse three. Jude had no such intention. It was important to him that he assured his readers of what they are in Christ – called, beloved ... and preserved – to remind them that they are His by election, affection, and preservation. This would give them comfort in knowing that their temporal experience was permitted as part of their infinitely greater and eternal experience.

Paul gave an expanded version of this when he wrote so reassuringly to the church in Corinth:

"And since we have the same spirit of faith, according to what is written, 'I believed and therefore I spoke,' we also believe and therefore speak, knowing that He who raised up the Lord Jesus will also raise us up with Jesus, and will present

us with you. For all things are for your sakes, that grace, having spread through the many, may cause thanksgiving to abound to the glory of God. Therefore we do not lose heart. Even though our outward man is perishing, yet the inward man is being renewed day by day. For our light affliction, which is but for a moment, is working for us a far more exceeding and eternal weight of glory, while we do not look at the things which are seen, but at the things which are not seen. For the things which are seen are temporary, but the things which are not seen are eternal."[1]

Having provided comfort by reminding them of what they *are* in Christ, Jude immediately added encouragement by speaking of what they *have* in Christ – *"Mercy, peace, and love be multiplied to you."* How graciously he set the scene, that what they needed through Christ was based on what they were and what they had in Him. In other words, he wanted them to know that contending flows from mercy, peace, and love being demonstrated through those who are called, beloved, and preserved. They needed to be emboldened by the same "spirit of faith" that drew its well-founded confidence from all that is written about the faithfulness of God and of His promises in the gospel of Christ.

Contend Earnestly for the Faith

On the basis of this loving introduction, Jude came straight to the point and shared what the Spirit of God had shared with him: *"I found it necessary to write to you."* How good it is when we truly are in touch with Him and able to say, *"It seemed good to the Holy Spirit, and to us,"*[2] knowing that we are equally able to say, *"It seemed good to us, being assembled with one accord."*[3] Like these leaders, Jude sensed a need and, as his word for necessity implies, felt distressed by it (see the use of the same word in 1 Corinthians 7:26 and 1 Thessalonians 3:7). Having already called them *"beloved,"* he not only felt for them in their need but also was able to address it by *"the love of the Spirit."*[4] But what was this Spirit-led necessity? It pinpointed that he must urge them to sense the urgency of contending earnestly for the

167

faith. Alerting them to the battleground of the faith is captured in the word *epagōnizesthai*, from which we get the thought of an agonising struggle.

His way of doing this was typically big-hearted. By *"exhorting"* (Gr. *parakaleō*: to call near or from beside) them, He wanted them to feel that he was close to the action, that his exhortation wasn't a shout from a distance, but meant he was close to them and calling alongside to comfort and entreat. He was well aware of what was going on among them and his approach was consistent with what Paul wrote to Philemon: *"Therefore, though I might be very bold in Christ to command you what is fitting, yet for love's sake I rather appeal [Gr. parakaleō] to you."*[5] In the same way, Jude appealed that his brethren should fight for what they believed, and it may be that he wondered if they had any fight left in them.

Had their spiritual energy been sapped by lengthy debate and argument? Had widening division weakened them? Or had they even been compromised by the manipulating influence of deepening friendships? It may be that fear kept them from countering heresy with truth. Being afraid of 'rocking the boat,' 'making matters worse,' or 'causing more trouble' could have seemed like good reasoning. They may even have become convinced that contending earnestly could be divisive; they could gain the core and lose the fringe. We have no way of knowing, but we do know that prolonged spiritual struggles deplete spiritual strength. False teachers know how to box clever, and those who defend the faith can be outwitted, out-thought and out-fought. All the more reason, then, that we show a willingness to fight for what we believe by learning how to *"fight the good fight of the faith"*;[6] not militantly, but biblically.

In 1965, two heavyweight boxers stepped into the ring in Lewiston, Maine, USA. Within two minutes of the first round, one was knocked down and promptly knocked out. He had been a contender, but not for long, and very quickly there was no fight left in him. Jude may have been concerned that his brethren had no fight left in them and were no longer real contenders. As

Paul weathered his difficulties, he was able to say, *"We are hard-pressed on every side, yet not crushed; we are perplexed, but not in despair; persecuted, but not forsaken; struck down, but not destroyed."*[7] Some have rephrased the last clause and applied it in boxing terms as "knocked down, but not knocked out."[8]

Half-hearted conviction never leads to wholehearted commitment, and losing ground never leads to gaining the victory. They would never gain ground against false teachers if they didn't believe, love and practice the truth of God. The way forward would be a battle in which they must be actively engaged in the struggle to defend *"the faith,"* which would involve being faithful to it and with it. This implies a serious contest, but not one of being contentious! Jude obviously meant everyone to take this on board, and that no one should opt out and leave it to others to do the thinking. Every believer has a responsibility to learn, love and live the doctrines of the Lord, which He Himself said we should teach and that, in doing so, He would be with us to the end of the age.[9]

Of course, some say that 2016 marked the birth of the post-truth era, and this has been defined as "Relating to or denoting circumstances in which objective facts are less influential in shaping public opinion than appeals to emotion and personal belief."[10] Nothing could be farther from the truth, and we need to go back to before The Fall in the Garden of Eden to find a pre-lie period. It was the spawning ground of questioning, *"Has God indeed said?"*, and the place where falsifying His word began. The truth of God is clear-cut and, as believers, we must never give the impression that our beliefs are hazy and woolly or as unsubstantial as what some know as cotton candy or candy floss.

Jude's audience battled with their version of post-truth, centuries later so do we, and we need to ask if our understanding of what we believe matches:

- all things - Matthew 28:20;

169

- the way - Acts 18:26;
- the whole counsel of God - Acts 20:27;
- the faith - Romans 1:5;
- the truth -Galatians 5:7.

They will, if we:

- observe all things (Gr. *tērein* - from the same word used in Jude v.1 and v.21): By guarding and keeping our eye on what the Lord has commanded;
- explain the way (Gr. *exethento* - set out and expound);
- declare the whole counsel of God (Gr. *anangeilai* - to announce or tell as a messenger);
- obey the faith (Gr. *hupakoēn* - listening attentively);
- obey the truth (Gr. *peithesthai* - trust, agree, have confidence).

Each generation, including our own, must re-establish and re-emphasise doctrinal truth. Unsound teachers must meet more than their match with *"sound doctrine"*[11] and *"sound words"*[12] presented by those who are *"sound in the faith."*[13] Each overseer should give a lead in this by *"holding fast the faithful word as he has been taught, that he may be able, by sound doctrine, both to exhort and convict those who contradict."*[14] Following his example, there comes a point when men and women of God should become intolerant of tolerance. As already mentioned in chapter 1, this means we seek peace with honour, not peace at all costs; and unity that doesn't tolerate the adversity that comes from those who treat uniters as dividers.

It's right that those who love the Lord should love what He loves. Do we hold and emphasise what God holds and emphasises? Do we share what He has shared? It's essential that we do this for polarised opinions cannot possibly speak for Him or be given by His Spirit. Very careful attention needs to be given whenever conflicting interpretations are made about anything in Scripture. The simple challenge is, are we being faithful to all that *"the faith* "[15] embraces?

Once for All Delivered

As we have already thought, God has given unchanging truth in the unchanging gospel of the unchanging Christ, and He has done it for all time, so we have every reason to trust the God who delivers. The real meaning is that He has surrendered it to us, that we in turn might be surrendered to Him.

- Once for all delivered (Jude 3) - **IT TO US;**
- To which you were delivered (Rom.6:17) - **US TO IT;**
- Who was delivered up (Rom.4:25) - **HIM TO US;**
- We are always delivered (2 Cor.4:11) - **US TO HIM.**

We have no idea how Jude's hearers responded, or how successful they were in healing believers who were damaged or in seeing false teachers won through the gospel. All we know is that his short letter was God's answer to the challenge. This was His remedy that should encourage the faithful, restore the fallen, and be able to convict the false. He could do no more than reflect the present-continuous implications in what Paul wrote to the church in Thessalonica: Keep on standing fast and keep on holding *"the traditions* [ordinances] *which you were taught, whether by word or our epistle."*[16]

A GORGEOUS ROBE

"Then Herod, with his men of war, treated Him with contempt and mocked Him,
arrayed Him in a gorgeous robe,[1] and sent Him back to Pilate"
[Gr. *lampros*: bright, clear, shining] (Lk.23:11)
"And they clothed Him with purple" (Mk.15:17)

Again and again, in constant, cruel jeering
These puny armies voiced their feeble scorn
Against the Man who knew His hour was nearing,
And taunted Him with royal robes and thorn.

For Jews, their kingly robe was bright and gorgeous:
A radiant garment made by men for men,
But while it shone, its glory was less glorious
Than heaven's Best who stood before them then.

The Gentile rulers saw this feeble effort
And tried to outperform what Jews had done.
Their purple robe was not designed for comfort,
But to demean the glories of God's Son.

Yet, none can divest Him of His own glory,
Nor can they invest any of their own;
This Kingly Man did this Himself more ably
By rising from His cross to fill the throne.

His rightful robe is clear, as clear[1] as crystal; (Rev.22:1)
His righteous clothing, whiter[1] than the light; (Rev.19:8)
The Root, the Branch, the offspring of King David, (Rev.22:16)
Heaven's great I AM eternally is Bright[1].

No *"gorgeous robe"* or *"purple"* can be fitting
Apparel for the glorious heavenly King;
The Saviour in Himself is the right clothing
And to Him Jew and Gentile need to cling.

(A. McIlree)

2.5 CONDEMNATION: ON THE BASIS OF 'WHAT'?

"For certain men have crept in unnoticed, who long ago were marked out for this condemnation, ungodly men, who turn the grace of our God into lewdness and deny the only Lord God and our Lord Jesus Christ. But these speak evil of whatever they do not know; and whatever they know naturally, like brute beasts, in these things they corrupt themselves. Woe to them! For they have gone in the way of Cain, have run greedily in the error of Balaam for profit, and perished in the rebellion of Korah. These are spots in your love feasts, while they feast with you without fear, serving only themselves. They are clouds without water, carried about by the winds; late autumn trees without fruit, twice dead, pulled up by the roots; raging waves of the sea, foaming up their own shame; wandering stars for whom is reserved the blackness of darkness forever" (Jude vv.4, 10-13).

* * *

Jude's salutation was all it took for a dividing line to be carved through the gathering, yet all he did was address the believers and no one else. Salvation always does this, of course; it confirms believers in their faith and in their security of being *"in Christ."* At the same time, it sets a spiritual division between believers and unbelievers, saved and lost, alive and dead, between light and darkness, the hopeful and the hopeless, between those who have been brought near to Christ and those who are far off, and between those who are true and those who are false.

When you love the Lord, and are loved by Him, the joy of being on the right side of these differences is very meaningful, yet many on the wrong side of the line find them completely meaningless. Before we go any farther, perhaps all of us should stop, either to feel the comfort of the following Scriptures as we read them or to sense their challenge if you have never known what it is to accept Christ as your Saviour.

- **In Christ** - *"There is therefore now no condemnation to those who are in Christ Jesus"* (Rom.8:1; 16:7);
- **Believers and unbelievers** - *"He who believes in Him is not condemned, but he who does not believe is condemned already, because he has not believed on the only begotten Son of God"* (Jn 3:18)
- **Saved and lost** - *"For the Son of Man has come to save that which was lost"* (Matt.18:11);
- **Alive or dead** - *"And you He made alive, who were dead in trespasses and sins"* (Eph.2:1);
- **In light or in darkness** - *"You were once darkness, but now you are light in the Lord"* (Eph.5:8);
- **Hopeful or hopeless** - *"Christ in you, the hope of glory"* (Col.1:27). *"Having no hope and without God"* (Eph.2:12);
- **Near or far off** - *"But now in Christ Jesus you who once were far off have been brought near by the blood of Christ"* (Eph.2:13).

Creepers, Condemned and Corrupt

The problem among Jude's readers was real. In fact, it was very threatening. Being well aware of this, like any shepherd who wants to protect his flock, he faced up to the predators. When he referred to them as *"certain men,"* he really was saying, "these kind of men" for he knew what they were. His approach is enlightening, to say the least, for, instead of addressing them directly, he kept speaking to the church. Everything he had said so far was to believers about believers, but now he speaks, not to, but about the false teachers. This was sound principle and good practice for, although these men had wormed their way into the gathering, they didn't belong to that church. Those who don't belong to Christ don't belong among Christians, and those who don't belong to the church, which is His body, can't possibly belong to the local assembly.

For this reason, Jude immediately sets up one of his defining tripods and exposes these men as creepers, condemned, and corrupt. They were creepers, because they *"crept in unnoticed."* Their craftiness is captured in the Greek word *pareisdunō*, which is three words put together: *para* means beside, *eis* means into, and *duno* means go down; so, like foxes stalking sheep, they crept down in beside those of the little flock. They crept in unnoticed, but didn't stay unnoticed for long! They came in intentionally, but were not intentionally let in. Their disguise was so good, and their deportment so sly and convincing, that they had deceived the shepherds and come in by stealth.

Sadly, this wasn't the only place that suffered from this kind of infiltration. In 2 Corinthians 11:13-15, Paul warned the church about *"false apostles"* who were deceitful workers and cunning enough to transform themselves into ministers of righteousness. As he thought of the hazards he had faced, he lists *"perils among false brethren"* with what he had suffered by imprisonment and flogging, shipwreck, robbers, dangers among Jews and Gentiles, and battling high seas.[1] If anyone knew how dangerous these men were, Paul did, and they were part of his *"deep concern for all the churches."* He had seen through their disguise and concluded that their end will be according to their works.

Jude was of the same mind and was clear that they *"long ago were marked out for this condemnation."* God always sees and knows what's in the heart and mind of everyone,[2] and nothing goes unnoticed by Him. When the Lord Jesus Christ was on His way to Calvary He faced *"certain"* – the kind of men – *"who bore false witness against Him."*[3] He was on His way to die for the ungodly,[4] yet Peter speaks in his second letter about *"the day of judgement and perdition of ungodly men."*[5] God has marked them out – He has written beforehand – that their day of reckoning is coming.

Sheep Among Wolves

In the meantime, the Good Shepherd says, *"I send you out as sheep in the midst of wolves."*[6] His commission sets His sheep at the centre of hostility, just as He was. Psalm 22 describes Him as being surrounded by bulls, lions, dogs, and wild oxen; and how they attacked, and roared, and snarled, and gored! Psalm 118:12 adds, *"they surrounded Him like bees"* with stinging words and insults, and so He promised His own, *"If they persecuted Me, they will also persecute you."*[7] But the Lord didn't only say what they would face, He told His disciples how to face them. In His own ministry, He never retaliated, not even *"When they hurled their insults at Him,"*[8] so He told them to *"be wise as serpents and harmless as doves."*[8]

This would guide what they said, and how they said it, which takes wisdom for reasoning and warmth for appealing. It takes both. This is the Christian's best defence. Being wise means we know the Word and what it means; being harmless means we know how to share it in the gentleness and love of our Saviour who was depicted by the turtledove in the burnt offering,[9] and by the bridegroom of the Song of Songs whose eyes were like doves.[10] However, we will be poorly equipped if we try to have one without the other. On its own, clear reasoning isn't enough; neither is warm appealing.

There are wolves who want to tear our reasoning to shreds, and some know the Bible well enough to mount their thought-out arguments, so we need to know God's Word better than they do. It's paramount, but we also need to know how to use it. Left to ourselves, we would be like Peter with his brandished sword in Gethsemane. In the place where the heart of the Saviour was moved so deeply, His disciple was ready to show that his mind wasn't harmless. We need the mind of the Spirit, if we want to share the mind of Christ. There's never any shortage of great debates, but we are not out to win the argument, we want to win the arguer!

Wolves Among Sheep

There's a big difference between sheep being in the middle of wolves and wolves being in the middle of sheep. The first is where we are meant to be, and the second is where they are not meant to be. In the first, we go to them; in the second, they "come to you."[11] The intentions are not mutual. The sheep want to see wolves changed by being drawn to life in Christ; the wolves want to see His sheep drawn away from Him and their love for Him killed off. The problem is that these wolves don't come among the flock looking like wolves; they come looking like sheep and looking for sheep. Around seven hundred years earlier, Zephaniah the prophet said that Jerusalem's judges were *"evening wolves that leave not a bone till morning."*[12] It was the same old story - they were wolves dressed as judges.

It was different in Nehemiah's day and, if anything, worse. It's bad when wolves come in unnoticed, but worse when they are invited in! With their captivity in Babylon over, the people were kept busy rebuilding the wall of Jerusalem, and even Eliashib the high priest was involved. By all appearances, he was living up to the meaning of his name, God will restore, as he built the Sheep Gate with its doors and wall and towers. What a force for good, yet tragedy was to come. The very man who built the Sheep Gate was the first to let in a wolf. Ironically, the man he welcomed was the one who taunted Nehemiah and the builders by saying, *"if even a fox goes up on it, he will break down their stone wall."*[13]

But, sadly, he didn't have to walk on it for he was allowed to walk through it. The wolf was allowed to enter the gate that was built as the entrance for sacrifices that were going to the altar, and, once inside, he was given a place of residence. Eliashib had become a close friend of Tobiah. Too close, in fact! The word used to describe their alliance is *qarowb*, a kinsman, as Boaz was to Naomi and Ruth,[14] but Eliashib and Tobiah were never kinsmen. To make a boarding place for the wolf, Eliashib emptied the storeroom that kept the meal offering, the frankincense, the tithes of grain, the new wine and oil, which were commanded to be given to the Levites and singers and gatekeepers, and the offerings for the priests.[15]

If ever two men failed to live up to the meaning of their names, they did. 'God will restore' and the 'goodness of Jehovah' should have been a merger that signified great things, but not at this price. This storeroom should have been a safe house for the service of God, in a safe passage from the doorkeepers at the gate to the priests at the altar. But the way was badly compromised, and this may have had its roots in a marriage between one of Eliashib's grandsons and a daughter of Sanballat. How sad it is when family relationships distort spiritual judgement!

With tears running down their faces, Paul left the elders from Ephesus on the beach at Miletus, and one of the sobering thoughts he left with them was that *"savage wolves will come in among you, not sparing the flock."*[16] He urged them to pay attention, to take care of themselves in their role as elders and of the flock God had given them. As part of this, from then on they would be on the lookout for wolves. How would they know them? The Lord Jesus said, *"You will know them by their fruits."*[17] They can be identified by what they are, what they do, and by what they have: by their nature, their tactics, and by what they produce. Paul says they are *"men of corrupt minds and destitute of the truth, who suppose that godliness is a means of gain. From such men withdraw yourself."*[18]

A Threefold Denial

Jude's concern was that his brothers and sisters needed help to identify the character and conduct of the false teachers among them. He was in no doubt that the grace of God meant nothing to them, and that they wanted to influence those to whom it meant everything. These men were indecent and their corruption corrupted God's truth and grace. One thing we can be sure of is that grace never condones sin, it condemns it; it never excuses sin, it accuses it. Their underlying problem was that they had never died with Christ and therefore couldn't die to sin! Only dying with Him lets us die to it. Even in the present day, some gospel preaching makes little of sin and repentance and much of love and forgiveness; little of lordship and much of freedom, little of change and much of professing. It mistakes free grace for cheap grace and, in its own way, changes *"the truth of God into a lie."*[19]

These men made an outright denial of who the Saviour is, and kept on actively rejecting grace as the only means of salvation. They denied Him as *"the only Lord"* – *ton monon despotēn* – meaning they refused to have His sovereign and absolute rule. They denied Him as Lord – *kurios* – by refusing to acknowledge His divine authority; and they denied Him as the Christ, the anointed Messiah. True believers have no difficulty in saying that He is the Christ,[20] but these men rejected His Deity and authority, the Master and His mastery. Their continuing condition dictated their continuing action, so they had nothing in common with *"common salvation,"* and no fellowship with God and Christ.[21] It could never be said of them, *"you all are partakers with me of grace,"*[22] or that they were *"partakers of the divine nature, having escaped the corruption that is in the world through lust."*[23]

Cain, Balaam and Korah

This is another of Jude's tripods, and it presents three aspects of failure that motivated the false teachers. They were defilers, rejecters and blasphemers, and in this triplet (Jude 1:8) they were identified with:

- A challenge to worship in Cain;
- A challenge to stewardship in Balaam;
- A challenge to leadership in Korah.

Each of these is an example of showing opposition to the will of God. Cain had no reaction until God indicated that He had found pleasure in Abel's offering, but had not seen the same in his. We know from Hebrews 11:4 that Abel's faith in God supported his offering, whereas it was absent in Cain. These early days were no different from now, in that faith is founded on what God has said, and we can assume that both sons heard something through their parents. Hebrews makes it clear that Abel's faith was the basis of his offering, and also was the foundation of his righteousness and witness. In Cain's lack of faith, all three were missing. On a personal level, he was like the people of Israel when they failed to enter God's rest because *"the word which they heard did not profit them, not being mixed with faith in those who heard it."*[24] God had seen the blood of Abel's offering, but, instead of bloodshed in Cain's offering, the only bloodshed was in his sin of killing his brother.

The absence of faith spoke loudly in Cain, and the sound of his faithless voice was as displeasing to God as his offering. In contrast to Cain's living without faith, Abel died in faith, yet even then a voice was heard for God was able to say, *"The voice of your brother's blood cries out to Me from the ground."*[25] What a hard way it was for Cain to learn that *"Without faith it is impossible to please Him."*[26] If only faith had awakened its expectation of God and caused him to cry out, like David, *"Deliver me from the guilt of bloodshed, O God."*[27] This was very relevant to the false teachers Jude was thinking about, for it described their hostility toward the believers that Jude commended. Cain was the first wolf to kill one of God's sheep, and instead of being convicted by the acceptance of Abel's offering, he resented it and deprived his brother from ever offering another. Undoubtedly, these false men had the same intention.

Like Balaam, they had their eyes on personal gain, but they certainly didn't set a precedent. Judas Iscariot had his eye on the bag.[28] Long before him, there was Elisha's servant, Gehazi, who certainly knew how to run greedily after Naaman for wealth he would never spend and clothes he would never wear.[29] In Balaam's case, his hand was reaching out to the bribing hand that brought *"the diviner's fee,"*[30] and he *"loved the wages of unrighteousness* [wrong-doing, RV]."³¹ He is a great example of the often misunderstood proverb, *"A man's gift makes room for him, and brings him before great men."*³² God knew that the temptation would be there, and gave an early warning of it when He said, *"You shall take no bribe, for a bribe blinds the discerning and perverts the words of the righteous."*³³ It has ruined individuals, but there were times when it permeated God's people too.

Micah was particularly burdened about it, and wrote, *"Her heads judge for a bribe, her priests teach for pay, and her prophets divine for money. Yet they lean on the Lord, and say, 'Is not the Lord among us? No harm can come upon us.'"* And then he added, *"The prince asks for gifts, the judge seeks a bribe, and the great man utters his evil desire; so they scheme together."*³⁴ How well these earlier failures summed up the craving of the false teachers who *"ran greedily"* after profit! Jude's word for them was *ekcheo*, which means "poured out," so they didn't suffer from the slight temptation of a dripping desire, but from a gushing urge for gain.

Their third resemblance was to Korah whose challenge to Moses and Aaron in Numbers 16 showed defiance at its worst. In blatant confrontation, they accused their mediator and high priest of unwarranted dominance, and claimed that both holiness and the LORD were as much among the congregation as with each of them. After God's judgement had fallen on two hundred and fifty leaders, the agitation stirred the people to further complaint, and by the end of that day the death toll had risen to almost fifteen thousand. It was brought to an end when Aaron, for the first and only time that we know of, ran among the people with a censer containing fire from the altar and incense.

It was a graphic demonstration of the fire from the altar of God and the fragrance of Christ combined in the urgency of atonement.³⁵ If only the false teachers had listened, and learned that man's rebellion has only two outcomes: either they fall under the judgement of God or their plague is stopped by acceptance of the sacrifice of the Lord Jesus Christ and the merits of His atonement. The sequel to Korah's sin was that their two hundred and fifty copper censers were gathered up and hammered into thin plates as a covering for the altar. From then on, there was a reminder on the altar for every offerer that sin's *guilt* had been judged. The only other record of thin plates is in Exodus 39:3 where gold was beaten into plates and fine wires, and then interwoven with the tabernacle's colours. In a very distinct way, God arranged for the gold to be worked into each fibre: in the blue, in the purple, in the scarlet, and in the white fine linen. In this way He foreshadowed Christ's heavenliness, kingliness, lowliness, and righteousness, with *glory* at the heart of each.

These two precedents occurred on the same day: the high priest ran, and the memorial of judgement was fixed to the altar. It's a noticeable omission in the four gospel accounts that, when the Lord Jesus Christ was on earth, there is no indication that He ever ran. He stood, walked, sat, knelt and lay, but no mention of anything that caused Him to run. However, when His work on earth was over, the letter to the Hebrews describes His entrance to glory at the end of chapter 6 as the Forerunner. What a difference! He was entering into the presence of God as High Priest, and the end of chapter 2 depicts His ministry as being *"able to aid."* This time, instead of the word *prodromos* for the Forerunner, He is presented by the word *boēēthēsai*, which means to help or succour. It's interesting that it includes the Greek word *theō* and gives the thought that He runs to help those who call. How lovely to think that Aaron is recorded as having run only once, in judgement, yet Christ our great High Priest is constantly seen as running for our blessing.

All three examples of Cain, Balaam and Korah held a powerful condemnation for these false men for each of them stood for falsehood in one way or another. Cain's attempt to please God in worship was false; Balaam's attempt to prophesy was false, and the whole basis of Korah's attempt to gain priestly service was false. Worshippers, prophets and priests need to be genuine, and all falsehood means living a lie. This brought judgement from God in each case and a loud warning to false teachers that they were guaranteed to face it too.

Rocks, Clouds, and Trees

With this tripod, Jude had no intention of leaving the false teachers with no idea of what God thought of them. He didn't hold back in the slightest and, as we would say, he knew how to call a spade a spade! We could be tempted to say, tongue in cheek, "Hey Jude, could you come to the point? Can you make yourself clear?" But there's no need for such irony for the real speaker is the Spirit of God. His hard-hitting lessons came in pairs from sea, land and sky, and they should have been deeply convicted by what He said.

1. They are rocks ... and raging waves

The New King James Version speaks about *"spots,"* but this relates to the Greek word *spilos* – a spot or defect. The intended word *spilas* refers to a reef or hidden rocks in the sea. The thought of hidden rocks allows us immediately to think of unnoticed things, just as these men had been, but they are no longer unnoticed. God has His own way of bringing things to light, and even hidden rocks can be brought to the surface! Jude senses that it's time for suitably gifted men to speak up. He would have known that among the spiritual gifts given to the church (1 Cor.12:28) was the particular ministry of *"administrations"* or, in other translations, *"governments."*

Both of these words can be rather misleading when we think of how we normally understand and apply them. The word *kubernēsis* is related to the helmsman or pilot (*kubernētēs*) of a ship. This implies someone who knows the currents and the undercurrents, the shallows, rocks and reefs, and is able safely to steer the vessel. He knew it was a time for spiritual helmsmen to pilot his brothers and sisters through troubled waters, and there are still times when the same spiritual skills are needed. Good helmsmen prevent shipwreck, and are God's antidote to false teachers. Their spiritual perception will detect menacing signs of danger and guide God's people clear of the shipwrecking intentions of evil men.

One version of the Scriptures (RSV) translates *kubernēsis* as "administrators," and this ambiguous connotation doesn't give the right sense at all. Naturally, there will be times when the practicalities of church funds, and correspondence need an administrator, but this is not what the spiritual gift implies. Unsaved men and women can be qualified administrators, but only redeemed men and women can be endued with the spiritual gift of spiritual navigation. As raging waves in a troubled sea, false men stir up lots of mire and dirt, and prevent peace.[36] Wild billows churn up all sorts of filth. As many beaches testify, disgrace has the habit of resurfacing! To its shame, church history shows that churches can testify to it as well, but our Chief Helmsman gives this assurance to those who take His word: *"Do not fear them. For there is nothing covered that will not be revealed, and hidden that will not be known."*[37]

2. Shepherds ... autumn trees

Jude's readers were in a battleground where those who were Christ-centred were under attack by those who were self-centred. To illustrate this, God says they were *"serving themselves,"* and His word for serving is the word *poimainō* – "shepherding." Instead of being God-appointed shepherds of the sheep, they were self-appointed shepherds of themselves. This was a fruitless exercise, for in their emptiness they were worse than the people of Israel whom the Lord portrayed as a barren fig tree. They had nothing but leaves, and these autumn trees were leafless as well as fruitless. And being rootless, they would remain so! In fact they were dead, pulled up by the roots and grounded in nothing, so they were twice dead: getting and giving nothing. Faith had never been sown in these ungodly men, so there could never be a harvest through faith. They were faithless and fruitless and must have looked so different from those who were planted in the house of the Lord! [38] It would make us wonder if leaders were emboldened to tell them so, by pointing out that Jude's letter had exposed them.

3. *Clouds … wandering stars*

Solomon said, *"If the clouds are full of rain, they empty themselves upon the earth,"*[39] but these men were empty. They were all bulk and no water, and Solomon had this kind of individual in mind when he went on to say, *"Whoever falsely boasts of giving is like clouds and wind without rain."*[40] They were bone dry, and there was only one reason for this: they had never been refreshed in Christ and couldn't refresh others. They were wandering stars, the opposite of those that were set in their galaxies by the Lord and by which men can set their compass. Of these, God has said, *"Lift up your eyes on high, and see who has created these things, who brings out their host by number; He calls them all by name, by the greatness of His might and the strength of His power, not one is missing."*[41] By contrast, meteors and comets that are nameless to God flash across the sky as its evidence of a fallen creation. What an apt description of false teachers who shoot off at tangents and go headlong into darkness! With much thankfulness to God, we take our place among His servants who have heard His desire, *"that you may become blameless and harmless, children of God without fault in the midst of a crooked and perverse generation, among whom you shine as lights in the world."*[42] And we do this knowing that, *"Those who are wise shall shine like the brightness of the firmament, and those who turn many to righteousness like the stars forever and ever."*[42]

ALL YOUR WAVES (*Psalms 42:7; 88:7*)
Like Him whose power was seen as much
In death, as in His infancy,
Waves in their birth, and in their death,
May never lose their potency;

Yet waves pre-set to sweep o'er Him,
And destined long before His birth,
Were formed while He was still in heaven,
Their deluge sent to crash on earth.

A course determined on the throne
By the eternal Trinity
Was fixed to end at Calvary's cross
On Christ 'mid man's brutality.

God's waves collided on Him there,
Each billow judgement-driven,
To bring us sinners to His cross
And to His throne in heaven.

As much as when in Galilee,
With waves and billow's bearing down,
He slept, unthreatened by the sea
That threatened those who were with Him;

Yet well He knew a greater storm
Would threaten Him, but not His own,
And give eternal rest to those
For whom He would for sin atone.

And now there is no storm to face,
The cross for Him, and us, is past.

The transient billows, by His grace,
Have given way to perfect peace.

Wave after wave, through precious blood,
Of peace secured, an endless flow,
Beginning in the heart of God
And ending in our hearts below.

His waves of wrath forever past,
His waves of peace forever last!
And what was birthed by Him above
Has birthed in us undying love.
(A. McIlree)

2.6 REVELATION: ON THE BASIS OF 'WHEN'?

Those who want to defeat their enemy must have victory with God. Jude certainly did, and his knowledge of how to handle false teachers flowed from his knowledge of God and His Word. Having charted their character with his tripods:

1. Cain, Balaam and Korah;
2. Rocks, clouds and self-serving shepherds;
3. Waves, stars and trees.

... he made a devastating assessment of them, but wasn't finished. The careful servant of God always makes sure that his view is well-founded, and it soon becomes evident to present-day disciples of the Lord Jesus Christ that divine revelation is to Jude's tripod what a laser level is to a surveyor's. Jude knew, and still teaches his readers, that withstanding false teachers and dismantling false teaching is inseparably connected to knowing what God has revealed. Shallowness gives no defence, so refuge must be found in the security of biblical revelation and reasoning.

Jeremiah wrote about Dedan and of how they were advised to *"dwell deep,"*[1] which meant they should find refuge in a place that was far from the fringes where they would be exposed to invasion. In a military sense, they were to dig themselves in, which is a graphic illustration of what believers should do. Living on the fringe of scriptural understanding leaves us vulnerable to attack, but the more we *"dwell deep"* the better we will be at contending earnestly for the faith. With this in mind, Jude presented three examples of how God has dealt with hostile opposition.

Unbelieving Israelites, Angels, Sodom and Gomorrah

One of God's great principles is that *"righteousness exalts a nation, but sin is a reproach to any people."*[2] The contrast is so stark: righteousness "lifts up" and sin is "wicked."[3] Jude's examples span earth and heaven, time and eternity, redeemed and unregenerate, and show the affront that sin is to the holiness of God. They also show a consistent response from *"Him who judges righteously."*[4]

The People

The adversary delights in alluring individuals into sin, but also does all he can to disrupt God-centred gatherings. Who would have thought that His people would have been so badly affected in their wanderings between the Red Sea and the Jordan? Even though the great Redeemer took them out of Egypt, this didn't take Egypt out of them, and unbelief robbed them of going into the land of Canaan. God took care of the advancing Egyptian army as it attempted to overtake them in their escape, and promised, *"The Egyptians whom you see today, you shall see again no more forever."*[5] Nevertheless, others came shortly afterwards, and it's on record that Amalek attacked their rear ranks: *"all the stragglers at your rear."*[6]

Once again, God promised that the memory of Amalek would be blotted out from under heaven for what they had done, yet the people had a much bigger lesson to learn. Their greatest enemy wouldn't attack from behind, but from within; they would become their own worst enemy until the wilderness became a graveyard. The book of Numbers tells its own story: in fact, it could be called the book of dwindling numbers!

- In chapter 14 -The influence of ten spies who brought back a "bad report" from Canaan was seen in a mass outbreak of rebellion among the people, to the extent they defied and rejected God and wanted to stone Joshua and Caleb. This resulted in God slaying the ten and condemning the whole generation to death in the wilderness, with the promise that only Joshua and Caleb would survive;
- In chapter 16- Two hundred and fifty men were killed for their part in Korah's rebellion, and fourteen thousand seven hundred died in the following plague;
- In chapter 21- An unknown number died after being bitten by fiery serpents;
- In chapter 25- Twenty-four thousand died in the plague that accompanied the sin at Baal Peor;
- In chapter 26:65- God referred to His earlier promise in chapter 14:29 that a whole generation would die and, true to His Word, only Joshua and Caleb survived of all who had been counted in the earlier census.

By referring his readers to God's dealings with the people of Israel, Jude left them in no doubt that He remains faithful to His Word, whether in blessing or in judgement. He had described the people as murmurers and complainers, and these are the words Jude would use in verse 16 regarding the false teachers (RV). He had reminded them of Balaam who, in spite of himself, had to tell Balak, *"God is not a man, that He should lie, nor a son of man that He should repent. Has He said, and will He not do? Or has He spoken, and will He not make it good?"*[7] This is the point that the false teachers should have taken to heart as soon as Jude stated they were marked out for condemnation. In their state of denying the Lord, it was irreversible. They also should have recognised that God thwarted Balak's plans, and would do the same with theirs. Had He not said, and would He not do? Moses' prayer in Psalm 90 holds a sad summary of Israel's wilderness experience: *"We have been consumed by Your anger, and by Your wrath we are terrified ... For all our days have passed away in Your wrath."*[8]

Angels

The greatest God-centred gathering the adversary ever disrupted was in heaven. Before the physical creation of Genesis 1, God created His angelic host with perfectly ordered ranks and seniority, and character suited to the Triune presence. Their harmony of character and purpose was wonderfully demonstrated when, in unison, *"the morning stars sang together, and all the sons of God shouted for joy"*[9] when the foundations of the earth were laid. Such was their response to seeing its Creator, and theirs, at work.

His mention of an innumerable company[10] refers to the present gathering around His throne of angels that are *"of God ... holy ... His ... mighty ... and elect."*[11] It is of this gathering that we read, *"He makes His angels spirits, His ministers a flame of fire,"*[12] meaning they instantly fulfil His will, and speedily like wind and lightning. They also are said to be *"ministering spirits sent forth to minister for those who will inherit salvation."*[13] This speaks of them fulfilling a dual role in their service: *leitourgika*, toward God in heaven like temple worshippers; *diakonian*, toward believers on earth as helpers on their journey to the salvation that is ready to be revealed in the last time.[14]

Before all this earthward service began, an even greater host surrounded the LORD of hosts until Satan led a rebellion that led to his fall. The Lord Jesus Christ said, *"I saw Satan fall like lightning from heaven,"*[15] which conveys how quickly he was judged and removed, along with those who were banished with him. John gives a graphic account in Revelation 12:4 when he says that the dragon's *"tail drew a third of the stars of heaven,"* and this may indicate the size of following he generated. If so, it shows the forces on which he has been able to draw throughout his efforts to topple the purposes of God on earth.

Paul has left us in no doubt about their activity in the heavenly places and how their influence lies behind the human face of opposition believers experience. We may feel that we are wrestling with human hostility, but he makes it clear that we are up against greater forces than men, beginning with the devil himself. Then Paul adds, *"For we do not wrestle against flesh and blood, but against principalities, against powers, against the rulers of the darkness of this age, against spiritual hosts of wickedness."*[16] They once belonged to Jehovah of hosts, but now they are hosts of wickedness who had forfeited:

- The glory of heaven for everlasting chains;
- Eternal light for eternal darkness;
- God-given liberty for Satanic bondage.

Peter reasoned that *"if God did not spare the angels who sinned, but cast them down to hell and delivered them into chains of darkness, to be reserved for judgement,"*[17] then judgement also awaits false teachers. Jude's comment is similar – *"And the angels who did not keep their proper domain, but left their own abode, He has reserved in everlasting chains under darkness for the judgement of the great day."* In telling us they *"did not keep their proper domain"* (Gr. *archē*), Jude means they didn't hold fast to the principality (Gr. *archē*) God had given them; and they are now principalities under the direction of the devil.

How persuasive the devil must be! It was one thing for him to enter the Garden of Eden to deceive Eve, quite another to operate among the host of heaven and spread his lies there in the belief of having an effect. Why did the omniscient God not challenge him as soon as the thought came into his mind or as he whispered it among other angelic beings? The only reason we can assume is that the eternal purpose of the Father, Son and Holy Spirit to redeem had already been formed, and that the fall of Satan was permitted in the sure knowledge of Their sovereignty that it would lead to His purpose being fulfilled.

Sodom and Gomorrah

Well could we, again, apply the stark contrast of Proverbs 14:34, but this time it is seen in looking at 'before and after' descriptions. When Lot looked at the landscape before him, he saw *"that it was well watered everywhere* [before the Lord destroyed Sodom and Gomorrah] *like the garden of the LORD, like the land of Egypt as you go toward Zoar."*[18] Twenty years later, according to Newberry, Abraham gazed on a very different scene when *"he looked toward Sodom and Gomorrah, and toward all the land of the plain; and he saw, and behold, the smoke of the land which went up like the smoke of a furnace."*[19] Sadder still, it never recovered. More than four centuries later, when God was about to speak to Moses about his death, He mentioned it again: *"The whole land is brimstone, salt, and burning; it is not sown, nor does it bear, nor does any grass grow there, like the overthrow of Sodom and Gomorrah, Admah, and Zeboim, which the Lord overthrew in His anger and His wrath."*[20] How could anyone want these in exchange for the lush conditions they had known? Barrenness and dryness instead of being well watered; and how could anyone want to lose the beauty and fertility that was like the garden of the LORD?

God's people had forfeited all the blessings associated with entering the land and His rest, a place they would never see,[21] angels forfeited their place around the throne of God and the holy atmosphere of His presence, the place and the Person they would never see again; and Sodom and Gomorrah lost conditions they would never reclaim. The people of Israel went after things that were false and ungodly; angels believed a lie from the father of lies[22] and turned from their only Master and Lord; and Sodom and Gomorrah went after the false pleasures of their filthy talk and walk.

Jude must have touched raw nerves as, by the leading of the Spirit of God, he highlighted the three areas of falsehood that the false teachers promoted among his readers, and as he fearlessly assured them of the impending wrath and judgement of God. Just as death, darkness and a day of reckoning, and fire were the lot of the people, angels, and Sodom and Gomorrah, so the false teachers were under the same condemnation. At the same time, the dear fellow-believers must have taken heart from all that applied to them:

- Like the people who fled from Egypt, they also had fled from bondage, having escaped the corruption that is in the world;[23]
- Like the angels who never fell, they were devoted to their only Master and Lord, Jesus Christ. Because of this, they also could rejoice in being *"of God ... holy ... His ... mighty ... and elect"*;[24]
- Like Sodom and Gomorrah in their former state, they were cultivated as God's tilled land[25] with its accompanying features of order, beauty, fragrance and growth being the testimony of their lives both individually and as a gathered company of the Lord's people.

What They Knew

So there was much to condemn the false and commend the faithful. Jude knew that they knew what he was speaking about, though this isn't clear in some versions. In verse 5, the New King James Version says, "I want to remind you, though you once knew this," but other versions make it clearer:

- ASV - *"though ye know all things once for all"*;
- NASB - *"though you know all things once for all"*;
- RSV - *"though you were once for all fully informed"*;
- NRSV - *"though you are fully informed"*;
- RV - *"though ye know all things once for all."*

By reminding them, Jude brought matters to the forefront of their minds so that they were more fully prepared *"to contend earnestly for the faith which was once for all delivered to the saints"* (RV) – and the point is, including to them!

What They Never Knew

Up until now, Jude has been reminding believers of what is recorded in the Old Testament Scriptures, but now there's a change. He moves from former revelation to fresh revelation by current inspiration, just as Paul did when he named Jannes and Jambres[26] as the magicians who opposed Moses in Exodus 7 and 8. Jude's new information must have carried enormous weight with the company of believers. Suddenly, they must have realised that Jude was sharing things that had never been heard before, and in this privilege they must have been greatly encouraged to handle their opposition.

Michael the Archangel

Jude's first disclosure enlightened them to the dispute that took place between Michael the Archangel and the devil about the burial of Moses' body. There is no mention of this in Deuteronomy 34, and its emphatic comment is, that *"He [God] buried him ... but no one knows his grave to this day."* God chose the resting place for the body of His servant and friend,[27] and the devil doesn't know the place. Had the devil buried him, God would have known the place, so even on this point Jude was stating that God is sovereign, and the devil isn't. Had the people known, he could have misled them into misplaced hero worship, venerating the man, and promoting pilgrimage to his grave. Jebel Musa, the mountain of Moses, is an example of this. Visitors can climb its 3,700 steps of repentance that were cut out by a monk, and on their ascent they can visit a monastery, a mosque, a chapel to Mary, the Spring of Elijah and the cave where the Lord is said to have visited him. Religious men love monuments and shrines, and the adversary has used them well to distract countless men and women from God and from true worship, not least in the case of Mary.

As Michael contended with the devil, he made no attempt to bring *"a reviling accusation"* against him. He had been there when Satan led his rebellion in heaven. He watched as he and his rebel angels were cast out of heaven. He had seen the supremacy of God and the sentence He passed on His adversary, but he made no reference to any of this. Nor did he make any judgemental remark on the devil's inability to know what God knows. Instead, he simply said, *"The Lord rebuke you!"*

What a lesson for these believers and for us! In the power of the cross, we have been delivered from one who is too strong for us,[28] and should be careful what we say about him. He and his angels are a mighty force, and well may we say, *"We have no power against this great multitude that is coming against us; nor do we know what to do, but our eyes are upon You."*[29] Protected by the whole armour of God and righteousness, we stand against the devil's methods, and with it we can *"withstand"* evil and *"resist"* him.[30] Both words are identical – *anthistēmi* – meaning we oppose him in the righteous character of our Lord Jesus Christ, but leave it to God to rebuke him. On this side of Calvary's triumph over the devil and his works,[31] we can trust Him to say it for us: *"The LORD rebuke you, Satan!"*[32]

What a lesson for false men, too! The One whom they denied is the One who censured the devil, and the debate ended with the potency of His word. How could they hear what Jude was disclosing about the devil's tactics and not take on board the implications for themselves? Jude knew the reason. While he knew there were things the assembly knew and didn't know, he also was aware what kind of men these were.

Brute Beasts

Sometimes, ignorance has a loud voice. Jude's description wasn't complimentary, but he knew how irrational and ferocious these men were. Put literally, his words could be translated as 'unreasonable animals,' and they were mixing with men and women of God who were threatened by their perverted and predatory ways. In verse 8, he says they are defilers, despisers and blasphemers who, as dreamers, live in the unreality of their false profession and teaching. They:

- **defile the flesh** - living in the filthiness of the flesh;
- **reject authority** - disregarding and despising Lordship, honour and worship;
- **speak evil of** - blaspheming and railing against authority, both earthly dignitaries and heavenly.

In contrast to the believers who knew what they knew and didn't know, these men blasphemed what they didn't know and their lives withered under the influence of what they did know. Natural knowledge darkened them in their darkness, yet spiritual knowledge never enlightened them for spiritual things are spiritually discerned and not received by the natural man.[33]

Enoch

In the same way that he received formerly undisclosed details from the Holy Spirit about Michael, Jude proceeds to share what he has been told about Enoch. Most of what we know of him is gleaned from the early chapters of Genesis. For instance, he walked with God for 300 years after the birth of his son, Methuselah, which may have marked a turning point in his life as a 65-year-old man.[34] During those three hundred years, he enjoyed communion with God and walked in step with His purpose, until the day came when it was as if he walked farther than ever. His Companion didn't change, but the scenery did as he left earth and was taken into eternity.

Peter describes Noah as a preacher of righteousness,[35] and now Jude indicates that Enoch was a preacher of judgement to come. The Genesis account of his life makes no mention of his prophetic ministry, yet Jude makes it clear that this was a vital part of his walk with God. The obvious truth is, of course, that if Enoch preached this message then he received it from God as he walked with Him, even though the timing of the event to which he referred was not made known to him. Even so, from his distant outpost of almost five and a half thousand years ago, he was specific about its purpose. He knew:

· **The Lord will come** – to reign on earth;
· **Who will come with Him** – with His saints;
· **Why He will come** – to judge the ungodly;
· **What He will judge** – ungodly deeds, ways, and speech.

The Lord Jesus Christ spoke about this in Matthew 13:41-43 when He said, *"The Son of Man will send out His angels, and they will gather out of His kingdom all things that offend, and those who practice lawlessness, and will cast them into the furnace of fire. There will be wailing and gnashing of teeth. Then the righteous will shine forth as the sun in the kingdom of their Father. He who has ears to hear, let him hear!"* It was later given to the apostle Paul to add that the time is coming, *"when the Lord Jesus is revealed from heaven with His mighty angels, in flaming fire taking vengeance on those who do not know God, and on those who do not obey the gospel of our Lord Jesus Christ. These shall be punished with everlasting destruction from the presence of the Lord and from the glory of His power, when He comes, in that Day, to be glorified in His saints and to be admired among all those who believe."*[36]

Ungodly

It's understandable that walking with God made Enoch very concerned about ungodliness, and the closer we are to God and his holiness the more we will be, too. He was concerned about ungodly people with their ungodly works done in ungodly ways, and the ungodly harshness of words spoken by ungodly sinners. Four times he emphasised the wicked and their wickedness, and Jude adds a fifth and sixth in verses 4 and 18 to describe the character and walk of these false men. He knew all about their works and ways and words and walk, exposing them as evil speakers, grumblers, complainers, flatterers and mockers.[37] They were master fault-finders, the ultimate example of those who complain about the speck in someone's eye while they have planks in theirs.[38] They were well known for their bulging vocabularies and puffed-up talk, as with smooth words and flattering speech they tried to deceive the hearts of the simple.[39]

These Are

It's impossible to miss Jude's opinion (see APPENDIX 2) – and the Holy Spirit's, too, since the letter came by inspiration through a man moved by Him – but we notice another tripod, as three times over he says, *"These are"*[40]:

- Natural, but not spiritual;
- Divisive, not united;
- Living, but not alive in the Spirit; born, but not born again.

Jude could have concentrated on reminding believers of what they were, and we are thankful for scriptures that do this.

- *"You were slaves of sin, yet ... you were delivered."*[41]
- *"You were once darkness, but now you are light in the Lord."*[42]
- *"You were like sheep going astray, but have now returned to the shepherd and overseer of your souls."*[43]

Instead, he expressed what is true and exposed what was false by leaving both sides in no doubt about this very dark cloud - *"These are."*

MEETING HIM

Rom.14:10; 2 Cor.5:10

How shall I meet my Saviour's face
When He and I at last retrace
My works before His judgement seat,
My service laid down at His feet,
Will His 'Well done' make it complete?

How shall I meet my Saviour's eyes,
That fire which proves and purifies:
A searching, penetrating gaze
That estimates my words and ways,
Will they be worthy of His praise?

How shall I stand before His throne?
My eyes cast down before His own?
Or shall it be with gold, not dross;
With joy, not grief; with gain, not loss;
I trace the triumph of His cross?

My Lord, my Saviour, glorious King,
Help me today prepare to bring
Some gold, and silver, precious stones;
Some sacrifice that gladly owns
And proves Your sacrifice atones.

Oh, may I meet my Saviour's smile,
Cause Him who died to reconcile
To view a work that's all His own –
Not mine, but His, and for Him done –
Then from His hand receive a crown.

(A. McIlree)

2.7 BENEDICTION: ON THE BASIS OF 'WHERE?'

"But you, beloved, building yourselves up on your most holy faith, praying in the Holy Spirit, keep yourselves in the love of God, looking for the mercy of our Lord Jesus Christ unto eternal life. And on some have compassion making a distinction; but others save with fear, pulling them out of the fire, hating even the garment defiled by the flesh" (Jude vv.20-23).

* * *

It's three thousand years since Solomon wrote, *"Better is the end of a thing than its beginning."*[1] Jude's short message proves this to be true, and yet it's noticeable that if the letter could be bent around to form a circle the end would connect in remarkable relevance with the beginning. We needn't be surprised for the same could be done with the whole canon of Scripture. Bend the whole Book into a circle and we will find that the theme in the opening chapters of Genesis, the first man with his bride in the presence of the tree of life, finds its counterpart in the closing chapters of the Revelation with the second Man, His bride and the tree of life. This is the divine order of inspiration, so there's nothing accidental about it and Jude would be the first to become aware of this as he penned his part. It was no random collection of sayings, but something closely interconnected, so that its purpose would be recognised firstly by him, then by those who received it, and ultimately by us. What a pity it would be if in our day we missed the integration that is presented to us in its layout!

Having begun with a salutation, which led into thoughts of salvation and the need for contention, he then gave a resounding condemnation of false teachers who had crept in unnoticed and much-needed revelation to strengthen the faithful. This was Spirit-given that they might be enabled to contend and overcome, and then be encouraged by a benediction that contains shades of what he had already shared.

It's easy to see, when Jude comes to the close of his letter, that he has become very adept at moving his tripod. What began in verse 1 with thoughts of being called, beloved and preserved is reflected in the content of the benediction where they are still beloved and kept. He did well, as an effective helper, to allay their fears by showing that he had made the essential first step of grasping the reality of their situation. This was vital for he didn't want to leave them there, but to lift them above it and to assure them that they could be lifted above it. So he began his benediction by fixing their eyes on the Trinity – the Holy Spirit, God, and the Lord Jesus Christ – and kept their eyes there at its end. It was a wonderful way, like balm to the soul, to let them know that, in spite of all their difficulties, a united God combined Their ministry toward them. Of all Jude's tripods, this is the greatest: the divine Tri-unity were working together for their blessing and comfort, which They sealed with a benediction that could be even more real to them than the hardships they faced.

It's interesting that the Holy Spirit is the first to be mentioned for there's a false notion that the Holy Spirit can be referred to as the third Person of deity. Deity has no third Person. In Matthew 28, we read about the Father, the Son and the Holy Spirit and it's this particular order that causes some to speak of the Lord Jesus as the second Person and the Holy Spirit as the third. Paul helps us to see this in the closing words of his second letter to Corinth: *"The grace of the Lord Jesus Christ, and the love of God, and the communion of the Holy Spirit be with you all. Amen."* We say "Amen" to the truth of this, and also to the order. He wasn't disagreeing with the Lord's order in Matthew 28 or suggesting that He is first, the Father second, and the Holy Spirit third.

Like Jude, he was not inferring any descending order, but rather Their equality. Jude was speaking about how all three are inseparably concerned and involved in helping them overcome the difficulties in their company. Louis Berkhof is at pains to show that the terminology of Person in the Trinity is not completely satisfactory, as it suggests separate identity, and no one is in doubt that the Trinity is one in essence. He points out the conversation that can take place between Father, Son and Spirit, and how hypostasis led to the term existentia as distinct from essentia. The upshot is that the matter is too profound, and notions of priority are misplaced.

Beloved ... Beloved ... Beloved

It's interesting to note what he said at the opening of his letter: *"You are called, beloved, and preserved,"* so we find the word *"beloved"* in verse 1, again in verse 3 and finally in verse 20. So it's one of Jude's tripods. The thought of being *"beloved"* is first expressed in relation to God's care for this gathering, and the next three occurrences is Jude's concern and affection for them. He was sharing in the divine affections of God toward this gathering, and they would become very much aware of that as they read the letter. Jude felt for them what Paul expressed to the church in Philippi: *"God is my witness, how greatly I long for you all in the affection of Jesus Christ."*[2] How wonderful to feel as He feels and to love as He loves. Is it possible? The Lord Jesus says, *"As the Father loved Me, I also have loved you; abide in My love,"* and we abide or continue in it by showing it to Him and to others.

Building ... Praying ... Keeping

At the opening of the letter, we see what God does for them and for us, but verses 20 and 21 speak about *"building"* in regard to what we do for ourselves. By saying, *"But you, beloved, building yourselves up on your most holy faith, praying in the Holy Spirit,"* he was introducing two thoughts to them. One was the triumph of the Person within them, for he wants them to know that the Holy Spirit, the Father, and the Son are their only means of victory. They alone are the source of all triumph. Just as the Lord Jesus Christ has ensured our salvation, our service is ensured by all three Persons working together as They did at the cross. Now, from the throne of God He wants to make known to them that the reality of God's power and presence ought to be sensed within them.

The Father's care should be known within them, and the love of the Lord Jesus Christ ought to be ministering to their own spirit through the Holy Spirit. So he was saying that, first of all, it's the triumph of the triune Person within, but it's coupled with the thought of triumphing in the triune purpose. Jude had two reasons for saying *"building yourselves up in your most holy faith,"* for two things were happening in this gathering. One was they were being impeded by false men; and, secondly, they were wrestling with an inward impediment that was self-inflicted, as some of them yielded to the spiritual effects of false teaching. This was a gathering of the Lord's people who had known the blessing of God in their salvation and of being brought together through baptism and addition into the joy of assembly service. Then these men crept in to this unsuspecting company of disciples who probably had rejoiced in their coming, until they saw the effect they were having on one and another.

Jude became aware there was something far wrong and intended writing to them about common salvation, but he knew this would be hard to achieve since some were not saved at all. Others who were saved had their joy diminished because of the impact these false teachers were making. As he thought of the Person and the purpose having an effect on them, he saw this triplet as being the essence of their spiritual survival.

- Building themselves up through constant devotion to constructive biblical teaching, which is the faith being lived by faith. It's not salvation followed by legislation; it's believing faith followed by faith in our beliefs;
- Praying in the Holy Spirit by maintaining a regular prayer life that is Spirit-led;
- Keeping themselves in the love of God, living in it and being obedient to it by keeping His commandments.[3]

These must lie at the heart of every believer's service, if we want to be building ourselves up, to keep on praying, and to keep on keeping ourselves in His love. The tense of the Greek verbs indicates an on-going commitment, so we should be consistently building, praying and keeping rather than haphazard. If God is your Keeper[4], He will never let you go, and our response should confirm that we want to keep up our devotion and never let it go. God has laid a sure foundation in each believer, but the problem is that some have an unsure structure. What he has laid can never be taken away, but these men were doing their utmost to take away the satisfaction and joy from their service.

It's always the adversary's aim that, if he doesn't keep us from forgiveness in God's salvation, he will do all he can to keep us from fulfilment in godly service. His aim, of course, is not only to deprive the believer, but also to keep you from giving satisfaction to the heart of God. The secret lies in our wanting to do what God has already done. In verse 1, He is the One who keeps; and in verse 21 we keep ourselves. In both verses, the word is the same – tēreō – which means to guard by keeping your eye on it. He is our guardian and there should be a corresponding keeping desire in the hearts of those He is guarding. We should be protective of all He protects. What a challenge this is! Are we genuinely keeping our eyes on preserving our love for the Lord and for His Word?

The purpose of building, praying and keeping is not only for the good of the person, but for edifying the whole assembly. We should be making it an edifice of building, praying, loving people, but we can't be this without being men and women of the Word. Paul spoke about *"the word of His grace, which is able to build you up."*[5] He also taught us to *"pursue the things which make for peace and the things by which one may edify another."*[6] He also reminds us that *"love edifies,"*[7] so the assembly should be a place where sharing the Word and showing love provide the right atmosphere for spiritual enjoyment and growth.

During the years of Israel's wilderness journey, there were men who carried the ark of the LORD on their shoulders. This meant they walked closely together, and at the end of their sojourn they waited together. The ark is a symbol of the exalted Lord Jesus Christ keeping us together in step with each other in collective testimony. With Him, we walk and wait, and worship; so we can readily link our *"most holy faith"* with the Man in the Most Holy Place. Just as our most holy faith is for the enriching of our corporate walk, the Most Holy Place is for expressing our worship through our great High Priest as the most holy Person. Jude wanted to encourage his readers to walk with the Lord in such a way that their prayerful adherence to the Word would be clearly evident to those whose sole mission was to upset them. It was only by maintaining a close relationship with Him that they could contend earnestly for the faith. It was for them to take care of the earnestness, and they could leave the effectiveness with God.

On some ... Some ... Others

Damage had already been done in this gathering. Some had been influenced by the persuasive arguments of the false teachers, and their confidence had been shaken. This prompted Jude to make this Christlike appeal: *"on some have compassion."* Once again, he was asking them to do what God had done for them. He had shown "mercy," and His mercy should make them merciful. Now it was being multiplied to them, so they ought to be merciful to their damaged brothers and sisters. This should have made an impact on those who caused the damage, as they saw mercy being shown by those who disagreed with them for letting it happen.

Not all versions of the Bible clearly show who had been affected. The English Standard Version says, *"And have mercy on those who doubt; save others by snatching them out of the fire; to others show mercy with fear, hating even the garment stained by the flesh"*; and the Revised Version translates it as, *"And on some have mercy ... and some save ... and on some have mercy."* They have done this because the Greek word *hous*, which can be translated as "some" or "others," is used three times in these verses. This meant three kinds of targeted help:

· The first was by showing mercy to those who were wavering, which allowed them to put God's mercy to good use, while causing them to enjoy the Lord's promise: *"Blessed are the merciful, for they shall obtain mercy"*[8];

· The second were those who needed to be forcibly hauled from the fire of heretical teaching. They had listened to false men, had played with fire, and needed strong hands to bring robust deliverance;

· The third needed mercy combined with a sense of alarm that those with a stained testimony, depicted by filthy garments, could defile those who were trying to help.

Their defilement didn't come from external staining that marred their outer garment, but from fleshly desires in the person that stained their inner garment (Gr. *chitōn*). When the Lord looked at the church in Sardis, He said, *"You have a few names ... who have not defiled their garments,"*[9] and He meant they had been blackened. His word to Laodicea was, *"I counsel you to buy from Me ... white garments,"*[10] so that they would stand out as being different. In other words, He wanted their testimony to be pure. Laodicea was well known for its flocks of black sheep from which black clothing was made, but the church should be well known for the whiteness of its purity.

Verse 22 shows that the damaged Christians could be seen in three different parts: those who were not seriously affected, those who were, and those who could defile anyone who tried to rescue them. Jude must have known there was a fourth part who remained faithful and that they were to be the rescuers. They had a big task, didn't they? All three approaches may still be called for in trying to rescue Christian lives from various kinds of damage. For some, being merciful will be enough; for others, it may take a firmer hand; and for some, it may be with fear that we try to win them back knowing that, being damaged, they may damage those who are trying to help. It's not enough to be well meaning in any of these. Each approach is different, but mercy and strength and fear are essential elements of Spirit-given help.

Trying to assist spiritual recovery is impossible without doing it in a spiritual way. We may know some who have been side-tracked. If so, what has been our response? Critical, judgemental or merciful? When Jude began by saying, *"Mercy, peace, and love be multiplied to you,"* he knew how much these would be needed in the recovery process. It was as if he were assuring them that, if they wanted to win their brothers and sisters, they should make sure that what they were receiving from God was what they were conveying to them.

There's a remarkable illustration of this in the days of King Jehoash in 2 Kings 12 when Jehoiada was priest. The temple had fallen into disrepair and there were obvious areas of damage that called for reinvestment and restoration. They needed to give in a very definite way for the renewal that some parts required and Jehoiada came up with an idea that had never been thought of before. He took a box, bored a hole in its lid, and set it beside the altar of God for collections that would go toward restoring damaged stones and woodwork. Things were not as they should be, but a young king and a priest found a way of giving the people a collective sense of responsibility and purpose.

With no precedent to follow, Jehoiada could have placed his box in a number of places, and we would have understood if he had set it at the gate of the temple. He chose the altar, the place of sacrifice, that pointed to the cross-work of the Lord Jesus Christ where He offered Himself for sin and for our common salvation. He even chose its north side, which in Hebrew means dark, gloomy and hidden, where the lamb was slain.[11] It's a very interesting thought that Jehoiada and the people knew that investing in the temple of God began at the altar of God, and we can apply the same principle. Those who share the temple character of a local assembly[12] also understand that their desire to invest in the people of God begins with our appreciation of the cross.

Does this hold a valuable lesson for us? Are we not aware of brothers and sisters who are like damaged stones and are badly in need of help? To what extent are we investing in the ministry of restoration? Thankfully it's not often that we have to talk with a brother or sister who is leaving the church or has to be removed from it, but in that conversation it's important that we discuss the Lord's provision of a way back. Even in a time of disappointment or disagreement, we need to start there so that their affections are won all over again by the man of Calvary. It's at that stage they need to know how they will restore their relationship with the Lord and restart building themselves up in their most holy faith.

This implies three things: willing acceptance of His teaching, consistent adherence to upholding it, and heartfelt allegiance. It also implies absorbing it, understanding it, and living by it in such a way that our manner of living is affected and conditioned by it. Jude's phrase is very meaningful for it really means that *"the faith"* of verse 3 has become "your faith." More than that, it means that *"the most holy faith"* has become our *"most holy faith,"* and this implies that its nature becomes ours. Yes, we know that God's truths are our guidelines for spiritual service, but they need to be more than that. They need to be our guidelines for spiritual character. His *most holy* faith should produce holiness, and His most holy *faith* should produce faithfulness. If so, the real impact of His teaching will be seen in the holiness of our faithfulness, and in the faithfulness of our holiness.

Sadly, some believers seem to believe that doctrine gets in the way of Christian living, without realising how essential it is. Paul made it clear to Timothy that doctrine accords with godliness,[13] so the doctrines of *"the faith"* produce holiness, faithfulness and godliness. Our goal, as individuals and as churches, is to permit and assist this Spirit-given discovery, and to help those who have fallen to discover it too. It's not only restoring them to faith; it's helping them to walk in the holiness of the faith, so that the joy of their salvation and service may be restored. There is nothing more powerful than holiness, yet there are Christians all over the world who are praying for power. We might pray for power and never grow in holiness, but if we pray and grow in holiness we definitely will grow in power. We need an overwhelming sense of the holiness of God to accompany all that we are individually and collectively. It will monitor our character and conduct; how we stand before a holy God, and allow others to see *"how holily and righteously and unblameably we behaved"*[14] toward them.

This is the kind of ministry Jude was thinking of as he surveyed a damaged gathering and its need for repair. He was the Jehoiada of his day appealing for restorers on behalf of his King, and yet he knew that what he called *"our common salvation"* wasn't common to all. False teachers had never *"begun in the Spirit,"*[15] so they couldn't continue in the Spirit; they also had no faith and no holiness. But there were others who started in the Spirit, and were not being made perfect in the Spirit. They had faith, but were not serving in the holiness of the faith. They had been affected by the adversary, conflicting thoughts were going on in their minds and hearts, and Jude had good reason to be concerned.

NOTHING BUT LEAVES
Matthew 21:19

He looked before He faced the cross
On a fig tree full and fair,
But the very thing He looked for most
Was the thing it did not bear.

And, in spite of all His mercy shown,
In spite of a heart that grieves,
It never turned from its fruitless ways
And gave Him "nothing but leaves."

He had traced their walk from early days,
In the call to Abraham;
He had seen their bondage overcome
By blood from the Passover lamb.

And the path God chose for His redeemed,
The chosen whom He receives,
They chose to despise His Lamb and Man,
And gave Him "nothing but leaves."

He looked on us as He bore His cross
With a longing still the same,
That those who claim to own His grace
Will honour and praise His Name

By showing the love we have for Him,
And the faith by which each cleaves.
Will we spend our days in fruitful growth
Or give Him – "nothing but leaves"?
(A. McIlree)

2.8 DOXOLOGY: ON THE BASIS OF 'WHOM?'

"Now to Him who is able to keep you from stumbling, and to present you faultless before the presence of His glory with exceeding joy, to God our Saviour, Who alone is wise, be glory and majesty, dominion and power, both now and forever. Amen" (Jude vv.24,25).

* * *

God always initiates His own rescue missions. He did it in Genesis 3 in His call to fallen Adam and Eve, He did it through the cross of the Lord Jesus Christ to provide the only means of calling fallen sinners to Himself, and Jude's doxology leaves us in no doubt that, in spite of his readers' present struggles, God would do it for them too. He began his short letter in the heights of the promise of the gospel, which assured them that they were called, beloved and preserved, and he ends by bringing them to greater heights in the prospect of glory.

Two verses capture the first for us, and the last two verses capture the second. Victory condensed in four short verses! In the mid-section of 21 verses lies an inspired message that deals with the heat of the battle, the darkness of the enemy, the deceit of false teachers, but not the defeat of the believer. The overall message that would be reinforced as the letter was read and re-read, was they were going from victory to victory, from the

Victor being with them to them being with the Victor.

His be the Victor's name
Who fought the fight alone;
Triumphant saints no honour claim,
Their conquest was His own.
(Samuel Gandy)

To Him Who is Able

Divine ability is unique, and each believer is assured of it through the power that God has demonstrated in the gospel. Eternal security is guaranteed. The means of saving grace was seen when the Victor of the cross *"offered up prayers and supplications ... to Him who was able to save Him from* [Gr. *ek* – out of] *death,"*[1] and the end is seen in His being *"able to keep."* The first has underwritten the triumph of the Saviour, and the second underlines the triumph of the saved. Both are integral to *"our common salvation,"* and every born-again believer is secure. The nature of the gospel confirms God's ability, and the word *dunamai* supports the certainty of the power Jude speaks of in his doxology. The same word is used in Paul's doxology in Romans 16:25,[2] and we also find it in Mark 2:7 where the scribes asked, *"Who can forgive sins?"* The word *dunamai* means they put a question over the Lord's deity by asking, *"Who is able to forgive sins but God alone?"*

During the time of captivity in Babylon, when Daniel was cast into the lions' den, King Darius spent a sleepless night before rushing to find out in the morning if he had survived. As soon as he arrived, *"he cried out with a lamenting voice ... 'Daniel, servant of the living God, has your God, whom you serve continually, been able to deliver you from the lions?'"*[3] To his relief, Daniel was unharmed and replied, *"O king, live forever! My God sent His angel and shut the lions' mouths, so that they have not hurt me."* His faith in God hadn't wavered, and he was living proof that *"our God whom we serve is able to deliver."*[4] Like Daniel, Jude never doubted God's ability, and he would

214

know that the God who shut the mouths of lions was just as able to shut the mouths of false teachers who were like wolves in sheep's clothing.[5]

To Keep You From Stumbling

Job called God *"the watcher of men,"*[6] and evidently trusted Him as his guardian and protector. So can we, for He hasn't changed. David knew this and pre-dated Jude by putting the words *"keep"* and *"preserve"* into the same verse when he wrote, *"You shall keep them, You shall preserve them."*[7] There's no doubt at all that God is able to keep His saints from tripping, in that He is able to deliver us *"out of"* them, but Jude's point is that God is able to keep us from going into them. What tremendous comfort this must have been to those who had been stumbled, and to us whenever we stumble too! His readers faced major obstacles for, apart from anything in their lives that could cause them to stumble, they had false teachers who were set on tripping them.

God can keep us from falling, from tripping and being tripped. Many a child of God lives with deep regret about falling into sin, and some never get over it. Memories of old failures can be an effective weapon in the hands of the adversary, and he's very good at raking up the past. If this is something you wrestle with, let God take it from you once and for all. He knows how the adversary uses these things to prevent us from knowing the peace and joy of His forgiveness, and the satisfaction of spiritual progress. We may even rake them up ourselves, but, once repented of and forgiven, He never will. His caring hand would rather erase such disturbing thoughts and help us to say, *"Do not rejoice over me, my enemy; when I fall, I will arise."*[8] God, in His mercy, gives a way of escape, and wants to remind us that there is a way back up when we fall.

It's also true, of course, that He cautions us, *"let him who thinks he stands take heed lest he fall."*[9] We need to be very careful that assuming we are above falling doesn't become the very thing that brings us down! Peter assures us that we *"are kept by the power of God"*[10]; Paul tells us that we are *"eagerly waiting for the revelation of our Lord Jesus Christ, who will confirm you to the end, that you may be blameless in the day of our Lord Jesus Christ."*[11] We are kept, are being kept, and always will be kept by our triune God.

To Present You Faultless

For false teachers to hear this promise being given to genuine believers resembles the position Judas was in when he heard some of the Lord's ministry in the Upper Room and had his feet washed without being *"completely clean."*[12] There's a big difference between being false and being faulty. It may be as you read this that you automatically think how your own faults have kept you from full involvement and enjoyment in your service for the Lord, and this may have led to feelings of inadequacy. God knows all about our faults and is well able to help us. In fact, He can do more with inferiority than He can with superiority. The superiority complex needs to be broken by Him, but He graciously reshapes any feelings of inferiority. None of us is adequate, and it wouldn't be a healthy sign if any Christian ever claimed to be.

All believers have faults, but all will be faultless on the day when we appear in His presence above. The struggle with sin will be over, and so will its stains for we will be, as the Greek says, *"amōmos"* – without blemish and blameless. Christlike, at last! He Himself will present us there. There will be nothing in us to displease Him, nothing to disappoint us, and nothing the adversary can defend. He was defeated at the cross[13] and will be again when everyone in *"the church, which is His body"*[14] – in the building, the body and the bride – stands perfected at His throne!

Before the Presence of His Glory

We began faith's journey by standing *before* Him in our guilt at the cross; we continue our service *for* Him by standing in his grace;[15] and we will finish our service by standing *with* Him in His glory. We are being taken from the grief of the cross to the glory of the throne. What a transformation! When we are raised at His coming, Christ will present (Gr. *paristēmi*) the church to Himself, and this means we will stand beside Him as a bride with her Bridegroom. We will be *"before the presence"* (Gr. *katenōpion*) of God, which means we will stand directly in front of Him as His Son presents the church to Himself, and we will have bodies that are like *"the body of His glory."*[16]

Some versions say, *"His glorious body,"* but the word is a noun, not an adjective, so in bodies like *"the body of His glory,"* we will stand *"before the presence of His glory."* We also know that great men of God in Old and New Testament days were deeply affected by the glory of God. In their earthly experience, some feared[17] and fell,[18] but, when the church enjoys her heavenly experience, the bride will stand. More than that, there will be *"exceeding joy"* (Gr. *agalliasis*).

The meaning of this was first expressed when Elizabeth heard Mary's voice and explained how *"the babe leaped in my womb for joy."*[19] John the Baptist was as yet unborn, but not unmoved. Peter captured its meaning in his first letter when he spoke of those who *"greatly rejoice"* (Gr. *agalliao*) in the anticipation of what is yet to be revealed at the Lord's coming. Later, he used the same word when referring to *"exceeding joy."*[20] The root thought means to jump for joy and, like John the Baptist, the lame man in Acts 3:8 was *"leaping"* as he entered the Temple praising God. Both are linked to unrestrained joy, and the same applies to the resurrected, glorified members of the church, which is His body. In their new bodies, with unlimited and uninhibited joy, there will be a sense of jumping for joy.

To God Our Saviour

Many versions translate this verse as, *"To the only God, our Saviour, through Jesus Christ our Lord, be glory, majesty, dominion, and authority, before all time and now and forever. Amen.*[21]

Be Glory

The glory (Gr. *doxa*: honour, praise, worship) of God consists of all the attributes of His character that radiate from Him in the full harmony of His Being. *"Through Jesus Christ"* indicates that He also is the brightness and outshining of God's glory.[22] The whole character of Deity has been made known through Him by means of His incarnation, ministry on earth, His death and resurrection. He is the only means by which the glory of God has been brought to us in the gospel, and the only means by which we are being brought to the glory of God.

Majesty

This refers to God in the greatness of His sovereignty, and Peter uses the related word *megaleiotēs* to express the magnificence, superbness, and splendour that belong to the perfection of God and His Son. We see God as *"the Majesty on high"* in Hebrews 1:3, and in chapter 8:1, with the Lord Jesus Christ at His side as co-equal in His majesty.[23]

There's a wonderful recognition of this at the beginning of Psalm 104 where the psalmist says, *"Bless the LORD, O my soul! O LORD my God, You are very great: You are clothed with honour and majesty, who cover Yourself with light as with a garment."* It's interesting to note that his words for *"clothed"* and *"cover"* convey the thought of being wrapped, and we can easily relate this to the Infant Jesus being *"wrapped in swaddling cloths"*[24] and then as a Man being *"wrapped"* in linen for burial.[25] When He came to earth in His birth, and was ready to leave it through His death, His wrapping followed the size

218

and contours of His frame, but how is the eternal God wrapped with honour, majesty and light? The question becomes even more interesting when we discover that the word for "garment" (*kasalmāh* from *salmāh* and *simlāh*) means "a dress that takes shape from what is under it."

The psalmist was speaking of God's pre-bodily form probably around a thousand years before the Saviour came, so he wasn't thinking of a garment taking shape from His body, but from His Being. His ministry and miracles were shaped by His nature and followed the content and contours of One who is in the form of God.[26] One hymn-writer says, "Through this dark vale of sorrow, He clothed with pity went," and he, too, was thinking of the clothing of His Being. When the woman touched the hem of His garment, she wasn't healed because there was something magical in the garment that covered His body. She drew power *"out of Him"* for she had reached far beyond the fringe of what covered His body to the garment that was shaped by the majesty of his inner Being.

Compassion is an attribute of Deity and Jesus showed it when He was on earth, in the same way as He caused people to see and hear the evidence of His omniscience, omnipotence, love and grace, which with all His other attributes, caused some to recognise Him as God manifested in the flesh. In all that He did through His bodily presence, the honour, majesty, and light of His inner Being shone out. When He said, *"I am the light of the world,"*[27] He was speaking as the eternal Being, co-equal with His God and Father, *"the brightness of His glory"*[28] and of the outshining of divine light from His nature. Through Him, and through the gospel, *"The light shines in the darkness,"*[29] and still takes shape from the nature of the *"I AM"*. No wonder Job said, *"He is unique, and who can make Him change?"*[30] Hallelujah! What a Saviour!

Isaiah's words in Isaiah 61:10 are like an echo of the psalmist, for they both spoke of the harmony between *"my soul"* and *"my God"*; and this helps us to see that our inner being is capable of blessing and rejoicing as it meditates on God. They give us real insight to the connection and communication between our inner being and His, just as we find them in Romans 8:16 where we read that, *"The Spirit Himself bears witness with our spirit that we are children of God."* From deep within our own being, we *"bless"* God, and the word *bārᵉchiy* conveys an attitude of kneeling down before Him in adoration. We sense how He is "clothed" (*lābāshᵉtā* from *lābash*), and as we apply Isaiah 61:10 to our own experience, He sees how we are clothed (*hilbiyshaniy* from *lābash*). The same thought is used of Him and of the redeemed, and we can take the lesson that, if His garment takes shape from what is underneath, so should ours for we have been "clothed" by Him. This will help others to see Christ in us and that we are "wrapped" up in Him!

> Let the beauty of Jesus be seen in me,
> All His wondrous compassion and purity;
> O Thou Spirit divine, all my nature refine
> 'Till the beauty of Jesus be seen in me.
> *(Albert Orsborn)*

Dominion

God's overall dominion is seen right at the beginning of our Bibles when we read what He said in Genesis 1:26, *"Let Us make man in Our image, according to Our likeness; let them have dominion ..."* By delegating dominion the Trinity showed Their own, but the day is coming when the Lord will come in His majesty. *"He shall speak peace to the nations; His dominion shall be 'from sea to sea, and from the River to the ends of the earth.'"*[31]

Power

This is the inherent power of Deity that is seen in God's control and authority over times and seasons,[32] in the Son's right to forgive sins,[33] and to give the great commission.[34] The same word is used in Luke 23:7 where Pilate heard that Jesus belonged to Herod's "jurisdiction" and sent Him to Herod.

Well might we say that He didn't belong to the jurisdiction of *"that fox,"*[35] but that the fox was under the jurisdiction of the Lamb! Having authority in heaven and on earth, the Lord's jurisdiction is much wider, and God *"will judge the world in righteousness by the Man whom He has ordained."*[36]

Both Now and Forever

The Greek phrase at the end of this verse falls into three parts of Jude's final tripod:

- *pro pantos tou aiōnos* – before all time;
- *kai nun* – and now;
- *eis pantas tous aiōnas* – and forever. Amen.

With these words, Jude completed his letter by emphasising that the Son is co-equal with the Father and co-eternal, and that the redeemed will be gathered Home. It is very evident that his benediction reinforced Christ's true nature to those who knew Him as their Lord and Saviour, while delivering a rebuke to the false teachers who were guilty of *"denying our only Master and Lord, Jesus Christ"* (Jude 1:4, RV).

DOXOLOGIES

In the New Testament, Paul, Peter, John and Jude introduce a doxology at different stages of their letters: sometimes, at the end; at other times, part way through. It is good for us to see that these are not interchangeable or random outbursts of praise to God, but rather meaningful exaltation with phrases that relate to the context. For instance, in Romans we find one at the end of eleven carefully reasoned chapters of gospel truth that led from the depravity of man, through the fundamental doctrines of grace, to the complete certainty of salvation provided by a sovereign God.

Paul is so masterly in his reasoning that we could stand in awe of his lawyer-like wisdom, and of how he concluded his whole presentation with a doxology that ascribes everything to the all-wise, all-knowing God who needed no assistance from angels or men. The wording of the doxology is perfectly suited to the redeemed giving glory to God for the wonder of His ways revealed in the Son and His ways. With a timely outburst of praise, he exclaims:

"Oh, the depth of the riches both of the wisdom and knowledge of God! How unsearchable are His judgements and His ways past finding out! For who has known the mind of the Lord? Or who has become His counsellor? Or who has first given to Him and it shall be repaid to him? For of Him and through Him and to Him are all things, to whom be glory forever. Amen."[37]

As the road south from Colorado reaches the border with New Mexico, the western horizon is filled by a magnificent view of the Southern Rocky Mountains. Their snow-capped peaks glow red in the sunset, and they are appropriately known as the Sangre de Cristo range, which means the blood of Christ. They are like a visual reminder of their spiritual counterpart in these eleven chapters in Romans. Paul lifts our eyes to focus on another range of mountain peaks that show what the precious blood of Christ has achieved. Well might we feast on lofty thoughts of how it has secured propitiation that satisfies the holiness of God and prevents His wrath being shown to everyone who believes; and absorb the marvel of how it also secures redemption that overcomes the sinfulness of the sinner. As we take in the heights presented in the great truths of the gospel, we also are led to repeat Paul's doxological song.

The relevance of a doxology is seen again at the end of chapter 16, which brings an end to the application of the first eleven chapters through the surrender and submission of the Christian's life. The opening appeal in chapter 12 – *"I beseech you therefore, brethren, by the mercies of God, that you present your bodies a living sacrifice ..."* – follows the doxology at the end of chapter 11 and precedes the unveiling of practical truth relating to spiritual gifts and other aspects of Christian service.

How could we ever stand at the end of these eleven chapters that are so filled with the wonder of the gospel and not be moved by this appeal?

> But we never can prove
> The delights of His love,
> Until all on the altar we lay;
> For the favour He shows,
> And the joy He bestows,
> Are for them who will trust and obey.
> *(John H. Sammis)*

The appeal leads into aspects of obedience that are to be shown by our conduct in the world and in the churches, and on into the appropriateness of the closing doxology:

"Now to Him who is able to establish you according to my gospel and the preaching of Jesus Christ, according to the revelation of the mystery kept secret since the world began but now has been made manifest, and by the prophetic Scriptures has been made known to all nations, according to the commandment of the everlasting God, for obedience to the faith—to God, alone wise, be glory through Jesus Christ forever. Amen."[38]

Another example is found in Paul's letter to the Ephesians. Right from his opening, we are lifted up to adore the One who *"has blessed us with every spiritual blessing in the heavenly places in Christ,"* and then we are introduced to how He has done this through His electing love, sharing His holiness, predestination, redemption, forgiveness, the mystery of His will, summing up all things in Christ, and guaranteeing our eternal inheritance. As in Romans, Paul applies body teaching in chapters 2 and 3 to our spiritual service before returning to the subject of spiritual gifts in chapter 4. In a nutshell, his message is that the blessings and character of *"the church, which is His body"*[39] should be seen in the churches, and this is crystallised in the doxology that follows. *"Now to Him who is able to do exceedingly abundantly above all that we ask or think, according to the power that works in us, to Him be glory in the church by Christ Jesus to all generations, forever and ever. Amen."*[40]

Jude's doxology is no less relevant to what he has been saying. Tripping and fault-finding were everyday realities among his readers, and he systematically addressed the hazards of their outlook in verses 1-23 before fixing their up-look in verses 24 and 25. What a contrast! He also set out to lift their spirits by reasserting the Saviour's rightful role, which the false teachers denied; and the fourfold character of His rightful place, which they despised (in v.8, dignitaries is Gr. *doxa* = glory). For himself as the writer, his closing benediction complemented and confirmed his opening salutation. It comforted his brothers and sisters and assured him, the boy from the same Nazareth home as the Saviour, that the servant also will be safe Home with his Master. Having followed his careful handling of scriptural truth and spiritual trials, we come to the end of his short and powerful letter and are ready to say as he did:

"Now to Him who is able to keep you from stumbling and to present you blameless before the presence of his glory with great joy, to the only God, our Saviour, through Jesus Christ our Lord, be glory, majesty, dominion, and authority, before all time and now and forever. Amen." [41]

TO HIM WHO IS ABLE

To Him who is able
To keep us – His called ones,
Preserved in Christ Jesus,
The saints of the Father –
To keep us from falling,
And faultless to set us
Before His bright glory
With fulness of joy.

To the Lord God, who keepeth
Midst sin and in weakness,
Whose wisdom alone is,
To God and our Saviour
Be majesty, glory,
Dominion and power,
Both now and for ever
Amen, Amen.
(Naylor)

FOOTNOTES

2.1 SALUTATION

(1) Acts 1:14 (2) Jn 15:20 (3) Matt.10:36 (4) Eph.4:10 (5) Lk.2:41-50 (6) Jer.18:18 RV (7) Phil.2:7 (8) 1 Pet.2:23 NIV (9) Matt.8:20 (10) The House of Christmas (11) Jas.1:17 (12) Jn. 1:46 (13) 1 Cor 2:8 (14) Phil. 2:7 (15) 1 Kin.8:27 (16) Ex.12:4 (17) 1 Cor.15:5-7 (18) Jn 14:22 (19) Jn 7:3-5 (20) Rom.11:34 (21) Jas.1:1; 2:1 (22) Mk.8:31 (23) Jn 9:4 (24) Acts 2:42 (25) Ps.55:22 (26) Lk.21:25 (27) Jn 15:19 (28) Ps.29:4 (29) Jas.1:18; 1 Pet.1:23 (30) Rom.5:6 ESV (31) Eph.2:5 (32) Eph.2:3; 5:8 (33) Phil.3:14 RV; 2 Tim.1:9; Heb.3:1 (34) Ps.32:8 (35) Prov.15:3 (36) Heb.4:13 (37) 2 Pet.1:1 (38) 2 Thess.1:5 (39) Rom.2:5

2.2 SALVATION

(1) 2 Cor.11:4 (2) 2 Thess.2:3,8 (3) 1 Jn. 2:18,22; 4:3 (4) 2 Thess.2:6,7 (5) 2 Thess.2:10 (6) Rom.1:1,9,16 (7) Rom.8:21 (8) Gal.5:1 (9) Mal.3:6 (10) Heb.13:8 (11) 1 Tim.1:10 (12) 2 Tim.1:13 (13) Job 13:7 (14) Isa.40:12 (15) Isa.52:7 (16) Rom.10:15 RV (17) 1 Thess.1:5 (18) 1 Cor.1:17 (19) Gal.1:10 (20) Job 13:7 RV (21) 1 Cor.9:22 (22) Gal.3:1 (23) Gal.2:20 (24) 1 Tim.3:16 (25) Col.1:13 (26) 1 Cor.9:23 (27) 2 Cor.5:20 (28) Jn 6:27 (29) Matt.28:19,20 (30) 1 Pet.1:2 (31) Matt.26:39; Mk.14:35 (32) Mk.1:19 (33) Prov.9:1 (34) Phil.1:27; Col.1:5,23

2.3 CONTENTION

(1) 2 Cor.4:13-18 (2) Acts 15:28 (3) Acts 15:25 (4) Rom.15:30 (5) Phlm.8,9 (6) 1 Tim.6:12 RV (7) 2 Cor.4:8,9 (8) MacArthur Commentary on 2 Corinthians (9) Matt.28:18-20 (10) Oxford Dictionaries (11) 2 Tim.4:3 (12) 2 Tim.1:13 (13) Tit.1:13 (14) Tit.1:7-9 (15) 2 Tim.4:7 (16) 2 Thess.2:15

2.4 CONDEMNATION

(1) 2 Cor.11; 23-28 (2) Isa.29:15; Jer.17:9,10; Ezek.11:5 (3) Mk.14:57 (4) Rom.5:6 (5) 2 Pet.3:7 (6) Matt.10:16 (7) Jn.15:20 (8) 1 Pet.2:23 NIV; Matt.10:16 (9) Lev.1:14 (10) Songs 5:12 (11) Matt.7:15 (12) Zeph.3:3 (13) Neh.4:3 (14) Ruth 2:20 (15) Neh.13:4,5 (16) Acts 20:29 (17) Matt.7:16 (18) 1 Tim.6:5 (19) Rom.1:25 KJV (20) Mk.8:29 (21) 1 Jn 1:3 (22) Phil.1:7 (23) 2 Pet.1:4 (24) Heb.4:2 (25) Gen.4:10 (26) Heb.11:6 (27) Ps.51:14 (28) Jn 12:6 (29) 2 Kin.5:20-27 (30) Num.22:7 (31) 2 Pet.2:15 (32) Prov.18:16 (33) Ex.23:8 (34) Mic.3:11; 7:3 (35) Num.16:39-50 (36) Isa.57:20,21 (37) Matt.10:26; see Job 28:11 (38) Ps.92:13 (39) Ecc.11:3 (40) Prov.25:14 (41) Isa.40:26 (42) Phil.2:15 (43) Dan.12:3

2.5 REVELATION

(1) Jer.49:8,30 RV (2) Prov.14:34 (3) Lev.20:17 (4) 1 Pet.2:23 (5) Ex.14:13 (6) Deut.25:18,19 (7) Num.23:19 (8) Ps.90:7,9 (9) Job 38:7 (10) Heb.12:22 (11) Gen.28:12; Mk.8:38, 13:27; 2 Thess.1:7; 1 Tim.5:21 (12) Ps.104:4; Heb.1:7 (13) Heb.1:14 (14) 1 Pet.1:5 (15) Lk.10:18 (16) Eph.6:11,12 (17) 2 Pet.2,4 (18) Gen.13:10 (19) Gen.19:28 (20) Deut.29:23 (21) Ps.95:11; Heb.3:11,16-19 (22) Jn 8:44 (23) 2 Pet.1:4 (24) Jn 1:12; Heb.3:1,2; Jude 14; 2 Cor.10:4; 1 Pet.1:2 (25) 1 Cor.3:9 RVM (26) 2 Tim.3:8 (27) Josh.1:2; Ex.33:11 (28) 1 Cor.1:18; Col.1:13 (29) 2 Chr.20:12 (30) Eph.6:11,13; Jas.4:7; 2 Cor.6:7 (31) Heb.2:14; 1 Jn 3:8 (32) Zech.3:2 (33) 1 Cor.2:11-14 (34) Gen.5:21-24 (35) 2 Pet.2:5 (36) 2 Thess.1:7-10 (37) Jude 8,10,16,18 (38) Matt.7:3 (39) Rom.16:18 (40) Jude vv.12,16,19 (41) Rom.6:17 (42) Eph.5:8 (43) 1 Pet.2:25

2.6 BENEDICTION

(1) Ecc.7:8 ESV (2) Phil.1:8 (3) Jn 15:9,10 (4) Ps.121:5 (5) Acts 20:32 (6) Rom.14:19 (7) 1 Cor.8:1 (8) Matt.5:7 (9) Rev.3:4 (10) Rev.3:18 (11) Lev.1:10,11; 4:33 (12) 1 Cor.3:17 (13) 1 Tim.6:3 (14) 1 Thess.2:10, RV (15) Gal.3:3

2.7 DOXOLOGY

(1) Heb.5:7 (2) See also Rom.1:16; 1 Cor.1:18; Eph.3:20 (3) Dan.6:20,21 (4) Dan.3:17 (5) Mat.7:15 (6) Job 7:20 (7) Ps.12:7 (8) Mic.7:8 (9) 1 Cor.10:12 (10) 1 Pet.1:5 (11) 1 Cor.1:7,8 (12) Jn. 13:10 (13) Heb.2:14; 1 Jn. 3:8 (14) Eph.1:22,23 (15) Rom.5:2 (16) Phil.3:21 (17) Isa.6:5; Lk.9:34 (18) Ezek.1:28; Matt.17:6; Rev.1:17 (19) Lk.1:44 (20) 1 Pet.1:6, 4:13 (21) ESV, NASB, NRSV, RSV; ASV, NIV & RV are substantially the same (22) Heb.1:3 (23) 2 Pet.1:16 (24) Lk.2:7 (25) Lk.23:53 (26) Phil.2:6 (27) Jn 8:12 (28) Heb.1:3 (29) Jn 1:5; 2 Cor.4:4,6 (30) Job 23:13 (31) Zech.9:10 (32) Acts 1:7 (33) Matt.9:6 (34) Matt.28:18-20 (35) Lk.13:32 (36) Acts 17:31 (37) Rom.11:33-36 (38) Rom.16:25-27 (39) Eph.1:22, 23 (40) Eph.3;20,21 (41) Jude v.25 ESV

APPENDIX 1: JUDE'S TRIPODS

1. Called, beloved, and preserved – v.1
2. Preserved (Gr. *tēreō*), keep (Gr. *tēreō*), keep (Gr. *phulasso*: keep) – vv.1,21,24
3. Mercy, peace and love – v.2
4. Mercy (Gr. *eleos*), mercy (Gr. *eleos*), compassion (Gr. *eleeō*: mercy) – vv.2,21,22
5. Beloved by Jude – vv.3,17,20
6. Marked out for condemnation – v.4. Turn the grace of God into lewdness, Deny the only Master and Lord, Jesus Christ
7. Lord, God and Saviour – vv.4, 25
8. The people, angels, Sodom and Gomorrah – vv.5-7
9. Defile the flesh, reject authority, and speak evil of dignitaries – v.8
10. Cain, Balaam and Korah – v.11
11. Rocks and waves, shepherds and trees, clouds and stars – vv.12,13
12. These are – vv.12,16,19
13. Sensual, cause divisions, not having the Spirit– v.19
14. Building, praying, keeping – as we wait – v.20
15. The Holy Spirit, the love of God, our Lord Jesus Christ – vv.20,21
16. On some (Gr. *hous*: others) have compassion – v. 22, 23, Some (Gr. *hous*) save out of the fire, Others (Gr. *hous*) detesting their defiled garments
17. Presented – faultless (v.24) – before His glory – with exceeding joy
18. Before all time (Gr. *pro pantos tou aiōnos*) – v. 25, and now (*kai nun*),

and forever (Gr. *eis pantas)*

APPENDIX 2: THE CHARACTER OF FALSE MEN

v.4

- Crept in unnoticed; Marked out for this condemnation;
- Ungodly men, who pervert the grace of our God into
- sensuality (ESV);
- Deny our only Master and Lord, Jesus Christ (ESV).

v.8

- These dreamers defile the flesh;
- Reject authority; Speak evil of dignitaries.

v.10

- Speak evil of whatever they do not know; and whatever they know naturally;
- Like brute beasts, in these things they corrupt themselves.

v.11

- They have gone in the way of Cain;
- Have run greedily in the error of Balaam for profit;

- Perished in the rebellion of Korah.

v.12

- These are rocks (spots) in your love feasts;
- They feast with you without fear;
- Shepherding (serving) *only* themselves;
- *They are* clouds without water, carried about by the winds;
- Late autumn trees without fruit, twice dead, pulled up by
- the roots.

v.13

- Raging waves of the sea, foaming up their own shame;
- Wandering stars for whom is reserved the blackness of darkness forever.

v.15

- To convict all who are ungodly ... their ungodly deeds ...
- committed in an ungodly way, and of all the harsh things which ungodly sinners have spoken against Him.

v.16

- These are grumblers, complainers;
- Walking according to their own lusts;
- They mouth great swelling *words*, flattering people to gain
- advantage.

v.18

- Mockers ... who would walk according to their own ungodly lusts.

v.19

- These are sensual persons, who cause divisions, not having the
- Spirit.

WHAT THINK YE OF CHRIST?

What think ye of Christ? is the test
To try both your state and your scheme;
You cannot be right in the rest,
Unless you think rightly of Him;
As Jesus appears in your view,
As He is beloved or not,
So God is disposed to you,
And mercy, or wrath are your lot.

Some take Him a creature to be,
A man, or an angel at most:
Sure these have not feelings like me,
Nor know themselves wretched, and lost;
So guilty, so helpless, am I,
I durst not confide in His blood;
Nor on His protection rely,
Unless I were sure he is God.

Some call Him a Saviour in word,
But mix their own works with their plan;
And hope He His help will afford,
When they have done all that they can;
If sayings prove rather too light,
(A little they own they may fail)
They purpose to make up full weight,
By casting his name in the scale.

If asked what of Jesus I think,
Although my best thoughts are but poor;
I say He's my meat and my drink,
My life, and my strength, and my store,
My Shepherd, my husband, my friend,
My Saviour from sin, and from thrall,
My hope from beginning to end,
My portion, my Lord, and my all.
(John Newton)

III

Boaz - Ruth's Redeemer, Bridegroom and Lord of the Harvest

The events of the book of Ruth are like a jewelled cameo woven into the fabric of Israel's chequered background – an interweaving of His grace, His call and His purpose. There is no shallow end to the story, as depths of despair at the beginning lead on to deepening delight, which causes us to exclaim, "Oh, the depth of the riches both of the wisdom and knowledge of God! How unsearchable are His judgments and His ways past finding out!"

3.1 INTRODUCTION

The story of Ruth has found an honoured place in literature, but, right at the outset, we salute its much more highly prized place in Scripture. The romance of literature can stand on its own, needing neither background nor foreground, and most authors would derive satisfaction if their particular book gained recognition for its individuality. The Bible is never like that. The revelation of Scripture is completely different. Unlike literature's independence, the interdependence of all scriptural content reveals that background and foreground are essential to each individual part, and that Divine authorship is satisfied by its overall harmony. Ruth's contribution beautifully reflects this. In fact, if we miss the wonder of its wider application, we miss its true relevance. The events of the book are like a jewelled cameo woven into the fabric of Israel's chequered background. The account of Ruth's arrival on the pages of God's Word is an interweaving of His grace, His call – so typical of His reaching out to Abraham, Rahab, and to Gentiles – and His purpose. So, during Israel's dull days, she is like a colourful butterfly emerging from a very drab chrysalis.

There is no shallow end to the story of Ruth, as depths of despair at the beginning lead on to deepening delight, which causes us to exclaim, *"Oh, the depth of the riches both of the wisdom and knowledge of God! How unsearchable are His judgments and His ways past finding out!"*[1] Her story is a revelation, yet the inscrutable wisdom of God allows certain details to remain hidden. When it was written, where, and by whom, fade into the unknown, but why it was written brings each enquiring reader closer to what may be more fully known of God. The stunning reality is that He had the record penned when, generations later, prophecy had become history, and the One to whom both are the same had the man after His own heart[2] reigning in Jerusalem.

Mr Newberry dates the Judges from 1425 – 1120BC and sets Ruth at 1322 – 1312BC, which would place her story around the time of Shamgar and Deborah. Others place it during the rule of Gideon, suggesting that the conditions mentioned in Judges 6:1-6 coincide with those referred to in the first chapter of Ruth. Whatever may be the timing of the story's historic setting, the genealogy at the end of chapter 4 indicates that the earliest the book could have been written was in David's lifetime.[3]

Merely tracing the beauty of each gripping chapter is not enough for it soon becomes evident that a higher hand lies behind the tragedy and unfolding triumph. It is the hand of Omnipotence, which Naomi claimed had gone out against her,[4] and from which she would receive so much blessing. It's the story of two great journeys: one, from Bethlehem to Moab; the other, from Moab to Bethlehem; the first, from faith to faithlessness; the second, from faithlessness to faith; one, away from God by hearts that were wayward; the other, toward God by hearts that were won. Irrespective of away or toward, believer or unbeliever, of belief or unbelief, spiritual direction always begins in the heart.

The tragedy of the first journey for three – Elimelech, Mahlon and Chilion – started and finished in the first five verses of chapter 1; the triumph for another three – Naomi, Ruth and Boaz – began in chapter 1 and lasted almost to the end of chapter 4. The final two verses crown the story of Boaz the redeemer and Ruth the redeemed, and anticipate the greater crowning of David, the king of Israel, through whom would come One whose crowning was greatest of all: Christ – God's King, and ours!

If we were looking at Abraham and Isaac's journey to Moriah in Genesis 22, apart from absorbing the actual event, we would see it as a foreshadowing of the Lord Jesus Christ's death at Calvary. In a similar way, the Spirit of God helps us to look beyond many Old Testament narratives to see their New Testament fulfilment, and there's outstanding value in doing this with the Book of Ruth. As we trace redemption's story in Ruth, the glorious light of the epistle to the Romans shines into the cameo and its foreshadowing follows its beam the whole way forward to the gospel of Christ.

Naomi and her family were characteristic of Israel as a nation, and their departure is symbolic of Israel's waywardness and unbelief. In Romans 9:1-5, Paul refers to their rejection of Christ and confesses: *"I tell the truth in Christ, I am not lying, my conscience also bearing me witness in the Holy Spirit, I have great sorrow and continual grief in my heart. For I could wish that I myself were accursed from Christ for my brethren, my countrymen according to the flesh, who are Israelites, to whom pertain the adoption, the glory, the covenants, the giving of the law, the service of God, and the promises; of whom are the fathers and from whom, according to the flesh, Christ came, who is over all, the eternally blessed God. Amen."*

Having made known his longing for them, and his mourning, he moved on in chapter 11:12 to give the outcome of their hardening: *"Now if their fall is the riches of the world, and their failure riches for the Gentiles, how much more their fulness."* Through Israel's fall, salvation has come to the Gentile, and Paul's message for them in verses 30 and 31 is, *"For as you once were disobedient to God, yet have now obtained mercy through their disobedience, even so these also have now been disobedient, that through the mercy shown you they also may obtain mercy."* At present, God is being glorified as many Jews come personally to Christ for salvation and follow the host who turned to Him both at and after Pentecost in Acts 2. They are what God calls, *"a remnant according to the election of grace"* in Romans 11:5.

Another day is coming, when the time of great tribulation is over and the Lord Jesus Christ appears to win them nationally, as Romans 11:26, 27 promises: *'And so all Israel will be saved, as it is written: "The Deliverer will come out of Zion, and He will turn away ungodliness from Jacob; for this is My covenant with them, when I take away their sins."*[5] God also promised in Jeremiah 23:8 to gather *"the descendants of the house of Israel from the north country and from all the countries where I had driven them. And they shall dwell in their own land."*

> Then from the east, and from the north,
> From every clime and strand,
> I have resolved to bring them forth,
> Back to the glorious land.

We can summarise a parallel of Ruth and Romans as follows:

- Elimelech and family leave Bethlehem - Their fall (Rom.11:25);
- Naomi returns, the only one of four - A remnant will return (Rom.9:27);
- Ruth reached by disobedient Jews - Gentiles reached after Jews' disobedience (Rom.11:30);
- Ruth obtains grace and mercy - Gentiles receive mercy (Rom.11:30);
- Ruth obtains redemption - Gentiles receive grace through redemption (Rom.3:24);
- Naomi blessed through Ruth - Jews' fulness, after God's riches to the Gentiles (Rom.11:12).

In the sovereignty of God, Ruth came to God, His people and His land, because a Jewish family had become estranged, and this is the teaching we find in Romans chapter 11 as Gentiles are brought to Christ because of an estranged Jewish nation. In His infinite wisdom, God has made it that we have been blessed through the Jew, since *"salvation is of the Jews,"*[6] and they will be blessed through the Gentiles. This is summed up in the final verse of Hebrews 11 – *"God having provided something better for us, that they should not be made perfect apart from us."* Bearing all this in mind, we will learn from the ways in which these four chapters fit into the purpose of divine inspiration. None of us should ever read it without seeing how *"profitable" it is "for teaching,"* that its ups and downs are good for *"reproof"* and *"correction,"* and that its spiritual triumph is designed to give us *"training in righteousness."* Paul emphasised these aims in 2 Timothy 3:16 and 17 (ESV) with the intention that *"the man of God may be competent, equipped for every good work."* Our prayer is that Ruth's journey to Boaz, and with Boaz, will provide each of these in our own journey to Christ and with Christ.

Nine characters will take up our attention:

- Elimelech (husband) - 'God is my King';
- Naomi (his wife) - 'pleasant, sweet';
- Mahlon and Chilion (their two sons) - 'sickly, weak' and 'pining, failing';
- Ruth (Mahlon's widow) - 'friend, companion';
- Orpah (Chilion's widow) - 'the nape of the neck' - from *'araph*: to bend down) - a practising unbeliever refusing to go forward;
- Boaz (a close relative) - 'In whom is strength';
- The closer relative (probably Elimelech's brother) - a non-practising believer refusing to go forward;
- Obed (Boaz and Ruth's son) - 'Servant'.

Ruth always follows the book of Judges in western Bibles, but the Jewish Scriptures, the Tanakh, have a different arrangement:

- The Torah (The Law): Genesis, Exodus, Leviticus, Numbers, Deuteronomy.
- The Nevi'im (The Prophets): Joshua, Judges, 1 Samuel, 2 Samuel, 1 Kings, 2 Kings, Isaiah, Jeremiah, Ezekiel, Hosea, Joel, Amos, Obadiah, Jonah, Micah, Nahum, Habakkuk, Zephaniah, Haggai, Zechariah, Malachi.
- The Kethuvim (The Writings) - Psalms, Proverbs, Job, The Song of Songs, Ruth, Lamentations, Ecclesiastes, Esther, Daniel, Ezra,

Nehemiah, 1 Chronicles, 2 Chronicles.

From the Kethuvim, five readings of the shorter scrolls called Megilloth are still reserved for certain festivals, and Ruth is elevated to a special place:

1. The Song of Songs – on the Feast of the Passover;
2. Ruth – on the Feast of Pentecost: Shavuot – the Feast of Weeks;
3. Lamentations - on the Fast of the ninth of Av (commemoration of the destruction of the Temple);
4. Ecclesiastes – on the Feast of Tabernacles;
5. Esther – on the Feast of Purim.

The story of Ruth stands in marvellous contrast to the book of Judges, which has just closed with the words, *"In those days there was no king in Israel; everyone did what was right in his own eyes."* The word *"right"* was normally a complimentary description, but its proper connotation of uprightness was lost when applied to their ungodly hearts and minds. In their case, it simply meant that they did what was convenient and self-pleasing, and that their twisted and crooked reasoning allowed them to think they were going straight. These were days in which Israel's relationship with God was inconsistent, as they rose to great heights and fell to great depths. Some of their leaders were like spiritual giants through whom He brought tremendous victories, yet the effects wore off and the people returned to their backsliding ways.

It's one of the wonders in the insect world that *"The locusts have no king,"*[7] but there was nothing commendable about the way in which God's people voiced their thoughts of a kingdom. What defiance they showed when they said to Samuel, *"No, but we will have a king over us,"*[8] and more so when they said to Pilate, *"We have no king but Caesar."*[9] These hostile expressions leave us in no doubt that the beginning and end of Israel's monarchy was marred by anarchy. History shows that mediocrity can so quickly descend into hostility in any generation, but these words together with defeat should never belong to the Christian's vocabulary, since Christ is the victor and victory is assured.[10] Ruth clearly demonstrates that: even in the darkest times when His people's testimony was at a low ebb, God was on the march, in His gracious sovereignty, doing *"whatever He pleases."*[11]

How significant it is, that the ultimate peak in Ruth's great story lifts our thoughts to David and not Saul, Israel's first king. This is significant in two ways: firstly, she was brought into the line of Judah of whom the prophetic word was, *"The sceptre shall not depart from Judah, nor the ruler's staff from between his feet, until Shiloh come; and unto him shall the obedience of the peoples be."*[12] *Saul was from the tribe of Benjamin, and therefore didn't belong to the kingly line that God had chosen for His Son to come. The second was that giving Saul as king was in response to the people's impatient demand of which God said, "I gave you a king in My anger, and took him away in My wrath."*[13] His eye was on the final word of Ruth's story – *"David"* – long before He called her into the mainstream of His purpose and, looking via the victor of Elah,[14] whom He declared the *"man after My own heart,"*[15] He saw the One who was *"born of the seed of David"*[16]: *"Son of David"* – guaranteed the throne – and *"Son of Abraham"* – guaranteed the cross.[17] The nation lived like Job's friends, speaking unrighteously for God,[18] but God often stepped in, just as the Lord did to rectify Peter's misuse of his sword!

In his delightful book, 'Ruth the Moabitess', Henry Moorhouse speaks of lessons we can learn from Old Testament pictures and suggests the following:

- A Jew's going into a far country in chapter 1 is like the parable of the lost son in Luke 15.
- A Gentile girl's being brought into the land of blessing and marrying Boaz by means of a Jew's backsliding is a picture of Christ obtaining a bride.
- After their marriage, the Jewess (Naomi) was blessed again, which points to God's New Testament dealings with Israel: they backslide,

Gentiles are blessed, the church is united to Christ, and then the Jews are blessed again.

God has woven the wonderful theme of the bride throughout the Old Testament. For example:

- Adam and Eve – a bride through blood: prior to The Fall and sinless;
- Isaac and Rebekah – a bride through the Spirit: after Moriah and substitution;
- Ruth – a bride for the lord of the harvest and redeemer;
- The Song of Songs – a bride for the shepherd-king.

By combining this sequence, we have a wonderful glimpse into the glorious means by which God will obtain a bride for His Son: by no lesser route than through the blood of His cross, shed for fallen sinners, and the gracious ingathering work of His Holy Spirit. One by one, like Ruth, we come as Gentile strangers from our ungodliness in a far-off place to meet our Redeemer, the Lord of the Harvest. In the purpose of God she was brought into the kingly line, and so have we[19]; and like the bride in the Song of Songs with her bridegroom, we rejoice in our bridal relationship with the good Shepherd and King of kings.

The harvest fields of Judah certainly stand in marked contrast to the battlefields of Judges, and we discover that God's giants can be found among those who followed reapers as well as among those who led warriors. By grace, we see a glorious parallel to Psalm 24:7, 8 where we read, *"Lift up your heads, O you gates! And be lifted up, you everlasting doors! And the king of glory shall come in. Who is this King of glory? The LORD strong and mighty, the LORD mighty in battle."* The same glorious Person, as God manifested in the flesh[20], was the speaker who said in John 4:35, *"lift up your eyes and look at the fields, for they are already white unto harvest"*. So His victory is twofold: He is King of the battlefield and Lord of the harvest field.

As we begin to absorb the overall wonder captured in four short, dramatic chapters, we acknowledge that its inspiration declares the mind of the Inspirer, its laws project the heart of the Lawgiver, and its prophetic purpose shows the power of the Sovereign. We also will see ourselves reflected in discoveries the Moabitess made because of the lovely man, Boaz, and, as we consider his many resemblances to Christ, we will lift our eyes to that lovelier Man and worship the God of all grace.

The Way of the Cross

Some of us stay at the Cross,
Some of us wait at the tomb,
Quickened, raised, seated with Christ
Yet lingering still in the gloom.

Some of us bide at the Passover Feast
With Pentecost all unknown:
The triumphs of grace in the heavenly place
That our Lord has made our own.

If Christ who had died had stopped at the Cross,
His work had been incomplete.
If Christ who was buried had stayed in the tomb,
He had only known defeat.

But the Way of the Cross never stops at the Cross,
And the way of the tomb leads on
To victorious Grace in the heavenly place,
Where the Risen Lord has gone.
(Annie Johnson Flint)

3.2 THE TIMING

"Now it came to pass, in the days when the judges ruled ..." (Ruth 1:1)

* * *

Only four books in the New King James Version of the Old Testament begin with the words, *"Now it came to pass"* – Ruth, 2 Samuel, Esther and Ezekiel – and each of them, in its own way, indicates that it's not the biblical equivalent of saying, "Once upon a time." The first time that God used the little word *"yᵉhiy,"* from which the phrase comes, is found in Genesis 1:3 where we read, "Let there be," "and there was," and on that occasion He changed darkness to light. In a very different sense, the same could be said about the opening phrase of these four books: Ruth was brought from the spiritual darkness of Moab into the light of God's grace[1]; Saul's death would herald the light of His greatness being made known through David as king[2]; Esther would be used along with her cousin, Mordecai, for the light of His goodness[3] to shine into the darkness of Haman's intended persecution of the Jews; and Ezekiel was the means of the brightness of God's glory[4] being made known to His people in the darkness of their captivity in Babylon. Such great events have never been forgotten.

248

Ruth

To this day, the little book of Ruth is brought to the forefront by being read in the Jews' annual feast of Shavuot, which believers in the Lord Jesus Christ know as Pentecost. She is well remembered as the Gentile whom God drew as a foreigner to marry a wealthy Jew, so it's appropriate that the annual celebration of Shavuot should be a voice to Jews of God's desire to spread the message of the cross to other nations and draw Gentiles to Christ through the gospel.

David

In current Jewish practice, "The Book of Psalms is divided into five parts, parallel to the Five Books of Moses. It is further subdivided into seven parts, one for each day in the week, and further divided into 30 divisions, for each day of the month. Many Jews make it a habit to say a portion of the Psalms every day after the morning prayers, thus completing all the Psalms in the course of a week or a month." (From The Complete Story of Shavuot).

Another example is found each year on Yom Kippur, the Day of Atonement, when Psalms are recited throughout the day. The Jerusalem Talmud, *Hagigah* 2.3, says: "David died on Atzeret [Feast of Weeks]." According to Jewish tradition, this means that he was also born on that day, "Therefore one reads the book of Ruth, in order to honour David on his birthday" (Rabbi Shlomo Yosef Zevin cites *Tevu'ot Shor* on Baba Batra 13b). Of much more spiritual value and importance are the verses in David's psalms that were fulfilled while the Lord was on the cross[5]:

- *"My God, My God, why have You forsaken Me?"*
- *"They divide My garments among them, and for My clothing they cast lots."*
- *"Into Your hand I commit my spirit."*
- *"He guards all his bones; not one of them is broken."*

Quotations fulfilled in the Saviour's crucifixion were succeeded by Peter's quotes from Psalm 16:8-11 and Psalm 110:1 in his message on the Day of Pentecost.[6]

* *"I have set the Lord always before me; because He is at my right hand I shall not be moved. Therefore my heart is glad, and my glory rejoices; my flesh also will rest in hope. For You will not leave my soul in Sheol, nor will You allow Your Holy One to see corruption. You will show me the path of life; in Your presence is fullness of joy; at Your right hand are pleasures forevermore."*

* *The LORD said to my Lord, "Sit at My right hand, till I make Your enemies Your footstool."*

Esther

* The book of Esther is read every year at their feast of Purim and, in contrast to Ruth, she was a Jewess who married a wealthy Gentile.

Ezekiel

* The people of Israel's return from Babylon is well documented in the books of Ezra and Nehemiah.

When the Judges Ruled

Divine order is vital among God's people, and He had already made this known in the appointment of Moses as mediator and Aaron as high priest. It's interesting that these were two brothers of the same father and that, together, they pointed forward to the only Son who is One with His Father. In the perfect will of God, His Son is the fulfilment of both. He is the Apostle, prefigured by Moses who stood before the people for God; and He is the High Priest, portrayed by Aaron who stood before God for the people.[7] In Moses' case, his father-in-law indicated that he was insufficient for the job and advocated his need of assistance.

With this in mind, he assured Moses, *"The thing you do is not good. Both you and these people who are with you will surely wear yourselves out. For this thing is too much for you; you are not able to perform it by yourself."*[8] This resulted in Moses choosing *"able men, such as fear God, men of truth."*[9] There's no doubt that these were men of ability, sanctity and integrity, but it's not clear whether God had initiated their selection or if it was only Jethro's considered opinion. He certainly invoked the name of God three times when he said, *"Listen now to my voice; I will give you counsel, and God will be with you: stand before God for the people, so that you may bring the difficulties to God."*

Whatever the rights or wrongs of accepting Gentile advice, we can be absolutely sure of one thing: the Lord Jesus Christ is uniquely able and needs none to help him as *"Mediator of the new covenant."*[10] Nor does He need others to assist Him as great High Priest for, as such, *"He is also able to save to the uttermost those who come to God through Him, since He always lives to make intercession for them."*[11] He is eternally adequate as Mediator *"by means of death"* – no other ever died to save lost sinners, therefore none can help; and He is eternally adequate as High Priest, since no other *"ever liveth"* (RV).

After the death of Moses, his role was passed to Joshua ($Y^e h\bar{o}shuwa$, meaning Jehovah saves), and Aaron's *"garments of ministry"*[12] were passed on to Eleazar, which means God is Helper. What a lovely Christlike combination! We could hardly miss noticing that the book of Joshua closes by referring to three burials – Joshua, Joseph and Eleazar – and how the triumphant testimony of these three godly men buried at home in the Promised Land allows the book of Judges to open against its faithful background. How different, then, that the book of Ruth should open with three burials – Elimelech, Mahlon and Chilion – and we note the tragic testimony of three men buried among ungodly men, far from home in the unfaithful background of a foreign land.

The time of the judges presents a line of saviours who pre-dated the appointment of a king. Within this orderly arrangement, God had a wonderful way of ensuring that, where He gives triumph, there will be a testimony to what His people have experienced. Rahab heard a detailed account of how they crossed the Red sea on dry land and of subsequent God-given victories.[13] Others heard, too. Whole nations heard. No wonder the people rejoiced as they sang, *"The people will hear and be afraid ... The mighty men of Moab, trembling will take hold of them; All the inhabitants of Canaan will melt away. Fear and dread will fall on them."*[14] Long before Ruth was born, her people were disturbed by what they had heard, and there was more to come in the days of the judges. What a variety of characters they were, yet we see glimpses of Christ in the meaning of many of their names:

- Othniel - "the force of God" - (1 Cor.1:24; 2 Cor.13:4);
- Ehud the Benjamite - "son of the right hand, united" (Ps.80:17);
- Shamgar - "the cup-bearer" (Matt.26:27; 1 Cor.11:25);
- Gideon - "the feller" (Heb 2:14; 1 Jn 3:8)
- Tola - "the scarlet worm" (Ps.22:6);
- Jair - "the enlightener" (Jn 1:4,5; 8:12; Eph.1:18);
- Jephthah - "he will open"(Lk.24:31,32,45; Acts 16:14);
- Samson - "the sunlight" (Mal.4:2; Rev.1:16).

Ruth may have heard of Israel's historic achievements, but it's unlikely she hadn't known about how Ehud ended Moab's eighteen years of rule over Israel by killing its king, Eglon, with a two-edged sword. Once again, it would be etched in the Moabite mind that their mighty men were no match for the mighty God. Just as He had depicted in Moses and Aaron glories that would be available in His Son, so we trace features of Christ in the judges He had chosen.

How could we fail to see that Jesus is our Othniel, 'the force of God' revealed

as *"Christ the power of God"*? He is our Ehud, who although a Benjamite –
a son of the right hand – is described as *"left-handed,"* which implies his
right hand was maimed or bound. Our Saviour is the Man of God's right
hand, yet He came as if manhood had limited Him. But, no: just as Ehud,
in apparent weakness, overcame his adversary with a two-edged sword,
so also the One who was crucified in weakness overcame our adversary. In
His humanity, He was God manifested in the flesh, still the Son of the right
hand and unlimited in power. Being made in our likeness never made Him
more vulnerable or less victorious for He *"shared in the same, that through
death He might destroy him who had the power of death, that is, the devil."*[15]

He is our Gideon, and we can say to Him, "You are our feller." Even in His
defencelessness and lowliness, as the One who said, *"But I am a worm, and
no man,"* He is our Tola; and He is our Jair through whom the eyes of our
heart are enlightened. Our hearts were closed to Him, yet He alone is their
opener. Perhaps, right now, it will be good for each of us to pause, just to
check if from a more personal point of view we are truly able to say, 'Jesus,
You are my opener. You are my force of God, my Son of the right hand, my
cup-bearer, my feller, my scarlet worm, my enlightener, and my sunlight.'
He is mightier than Samson, and much brighter, for God *"has shone in our
hearts to give the light of the knowledge of the glory of God in the face of Jesus
Christ."* These and other judges were God-given deliverers, yet His people
slumped from deliverance to defeat as they came and went. They were
overcome until their saviour overcame, and so were we until our Saviour
came to prove that He was waiting to deliver us.

Two glad services are ours,
Both the Master loves to bless.
First we serve with all our powers –
Then with all our feebleness.
Nothing else the soul uplifts,
Save to serve Him night and day,
Serve Him when He gives His gifts –
Serve Him when He takes away.

(C.A. Fox)

The day also is coming when, *"He who scattered Israel will gather him, and keep him as a shepherd does his flock. For the Lord has redeemed Jacob, and ransomed him from the hand of one stronger than he. Therefore they shall come and sing in the height of Zion, streaming to the goodness of the Lord."*[16] From days much darker than were known in Moab, the redeemed of Israel will be brought back to God as the fullest answer to Naomi's homecoming to Bethlehem and to Him. All twelve tribes will come like tributaries of a river merged into one, and they will flow more spontaneously than ever was known in days when they went up to Jerusalem for the feasts of Jehovah.

As the word $w^e n\bar{a}h^a r\bar{u}$ implies, they will be sparkling like a river with the glow of sunlight on its surface for the goodness of the LORD, their Redeemer, will be shining on them as He sees them drawing near and acknowledges that they are not appearing before Him empty-handed[17] or empty-hearted. They used to sing the Songs of Ascents, songs of the going up composed of Psalms 120 to 134, as they journeyed, and as they neared Jerusalem they would hear the welcoming sound of the Temple singers, but this time they will meet the Singer of Hebrews 2:12 and hear the welcome of their Saviour.

Careless seems the great Avenger; history's pages but record
One death-grapple in the darkness 'twixt old systems and the Word;
Truth forever on the scaffold, wrong forever on the throne —
Yet that scaffold sways the future, and, behind the dim unknown,
Standeth God within the shadow, keeping watch above His own.
(James Russell Lowell)

3.3 THE DECISION

"Now it came to pass, in the days when the judges ruled, that there was a famine in the land" (Ruth 1:1).

* * *

God's promised response to order and disorder was embedded in His law: He blessed the former and judged the latter. It is clearly set out in Leviticus 26, and excerpts from verse 3 to 20 show how clear-cut His conditions were:

"If you walk in My statutes and keep My commandments, and perform them, then I will give you rain in its season, the land shall yield its produce ... Your threshing floor shall last till the time of vintage, and the vintage shall last till the time of sowing; you shall eat your bread to the full ... You will chase your enemies, and they shall fall by the sword before you ... You shall eat the old harvest, and clear out the old because of the new ... I will walk among you and be your God ... But if you do not obey Me ... you shall sow your seed in vain ... for your land shall not yield its produce ..."

This was fulness at its best. There would be such abundance that bringing in last year's crop would keep them busy until next year's sowing. Feeding from the past harvest would have a surplus rather than a shortage, and their storehouses would need to be emptied to make room for the incoming crop. God's earlier promise of unceasing *"seedtime and harvest"*[1] was wonderfully harnessed to His later assurance of grain from the threshing floor and wine from the vintage, which coupled promised feeding with promised joy. His abundant supply meant that hands and hearts should be full, not only for themselves, but for Him. In return for His rich blessing, a tenth of their produce was given to the Levites to sustain them in their priestly service and they, in turn, offered a tenth of that as a heave offering to God.

As they did this, His response was, *"And your heave offering shall be reckoned to you as though it were the grain of the threshing floor and as the fulness of the winepress."*[2] This meant that, out of their fulness of joy, He received fulness of joy, and so the cycle of blessing was complete: they were blessed by His giving, and He was blessed by theirs. It was like an Old Testament example of New Testament believers being able to say, *"Blessed be the God and Father of our Lord Jesus Christ, who has blessed us."*[3]

The people of Israel were triply blessed in the ways God provided for their needs. In Exodus 15:26, He took care of their sickness by saying, *"I will put none of the diseases on you."* In Leviticus 26:7, He took care of their security by assuring them, *"You will chase your enemies."* And in Isaiah 1:19, He added to His earlier promises of plentiful harvests by taking care of their satisfaction by saying, *"If you are willing and obedient, you shall eat the good of the land."* How then could couples like Elimelech and Naomi be confronted with conditions that prompted their decision to go elsewhere?

Famine in the Land

There should be no lack in God's land. It should be renowned for its fulness and fruitfulness. Oh, if only His churches were well known for the richness of their feeding. Is your assembly like that? God wanted His land to be a place of storehouses, and it's essential that His house takes character from that. Every assembly should have the spiritual wherewithal to keep its storehouse amply filled, and there's something far wrong if His Word is in short supply.

This brings us to consider the sad statement that He made through Amos: *"'Behold, the days are coming,' says the LORD God, 'that I will send a famine on the land, not a famine of bread, nor a thirst for water, but of hearing the words of the LORD. They shall wander from sea to sea, and from north to east; they shall run to and fro, seeking the word of the LORD, but shall not find it.'"*[4] May God keep us from ever experiencing a famine for "hearing" His Word, from times when either personally or collectively there is no hunger to hear it or for the impact of having it expounded. This is the worst of all famine. It's one thing to deprive the stomach, quite another to starve the soul. Amos was urged to *"Go ... Flee to the land of Judah. There eat bread, and there prophesy. But never again prophesy at Bethel."*[5]

No bread in Bethlehem, the House of Bread; and no word from God in Bethel, the house of God. If they had been asked why they didn't want to hear from Amos, they may have said that they never got anything out of it, and that would have revealed more about the hearer than the speaker. Our prayer meetings should be times of pleading that God will never stop speaking through His servants, that they always will have something from Him to say; and our teaching meetings should be times of hearing what He has to say. We should graciously encourage one another that there be no shortage of speakers and no shortage of hearers.

> Master, speak; Thy servant heareth,
> Waiting for Thy gracious word,
> Longing for Thy voice that cheereth;
> Master, let it now be heard.
> I am listening, Lord, for Thee –
> What hast thou to say to me?
> (F.R. Havergal)

We need the spirit of Elisha who, in a time of acknowledged dearth, immediately told his servant, *"Put on the large pot, and boil stew for the sons of the prophets."*[6] His sense of trust in God made him see beyond the famine, not to a small pot, but to a great one; and not to a cold meal or a reheat, but to something freshly cooked and hot. This holds a valuable lesson for any like the Scottish minister who was criticised for giving "Caul kail het again," meaning he repeated an old sermon, like reheated food. Elisha's story is covered in four verses, during which his intended meal became deadly, yet he was equal to this, too, and provided the remedy by calling, *"Then bring some flour."*

The New King James Version translates the next phrase rather tamely: *"And he put it into the pot,"* but this fails to convey the urgency of his action. Other versions say he "cast" it in, and some say that he "threw it," and they capture the meaning of the word *wayyashlēk.* The urgency of his calling, when Elijah *"threw his mantle on him"*[7] – he didn't 'put it on him' – went on to become the urgency of his service, and we see this when he *"cast in the salt"* to heal the bitter water[8] and *"cut off a stick, and threw it in"* to retrieve the sunken axe head.[9]

May God help us to be equal to the task in our day. Thank God for men like Elisha who face up to reality and take the initiative to do something about it! As a man of God, he would have been well aware why there was a famine in the land, and for that reason he acted by faith. But what happens when there are no Elishas? Perhaps, we can glimpse an answer in the opening verses of Jeremiah 14 by wondering at the nobles' lack of reality. A few questions will be enough to tell us what sort of men they were.

* Had they completely overlooked the fact that dearth and drought were signs of God's disapproval? Had they forgotten His warning? - *"'I will give you the rain for your land in its season, the early rain and the latter rain, that you may gather in your grain, your new wine, and your oil. And I will send grass in your fields for your livestock, that you may eat and be filled.' Take heed to yourselves, lest your heart be deceived, and you turn aside and serve other gods and worship them, lest the Lord's anger be aroused against you, and He shut up the heavens so that there be no rain, and the land yield no produce, and you* *perish quickly from the good land which the Lord is giving you.*"[10]

* Could they not read His displeasure on their parched land?

* Did they fail to see that no rain, no grain and no grass meant that He had withheld them?

They were supposed to be the excellent, yet they failed to show that, *"As for the saints who are on the earth, 'They are the excellent ones, in whom is all my delight.'"*[11] It wasn't the first time that nobles had failed for Nehemiah 3:5 speaks of those who shared in the effort of rebuilding the wall, *"but their nobles did not put their shoulders to the work of their LORD."*

* Was it beneath their dignity? And was it for the same reason that their successors *"sent their lads for water,"* to spare their blushes? Did they think they were above getting their hands dirty, and beneath them to have their hearts cleansed?

* Why send lads when the futility was so obvious? Young people, even in our day, may have their weaknesses, but the onus is never on young people when there's no refreshing feeding among the people of God. Leaders must lead, and feeders must feed!

Israel's mercurial state in the time of the judges made the downside of Leviticus 26 a reality. The people ceased walking with God and He stopped walking with them. They had disregarded His order and gone beyond the boundary of His promise: "If you walk … I will walk," so blessing changed to judgment. Famine ravaged the land, not only Bethlehem itself, yet being there depicted the poverty of the nation by emphasising famine in the House of Bread. God had taken the *Lechem* out of *Bēth Lechem*. Bethlehem is referred to as *"Bethlehem, Judah"* in verse 1, which distinguishes it from the other Bethlehem in the territory of Zebulun[12] and the family are described as *"Ephrathites of Bethlehem"* in verse 2.

This attributes fruitfulness to the place, but they would never be able to say, like Joseph, *"God has caused me to be fruitful [pārāh, linked to Ephrathah]in the land of my affliction."*[13] Truest fruitfulness came to Bethlehem when the Saviour was born there, of which Micah says, *"But you, Bethlehem Ephrathah, though you are little among the thousands of Judah, yet out of you shall come forth to Me the One to be Ruler in Israel, Whose goings forth are from of old, from everlasting."*[14]

Militarily and agriculturally, God was the means of their protection and production, and everything was governed by this one rule, "If you walk ... I will walk." But notice the change in His wording in these verses: He began by referring to "the land" and ended by calling it "your land." The Lord Jesus Christ made a similar change when He referred to the Temple in Jerusalem as "My house" and as "Your house."[15] How tragic it is when there is no evidence of His presence or blessing and when what was His simply becomes ours! This was a real danger in places such as Ephesus and Laodicea[16] where those who had been called into churches that belonged to God risked being at the stage when they would merely speak of them as "our church." The land, first and foremost, was His, and those in the land must live as being His. The assemblies, first and foremost are His, and those in them must live as being His. Only then can we say, as in the words of Psalm 85:1 and 12, *"LORD, You have been favourable to Your land; ... Yes, the LORD will give what is good; And our land will yield its increase."* His first, then ours!

When we walk with the Lord
In the light of His Word,
What a glory He sheds on our way;
While we do His good will,
He abides with us still,
And with all who will trust and obey.
Then in fellowship sweet
We will sit at His feet,
Or we'll walk by His side in the way;

What He says we will do;
Where He sends, we will go,
Never fear, only trust and obey.
(John Henry Sammis)

Famine in the Heart

Others went through difficult times too. When King Saul *"inquired of the LORD, the LORD did not answer him, either by dreams or by Urim or by the prophets."* God was completely silent: no answer was given within himself, the high priest had nothing to say to him, nor did the prophets. The truth was, the LORD had departed from him,[17] and had stopped communicating with him. Had he possessed the spiritual sensitivity of his successor, David, he would have cried out to God, *"O LORD my Rock: Do not be silent to me, lest, if You are silent to me, I become like those who go down to the pit."*[18]

With the insensitivity that comes from famine in the heart, Saul took his problem elsewhere, and his solution was to disguise himself and go to consult a witch. What a ludicrous move for a man who was head and shoulders above everyone else! It wouldn't take a witch to see through his disguise, but it would seem she didn't. She was supposed to be able to see into the future, yet she couldn't see through a disguise!

When Samson caved in to Delilah's questions and his hair was shaved off, *"he did not know that the LORD had departed from him."*[19] The sad thing was, he didn't know the difference. He had given in to a temptress and ended up bald, blind, and captured by the Philistines. King Hezekiah was another from whom God withdrew, *"in order to test him, that He might know all that was in his heart."*[20] How sad it is when those who should know better don't realise that when God withdraws He withholds.

We were thinking a moment ago of the church in Ephesus in Revelation 2 that risked having its lampstand removed. Would those in it have known any difference if it had been, or would they just have gone on as normal? The church in Sardis had a name of having life, yet it was dead. If the lampstand had been removed from Ephesus, would they not also have had a name of having light? Jeremiah spoke about the heart being deceitful,[21] and famine in the heart will make it even more so. Our Bibles give ample proof in both Old and New Testaments that, individually and collectively, it's possible to live with pretence.

God wants us to be real about our relationship with Him and to know the reality of His relationship with us. We reach times of spiritual crises when we turn away from Him, and are at a very serious crossroads if He ever needs to turn away from us. Yes, there can be times when we lose the assurance of knowing He is there for us, and He might be testing us to see what is in our hearts. At that point, we need to show that we have a heart for Him, and for what is His. If repentance is needed, there will be no hesitation when there is no famine in the heart.

Famine in the Home

Now it was Elimelech's turn. The famine was national, so there was no solution north or south. They were testing times, and he failed the test. This was no overnight, spur of the moment reaction. If we could have eavesdropped at the door of their home, we may have heard the process of this family's discussion, decision and departure. They might well have said, "We can't cope with this any longer. We have had enough. Staying here would be pointless. Anywhere will be better than here. The boys agree. Let's go." All four *"went."* Yes, they walked away, but the implications given by different forms of the word *hālak* are more serious than that. They wandered from their true home and vanished from their place among God's people in the land like the cloud that disappears and vanishes in Job 7:9.

Two valuable lessons can be learned from this kind of procedure. When we feel it is bad 'here' where God has called us, we should remember that it is much worse 'there' where He is not honoured. Furthermore, family decisions do not excuse us from personal responsibility or free us from individual accountability to God. The word *"dwell" (Heb. gūr)* is translated differently in Numbers 22:3 where we read, *"Moab was exceedingly afraid."* It also means to go in fear as a stranger, to turn aside from the road, or to shrink in fear, and may indicate that this family had serious reservations and were afraid of what lay ahead. They had every reason to be for they left *"Bethlehem"* - the house of bread, and *"Judah"* – the place of praise,[22] thanksgiving,[23] and confession,[24] and went to *"Moab"* which originated from the son of Lot after his incest with one of his daughters.[25]

Another interesting connotation from the word *gūr* is found in Psalm 33:8 where the psalmist says, "Let all the inhabitants of the world *stand in awe* of Him." Whatever could there be in Moab that would cause them to stand in awe other than with a sense of fear? They were turning their backs on Bethlehem and God's land where they could stand in awe of Him in true reverence, but there would be nothing to revere in Moab. When they "went," did they intend only to be visitors who would retrace their steps at the first opportunity? If so, they sound a loud warning to believers who assume that departure from God will be a temporary measure they can put right whenever they please.

Ten years in Moab testify to how short-sighted faithlessness is for it proved to be a decade in which the absence of faith's long-sightedness deprived them of enjoying the Passover and engaging in the other feasts of Jehovah.[26] Three deaths show that permanence can easily be masked by temporary intentions, which fail to take into account that repentance can't be guaranteed or pre-arranged. There would be no shortage of sorrow for them in Moab, but it wasn't of the godly sort through which God in His goodness grants repentance.[27]There would be tears over three coffins, and later at the crossroads when Orpah decided to give up the journey to Bethlehem and return to Moab, but not tears of contrition.

The famine in the land had triggered a famine in their hearts until it became a famine in the home for the whole family, and what a loud warning this is that dearth in the church can lead to dearth in our Christian homes! It can be the other way around, of course. Is it not true that our hearts and homes determine the state of the church? Our struggles affect us. Elimelech and Naomi's natural struggle became spiritual: faith decreased and fear increased. Had David been among their predecessors instead of their successors, they could have taken his advice, *"Trust in the LORD, and do good; dwell in the land, and feed on His faithfulness."*[28] They also could have taken the rebuke from Solomon had they been able to read, *"For the upright will dwell in the land, and the blameless will remain in it."*[29] It's a wonderful promise to many, and an indictment for others like Elimelech and family. They didn't "remain," so they couldn't claim to be "upright" or "blameless."

More than three thousand years have passed since then, but this doesn't reduce the need to ask, "As they prepared to leave and finally made their exit, did anyone urge them not to go?" Maybe they did: perhaps not. Either way, there's a lesson for us. Our love for the Lord, and for our brothers and sisters, should make us want to help some toward better decisions and to reassure them that God still says, *"If you walk … I will walk."*

Lord, Thou hast made Thyself to me
A living, bright reality,
More present to faith's vision keen
Than any earthly object seen;
More dear, more intimately nigh
Than e'en the closest earthly tie.

And Thou, blest vision of my soul,
Hast made my broken nature whole;
Hast purified my base desires,
And kindled passion's holiest fires;
My nature Thou hast lifted up,
And filled me with a glorious hope.

Nearer and dearer still to me,
Thou living, loving Saviour be;
Brighter the vision of Thy face,
More charming still Thy words of grace;
So, life shall be transformed to love,
Thy grace and mercy more to prove.
(Charlotte Elliott)

3.4 THE CONSEQUENCE

"And a certain man of Bethlehem, Judah, went to dwell in the country of Moab, he and his wife and his two sons. The name of the man was Elimelech, the name of his wife was Naomi, and the names of his two sons were Mahlon and Chilion—Ephrathites of Bethlehem, Judah. And they went to the country of Moab and remained there. Then Elimelech, Naomi's husband, died; and she was left, and her two sons. Now they took wives of the women of Moab: the name of the one was Orpah, and the name of the other Ruth. And they dwelt there about ten years. Then both Mahlon and Chilion also died; so the woman survived her two sons and her husband" (Ruth 1:1-5).

* * *

Like it or not, decisions have consequences. We know that, don't we? It's as old as Eden. As individuals, Eve and Adam saw and thought, made their decisions, and ate. Their foreseen consequences should have included God's forewarning about eating of the tree of the knowledge of good and evil: *"in the day that you eat of it you shall surely die."*[1] Their unforeseen consequences meant they didn't even have the knowledge that they would attempt to hide out of sight of the Omniscient, and have lost the desire to be with Him. Both actions were an admission that His promise had been fulfilled: spiritually, they had died. We know, of course, that God went after them and that, even though they were removed from the Garden of God, He had a plan to bring man back into fellowship with Himself.

Elimelech and his family were like a re-run of this. Individually, they saw and thought, they made their decision, and acted. Were they blind to the foreseen and the unforeseen or was their consideration of these outweighed by a decision about bread? One thing is sure, the adversary didn't make truth and the God of truth a priority as he helped them to read his faulty scales, and the perceived imbalance made them decide to leave His land. Bread tipped the scales! Like Adam and Eve, this family were in it together, yet sin always has made man individually accountable to God.

They would have admitted that lack of bread was their reason for leaving, but they would have been more honest had they admitted that the real reason was lack of love. They were like the church in Revelation 2:4, and God could have said to all four of them, *"Nevertheless I have this against you, that you have left your first love."* Sadly, we never see things the way God sees them when we turn away from Him and His service. Other things get the blame, even other people, yet God knows that the underlying cause is in the heart, not the feet. Paul had been able to say of this church in Ephesus, *"I heard of your faith in the Lord Jesus and your love for all the saints,"* but this changed. The same probably could have been said of Elimelech and his family, but their outlook changed too, and apparently neither God nor the people of God were good reason to stay.

The consequences were hard-hitting: three men lost their lives, three wives lost their men, and one widow lost the joy of being a mother. How right Solomon was when he said, *"The way of the unfaithful* [plural participle of *bāgad*] *is hard."*[2] They were a snapshot of what God sometimes saw in His people: He *"made the tribes of Israel dwell in their tents. Yet they tested and provoked the Most High God, and did not keep His testimonies, but turned back and acted unfaithfully* [from *bāgad*] *like their fathers."*[3] However, just as Genesis 4 shows that God received something acceptable from Abel after the crisis of Eden, Ruth 1 opens up the wonderful foreshadowing of how He would gain something out of Elimelech and Naomi's loss. Not only would Naomi point to His bringing Israel back to Himself, but that Ruth would show his purpose in drawing Gentiles to the Redeemer.

Already, at the beginning of this chapter, there is a compelling lesson to be learned: if we are tempted to turn aside from our Christian path, we should be honest about what distracts us from God. For Adam and Eve, it was fruit; for Elimelech, Naomi and their sons, it was bread. What will it be for us? What is it for you? Whatever it was for them, look at it this way: was it worth losing fellowship with God over their one-off enjoyment of fruit? They certainly never tasted it again, so it was a fleeting and seeming gain followed by permanent loss. Was it worth losing fellowship with God and His people for bread? Three men were an Old Testament proof that, *"Man shall not live by bread alone."* They had that in Moab and died, but failed to live *"by every word that proceeds from the mouth of God."*[4]

What appeals to you that outweighs your relationship with God? A partner who doesn't know the Lord? A job that will make you give up your Christian principles? Or are you just attracted to the world and its worldly ways? Yes, you may be tempted to think that God could bring something good out of it, but the truth is that Adam and Eve didn't think of that before they forfeited the garden. Neither did Elimelech and his family before forfeiting the land, and neither should we before going our own way. Wrong decisions have the ability to delude, and consequences can be serious. In the case of the prodigal son, he came back to his father with a lot of regret, yet he soon discovered that eating the "fatted calf" was much better than "pods."[5]

God keep us from the prodigal's appetite. Luke 15:16 tells us that, *"he would gladly have filled his stomach with the pods that the swine ate,"* and that was tragic for a Jew. Pigs should have been farthest from his mind, and the law should have kept them off his diet, since it stated in Leviticus 11:7, *"the swine ... is unclean to you."* The problem was, he wasn't prepared to make the law personal and say, "the swine is unclean to me." Poor spiritual judgment can have an effect on the Christian's desires, too, and the world has its own way of catering to them. Many Christian lives have been damaged, and some ruined, by craving wrong things in wrong places with the wrong company. The truth is, it never runs out of "pods."

God is My King

When Elimelech was born his parents' choice of name probably voiced their own conviction and aspirations for him, that he would live up to its meaning – 'God is my King.' Each time they called his name they announced that God is Sovereign; more than that, they would have testified their desire that he would acknowledge God as Sovereign by submitting to His rule. The meaning of his name is quite significant, but the record of the book of Ruth shows that he didn't live up to it and lost his desire to be subject to Him. Like those who called Jesus "Lord, Lord" and failed to do what He asked, Elimelech answered to the name of "God is my King" without showing that He reigned as Monarch in his heart. He exchanged Canaan for Moab and went to live in different surroundings with its different gods where his God and King was not accepted as Sovereign.

The meaning of Elimelech's name combined with Naomi's – sweetness – sound like symptoms of an ideal spiritual relationship with God. Sweetness is sure to reign where God's sovereignty is acknowledged, but going to Moab was equally symptomatic that where there is no submission to Him sweetness will vanish, too. The names he and Naomi chose for their sons didn't reflect the godly ambition of his parents, and this may indicate a lower sense of God already existed in his way of thinking. David said, *"The LORD sat enthroned at the Flood, and the LORD sits as King forever,"*[6] but not in Elimelech's heart.

If only, like others, he had stayed in God's land without bread rather than in a land with bread but without God! Mahlon (from *chālāh*) implies thoughts of being sick, weak, diseased, infirmity, worn out, and wounded; and Isaiah alluded to the root meaning of his name when he spoke about the inhabitant of Jerusalem not saying, *"I am sick"* (from *chᵒliy* and *chālāh*).[7] He had begun his prophecy by saying, *"The whole head is sick, the whole heart faints,"*[8] and Paul gave a New Testament counterpart when he wrote, *"many are weak and sickly among you, and many sleep."*[9]

Sadly, it wasn't long until Elimelech, together with his weak and sickly sons, also slept the sleep of death.[10] Chilion suggests wasting, pining, failure and destruction. Both names may refer to illness during infancy, but, whatever the reason, together with Elimelech's failure they combine to represent the poor spiritual condition of the people of Israel during the time of the judges. Isaiah also uses the thought of Chilion's name when he says to Israel, *"A remnant of them will return; the destruction [killāyōn]decreed shall overflow with righteousness."*[11] One commentator has written, "The word *killāyōn* from *kālāh* to complete, to finish, to waste away, vanish, disappear, denotes a languishing, or wasting away, as in disease; and then "destruction" or that which "completes" life and prosperity" (Albert Barnes). So Mahlon and Chilion's names, not only join to describe their poor physical health, but are combined by the Spirit of God to depict the people of Israel's poor spiritual health.

God is King

Elimelech's departure and demise teaches us that it's possible for "God is my King" no longer to be true, but one statement stands eternally true: "The LORD is King." With the waters of the Red Sea victoriously rolled over their enemies, the children of Israel concluded their song with the words, *"The LORD shall reign forever and ever."*[12] Around four centuries later, the psalmist wholeheartedly agreed: *"The LORD is King forever and ever."*[13] Difficult times may come and go, times may change, but He is unchangeable.

After hearing that five-year-old schoolchildren in his sister's class didn't believe in God, a four-year-old boy was asked what he thought about Him. He started off, "God is beautiful, and He made me." Suddenly remembering part of the answer to the fourth question in the Westminster Shorter

Catechism, he added, "God is Spirit, infinite, eternal and unchangeable." How true! At the end of his Lamentations, Jeremiah wrote over what was a very dark time for God's people, *"You, O LORD, remain forever; Your throne from generation to generation."*[14] Yes, He is enthroned in heaven from generation to generation, yet not every generation will show that He is enthroned on earth in their hearts.

She was left

What sad words! Naomi "was left" without her husband and in the burden of her widowhood it wasn't long until Mahlon and Chilion who had married Ruth and Orpah also died, and their deaths meant that, yet again, she "was left."[15] God always makes sure that something is "left," and Naomi is an example of His purpose in delivering a "remnant" of His people. Ezra spoke of it when he thought of those who returned from captivity in Babylon and attributed their escape to God's grace being shown to a "remnant."[16] Almost three centuries earlier, Isaiah had rested on the thought that *"the remnant who have escaped of the house of Judah shall again take root downward, and bear fruit upward"*[17] Naomi was of the house of Judah, and God was about to unfold how important her return would be.

As we shall see later, uppermost in the mind of God was the foreshadowing she gave of those from the people of Israel who respond to the call of the gospel of Christ and show that they are among the *"remnant according to the election of grace."*[18] He also looks forward to a coming day when *"The Redeemer will come to Zion, and to those who turn from transgression in Jacob."*[19] On that day, they will look on Him whom they pierced,[20] *"And he shall be their peace."*[21] He is the long-promised One of Bethlehem Ephrathah, *"The One to be Ruler in Israel, Whose goings forth are from of old, from everlasting"*; and then Micah adds, *"Therefore He shall give them up, until the time that she who is in labour has given birth; then the remnant of His brethren shall return to the children of Israel."*

Naomi's sons had married two Moabite women, Orpah and Ruth, and although Moab was not specifically mentioned in Deuteronomy 7:3, both Ezra and Nehemiah included Moab's women as being unsuitable wives for men among the people of God.[22] Forging wrong bonds in the place of bondage was an additional tie to Moab, marriage to their people meant marriage to the place, and they settled down to a future in Moab. Fear had gone, adjustments had been made, they no longer felt like strangers, and were at home in Moab until they died there. The *Targum* says, "And because they transgressed the decree of the word of the Lord, and joined affinity with strange people, therefore their days were cut off."

Staying in Moab for ten years was a mistake, but it is easy to make other mistakes after an initial error: like telling another lie to cover up the first one! The mistake of becoming unsettled in Bethlehem and leaving it led on to becoming settled in Moab and never leaving it. Straying was wrong, and staying was wrong. These young men squandered ten years – wasted years. It's a sober lesson, for it's one thing for us to use the world, but quite another for the world to use us. Another solemn lesson has to be learned: God can take us away from what we get in the world without asking our permission, but the world can never take what we get from God without our permission.

It's not possible to settle in Moab and be settled with God at the same time! Scripture gives us some clear examples. In Judges 3:14, *"the children of Israel served Eglon king of Moab eighteen years,"* until Ehud slew him and delivered them. In 2 Samuel 8:2, David *"... defeated Moab. Forcing them down to the ground ..."* In Psalm 60:8, God said, *"Moab is My washpot."* He saw it as being like a vessel for menial use, such as a slave washing his master's feet, and subdued before a conquering God. Jeremiah wrote, *"Moab is destroyed."*[23] To their shame, Elimelech, Mahlon and Chilion didn't defeat, destroy or conquer Moab. Instead, Moab defeated, destroyed and conquered them! Moab meant different things to different people, but it was to David what it was to God – a place to be conquered. Spiritually, it's a lesson for us that either it will defeat us or we will defeat it. We can rejoice that David's greater Son has conquered sin and death for us, but we have to learn to conquer worldliness for ourselves. We will see this clearly in our next chapter when Orpah shows that although she was out of Moab, Moab wasn't out of her. It will be equally clear that although Ruth wasn't yet in Bethlehem, Bethlehem definitely was in her.

We don't know how they blended in, but they must have been rather conspicuous when they arrived there looking out of place as Jews among Moabites. They would have been seen to be different, almost as different as Achan if he had worn in Israel the Babylonian garment he stole at Jericho.[24] But they couldn't remain different and blend in at the same time. Something had to go, and no doubt they let go what was precious to God, and should have meant most to them.

Sometimes, Christians merge into worldly ways for the same reason: they lose the will to be different and leave their *"first love."*[25] Many years ago, on a dark night in South India, two of us went looking for a Christian family whose address we didn't know, except for the general area where we knew they lived. Hoping that someone local to the neighbourhood could help, we stopped in a dimly lit street to ask an Indian lady. At first, we drew a complete blank, until we told her that our friend's parents were active Christians. Suddenly, a light went on in her mind: "Oh, that will be the woman in the white sari!" And she told us exactly where we would find her and her family. She was remembered for being different, and so should we.

I Look Not Back

I look not back; God knows the fruitless efforts,
The wasted hours, the sinning, the regrets.
I leave them all with Him who blots the record,
And graciously forgives, and then forgets.

I look not forward; God sees all the future,
The road that, short or long, will lead me home,
And He will face with me its every trial,
And bear for me the burdens that may come.

I look not round me; then would fears assail me,
So wild the tumult of earth's restless seas,
So dark the world, so filled with woe and evil,
So vain the hope of comfort and of ease.

I look not inward; that would make me wretched;
For I have naught on which to stay my trust.
Nothing I see save failures and shortcomings,
And weak endeavours, crumbling into dust.

But I look up - into the face of Jesus,
For there my heart can rest, my fears are stilled;
And there is joy, and love, and light for darkness,
And perfect peace, and every hope fulfilled.
(Annie Johnson Flint)

3.5 RETURNING TO THE LAND

"Then she arose with her daughters-in-law that she might return from the country of Moab, for she had heard in the country of Moab that the LORD had visited His people by giving them bread. Therefore she went out from the place where she was, and her two daughters-in-law with her; and they went on the way to return to the land of Judah. And Naomi said to her two daughters-in-law, "Go, return each to her mother's house. The LORD deal kindly with you, as you have dealt with the dead and with me. The LORD grant that you may find rest, each in the house of her husband." So she kissed them, and they lifted up their voices and wept.

And they said to her, "Surely we will return with you to your people." But Naomi said, "Turn back, my daughters; why will you go with me? Are there still sons in my womb, that they may be your husbands? Turn back, my daughters, go—for I am too old to have a husband. If I should say I have hope, if I should have a husband tonight and should also bear sons would you wait for them till they were grown? Would you restrain yourselves from having husbands? No, my daughters; for it grieves me very much for your sakes that the hand of the LORD has gone out against me!"

Then they lifted up their voices and wept again; and Orpah kissed her mother-in-law, but Ruth clung to her. And she said, "Look, your sister-in-law has gone back to her people and to her gods; return after your sister-in-law." But Ruth said: "Entreat me not to leave you, or to turn back from following after you; for wherever you go, I will go; and wherever you lodge, I will lodge; your people shall be my people, and your God, my God. Where you die, I will die, and there will I be buried. The LORD do so to me, and more also, if anything but death parts you and me." When she saw that she was determined to go with her, she stopped speaking to her" (Ruth 1:6-18).

* * *

With the weight of three deaths and three widows on her shoulders, Naomi must have wondered, "What should I do now? Where is God in all this? Where do I go from here?" Job knew that a meaningful part of his ministry was that he *"caused the widow's heart to sing for joy,"*[1] but who was there to make Naomi's heart sing? David's assurance in Psalm 68:5 wasn't available to her, yet the God of whom he spoke was always available as *"a defender of widows ... in His holy habitation."* Ruth and Naomi would find out how true this is after they reached Bethlehem, and, long before it was written in Psalm 146:9, each of them would prove that *"The LORD watches over the strangers; He relieves the fatherless and widow."* When news came that He had returned to bless His people, she knew what to do, and the comments are so informative: *"Then she arose ... for she had heard ...Therefore she went."*

Isn't it so typical of human nature that three deaths hadn't been enough to send Naomi back to Bethlehem, but the news of bread did? So the start of her journey back there was probably based on the wrong reason. It would have been much more meaningful if she had been prompted only by hearing the greater news *"that the LORD had visited His people,"* and not by hearing that *"the LORD had visited His people by giving them bread."* The next verse sums up her motive: *"Therefore she went out from the place where she was."* She left because there was no bread, and went back because there was bread. How sad! It's like going to church for help that's practical or social, rather than for what's spiritual! However, it did mean that His people's condition had changed: they were walking with God and providing the right spiritual climate for a new convert and a homecoming believer. The same is needed today. Churches should always be ready for the Lord to add those in whom

He is working.

Naomi wasn't there when Jehovah came to bless – just like John 20:24 where *"Thomas ... one of the twelve, was not with them when Jesus came."* Even today, some dear Christians learn by hearsay what faithful saints learn by first-hand experience, because they ignore the warning, *"not forsaking the assembling of ourselves together, as is the manner of some."*[2] They not only miss the gatherings of the Lord's people, they miss out when He comes in blessing. However, a sovereign God has a sovereign purpose, which means there is a way back. Hard lessons can be learned from lean times, from departure and disappointment, and Naomi learned that, no matter how far you go or how long you stay away, He can provide the way back. The lure of the world might be like the decaying corpses that appealed to Noah's raven in Genesis 8:7, but Naomi's homing instinct kept her from finding true rest.

Some Christians find it even harder than she did for they are like doves that choose to fly with ravens! As Dr Andrew Bonar put it, "I look for the church and I find it in the world. I look for the world and I find it in the church." This leads us to draw a very distinct conclusion: Elimelech's failure wasn't due to another attack by Moab. It didn't result from outward conflict, but from inward collapse. Similarly, with churches today: on the whole, decline isn't caused by an increase in outward foes, but by a decrease in inward faith. In other words, it's not resulting from what we are facing, but on what we are turning our backs!

Following Naomi's response, it says of Orpah and Ruth, *"they went with her."* What a lovely phrase, and it conveys a bit more than simply going with each other. Like the word *"went"* in verse 1, they walked away and vanished together from Moab. But the picture of going *"with her"* brings them even closer for the word *'imāh* comes from the word *'amam*, which Dr Strong says can mean to overshadow by huddling together. We don't know how far they went until Naomi voiced what was troubling her.

Go, return …Turn back …Turn back

We can't know for certain why Naomi was so persistent. Perhaps, she didn't want to take the evidence of her wayward and costly ten years back to Bethlehem. Was she so ashamed? Was she testing them? Or was she an Old Testament example of trying to find out if someone was there only for the loaves and fish? How tragic it was that she should do her utmost to turn them back and drive them away from the way to Judah, the pathway to praise! This was discouragement wrapped in a kiss, desertion concealed by affection, and a deception that they could find the Lord's kindness, comfort and rest in the place where she couldn't. No wonder they *"wept"* (Heb. *bākāh*), lamenting and mourning at the very thought of parting. This was their personal *"valley of Baca,"*[3] induced by an Israelite and not a fellow-Moabite.

No doubt her kisses were sincere, but they masked the deeper reality that she was prepared to lose the only link with her boys, probably because she had lost her spiritual vigour. Ten years had drained her of faith's dependence and she had no vision of the possibilities of God for her daughters-in-law. Her kisses may have been warm, but her heart was cold. She was shaken in her faith, so couldn't help theirs! She may have thought they had built up hopes that would end up with raised expectations being dashed. Was that her reason for saying, *"If I should say I have hope"*?

Jews refer to their hope as their *'tiqvah'* – and Rahab, the stranger, visibly bound her *"scarlet cord"* (*tiqvah*) in the window. Yes, she had hope, a hope that brought her right into the heart of things to settle in Israel with a real sense of belonging. What she didn't know was that God had brought her into the mainstream of His purpose, as we find in Matthew 1:5 which says, *"Salmon begot Boaz by Rahab."* Elimelech and Naomi would have known this for she was able to say, *"This man is … one of our close relatives."*[4] Rahab's hopes were more than fulfilled, and Ruth's would be too when this stranger met the earlier stranger's son!

279

Other possibilities are that she feared they were merely excited by the prospect of going to a foreign country to experience a different culture and customs, and thought they could regret it; or she wondered if they would be accepted among God's people and survive having their new religion tested in its homeland. She may even have been reflecting on how her family had left its inheritance and treated it so cheaply, and wondering if strangers would pay the price of commitment to God's service. Is it not also true in our case that those who prize their spiritual inheritance will encourage others to experience it too, while those who don't will fail to urge them on? Whatever her motive was, her three attempts to persuade them were attached to three different reasons.

1. The LORD would look after them (1:8);
2. There was no hope of future husbands (1:11-13) – limiting God;
3. They and their gods had no place among her people (1:15).

Having declined Naomi's first appeal, this time Orpah decided to go back and, with her kiss leaving its final imprint of fading affection, she disappeared over the horizon, out of their lives and from the pages of God's Word. Among the thoughts connected to Orpah's name, Dr Strong links it to the words 'oreph and 'āraph, which refer to "the back" and "to bend downward." At the turning point of her journey, it was as if she bent downward to write "Orpah" in the dirt with her back to Bethlehem and her face toward Moab. In doing so, she prefigured her nation's action in Jeremiah 48:39, *"How Moab has turned her back with shame!"*

Sadder still, God had already described Israel's response to Him in a similar way in Jeremiah 2:27 – *"For they have turned their back to Me, and not their face."* Saddest of all, we read in John 6:66 that *"many of His disciples went back and walked with Him no more."* We may find it hard to think of Orpah turning her back on Naomi, but how can we even begin to take it in that these men turned their back on the Saviour? They saw Him, they heard Him, yet, Orpah-like, they turned away from being in the presence of God manifested in the flesh. How could they have been so privileged, and decide to face the other way?

What we have to recognise, of course, is that we can see ourselves in Orpah and in these men, and it may be as you read this that the Lord is asking you, as he asked others in John 6:67, *"Do you also want to go away?"* Are you tempted to give up, because you are disappointed or disillusioned? Yes, it can happen, and it may be happening to you, but turning your back is not the answer. Much better to be like Jephthah in Judges 11:35 and say, *"I have given my word to the LORD, and I cannot go back on it."* By contrast, Ruth *"clung"* to Naomi with a bond that was first intended for married men who would *"be joined"* or *"cleave"* to their wives.[5] It is such a strong bond that Isaiah 41:7 translates it as *"soldering"* – fused and united as one.

Even so, Naomi remained determined and tried once more to dissuade Ruth: "Look, your sister-in-law has gone back to her people and to her gods; return after your sister-in-law." This must have been an unbearable thought for Ruth: back to the culture, customs and confusion of Moab among its people and their practices. It was unthinkable. Their main deity was Chemosh: *"the destroyer, subduer, or fish-god, the god of the Moabites (Num.21:29; Jer.48:7,13,46). The worship of this god, "the abomination of Moab," was introduced at Jerusalem by Solomon (1 Kin.11:7), but was abolished by Josiah (2 Kin.23:13)"* (Easton's Bible Dictionary).

Naomi's reasoning on the basis of Orpah's decision inferred that they would lack company and that there would be none of their own kind, but she overlooked the fact that anyone could feel at home among the people of God. Orpah had been encouraged to go back to idolatry by an Israelite, but when Naomi urged Ruth to "Look" she made it clear that her *look* was fixed in the opposite direction. Naomi had influenced her sister-in-law, but she would not influence her. Orpah couldn't resist the temptation to go back, and Ruth was irresistibly drawn to go forward! Thoughts of *"her mother's house"* and *"the house of her husband"* appealed to Orpah, but neither *Bēt* 'immāh nor Bēt 'iyshāh attracted Ruth. There was only one thought in her mind – Bēt Lechem, the house of bread.

Entreat me not to leave you

Orpah had shown the genuineness of her affection and the shallowness of her conviction, whereas the genuineness of Ruth's affection was sealed in the fulness of her conversion. Hers was a perfect surrender. There was more in her heart than a fondness for Naomi; it was set on the home of faith in the only true God and of love for Him and His laws. She knew that going back would be taking away her inner sense of the call of God of which she had become so convicted, and she knew that going back would silence the voice of repentance that was burning in her heart. Turning to Naomi, she made an appeal that could come only from the heart of a woman in whom God was deeply at work. Evidence flowed from her as she spoke those momentous words:

"Entreat me not to leave you, or to turn back from following after you; for wherever you go, I will go; and wherever you lodge, I will lodge; your people shall be my people, and your God, my God. Where you die, I will die, and there will I be buried. The LORD do so to me, and more also, if anything but death parts you and me."

She had made a spiritual calculation and knew that going back would have meant a lost opportunity to enjoy:

- Direction – *"wherever you go, I will go;"*
- Communion – *"wherever you lodge, I will lodge;"*
- Union – *"your people shall be my people,"*
- Submission – *"and your God, my God."*
- Anticipation – *"Where you die, I will die, and there I will be buried."*

Submission held all five certainties together and, wisely, Naomi made no attempt to alter what she had said. What a lesson! When God is at work in a person's heart, there's no need to tell them what to say. There's nothing sweeter or more precious in evangelism than hearing the spontaneous prayer of a newly convicted sinner. Not all will be as eloquent as Ruth, no two will say the same, but the plea from genuine hearts, no matter how faltering, will complete the Spirit's work. It's the voice of repentance composed in the troubled sinner's own heart, not by a concerned believer. Ruth knew nothing about the road she was going or what her lodging place would be like; she knew very little about the people or what her burial place would be like; but she knew God and what He was like. In fact, her word for God is very revealing. Twice she used the word Elohim, a plural name for the triune God, yet she never dreamt that He was calling her into the line that would lead to the incarnation of His Son. What she did see was that even death would not separate her from Naomi. She had the vision of being faithful unto death, and such was faith's grand anticipation that she grasped the reality of being gathered to her people, like Abraham, Isaac and Jacob,[6] Aaron and Moses,[7] Joshua[8] and David.[9] There is no mention of her ever kissing Naomi, but such words on her lips made a kiss redundant! She also confirmed her promise by calling on God to judge her if she ever went back on her word, which was an oath invoked by others in Israel.[10] Ittai also made a similar statement to David.[11]

Ruth's pledge shows that her allegiance to a person, a place, and a people had its higher focus on God. Take Him out of it, and she cannot say, *"your God, my God,"* and identifying with *"wherever you go … wherever you lodge"* and *"where you die"* is completely futile. Naomi was to Ruth what Israel and the law are to the Christian. As far as Israel is concerned, "their fall is the riches of the world"; and we value the law as being the tutor that brought us to Christ.[12] Alas, Naomi in her disturbed state probably missed that her daughter-in-law had so eloquently echoed God's covenanting promise in Leviticus 26:12, *"I will walk among you and be your God, and you shall be My people."* Totally different from Orpah, Ruth knew how serious it was to make a pledge in His name and is an outstanding example to believers who make a commitment in baptism that they will not return to their old lifestyle or habits.

She had not the slightest idea of what the way would be like, she had very little idea of what the people would be like, and she had no idea whatsoever of what her life's content or her death would be like, but she put her hand into the hand of God knowing what He is like and that was all that mattered. There might be decline. That doesn't mean to say that you have to decline. There might be casualties round about you; that doesn't mean that you have to become one. Ruth stood at that moment of crisis and gave her firm commitment under the calling of God, inside the purpose of God, responding irresistibly to the grace of God. And she moved towards her objective – Bethlehem, even though she had never seen it before. She was determined. Her determination registered with Naomi for *"When she saw that she was determined to go with her, she stopped speaking to her."* There is quite a contrast here. Ruth was *"determined"* (*hit'amēts* – to stiffen one's self firmly upon a thing (Keil and Delitzsch Commentary on the Old Testament); and Naomi *"stopped speaking"* (*chādal* – to be flabby). What a difference! Ruth's resolve was strong, but there was no robust response from Naomi. Her reasoning was so weak that she was left with nothing to say. Speechless and silent, she had no words of thanks, of approval, or of praise to God. At this juncture of their journey, Ruth demonstrated that she had defeated Moab. It was destroyed and it had lost its appeal.

G. F. Dempster wrote a book called, 'Touched by a Loving Hand,' and this title could be written over the story of Ruth. There are particular words woven into it that we find a dozen times in chapter 1, once in chapter 2, and twice in chapter 4, and they all come from the little word *shūb*. In the course of chapter 1, it is translated as "return," "turn," and "gone back," all of which refer to Naomi and Orpah's intentions. In chapter 2:6, it refers to Ruth's volition in accompanying Naomi to Bethlehem. However, there's a major change in its use in chapter 1:21 where Naomi acknowledged that the LORD *"has brought me home again."* It was His work. What an admission, even though she felt "empty"!

Finally, we find it again in chapter 4:15, this time translated as "a restorer" for Naomi. Not only had God turned her back to Himself, He provided another to be the restorer that she could never be for herself. Is this not the best of all encouragement? There's never a right time to turn away from God, but it's always the right time to turn to Him or to turn back to Him. If you have turned away, let him bring you back, and you will be able to put the same word into your life and say with Psalm 23:3, *"He restores my soul."*

> Hast thou heard Him, seen Him, known Him?
> Is not thine a captured heart?
> Chief among ten thousand own Him,
> Joyful choose the better part.

> Idols once they won thee, charmed thee,
> Lovely things of time and sense;
> Gilded thus does sin disarm thee,
> Honeyed lest thou turn thee thence.

> What has stripped the seeming beauty
> From the idols of the earth?
> Not a sense of right or duty,
> But the sight of peerless worth.

> Not the crushing of those idols,
> With its bitter void and smart;
> But the beaming of His beauty,
> The unveiling of His heart.

'Tis the look that melted Peter,
'Tis the face that Stephen saw,
'Tis the heart that wept with Mary,
Can alone from idols draw:

Draw and win and fill completely,
Till the cup o'erflow the brim;
What have we to do with idols
Who have companied with Him?
(Miss Ora Rowan)

3.6 WALKING TOGETHER

"Now the two of them went until they came to Bethlehem. And it happened, when they had come to Bethlehem, that all the city was excited because of them; and the women said, "Is this Naomi?" But she said to them, "Do not call me Naomi; call me Mara, for the Almighty has dealt very bitterly with me. I went out full, and the LORD has brought me home again empty. Why do you call me Naomi, since the Lord has testified against me, and the Almighty has afflicted me?" So Naomi returned, and Ruth the Moabitess her daughter-in-law with her, who returned from the country of Moab. Now they came to Bethlehem at the beginning of barley harvest" (Ruth 1:19-22).

* * *

Bethlehem! They would have seen it as it appeared on the horizon, with differing thoughts being kindled in them as it gradually became nearer and clearer. Recognisable to Naomi, as she wrestled with mixed thoughts of leaving and arriving, it was unrecognisable to Ruth, as she rested in her thoughts of leaving Moab and forming first impressions of her new homeland. They were together in the House of Bread to be blessed in its fulness, and together among Ephrathites to be blessed in their fruitfulness. Chapter 1 opens with a family who took their eyes off God and left Bethlehem, and it ends with God setting His eyes on Naomi and bringing her back to Bethlehem. More than that, as Ruth's story portrays, He had His eyes fixed on a brighter horizon that Jew and Gentile would be called to discover in Christ.

Paul spoke well of Him in Romans 1:4 when he described Him as being *"of the seed of David according to the flesh, and declared* [Gr. *horisthentos* from *horizō*] *to be the Son of God with power."* Through the Saviour's incarnation, crucifixion and resurrection, God has "declared" or shown His Son to be the horizon of His purpose and, like Naomi and Ruth, He will draw both Jew and Gentile to Him. Through saving grace, they enter into the blessing of the bread of heaven in the true Bethlehemite, and into the greater fruitfulness of the true Ephrathite.[1]

All the city was excited

Ten years away from God and His people had taken their toll and, without knowing how harrowing these years had been, the womenfolk didn't hide their surprise and shock. They probably deduced by seeing two lonely women that Elimelech, Mahlon and Chilion were no more. One thing was certain, three-quarters of her family were missing. She hadn't come back the way she went, so it was understandable that there should be the noise of commotion and uproar after such a long separation. The New King James Version says they were "excited." We should love that word when it means a spiritual excitement in the service of God.

Perhaps, we have known similar times when a brother, sister or whole family has gone away from the Lord and sad experiences have left their mark. At that point, God entrusts them to the gatherings of His people for their spiritual needs to be understood, and met. It's a time for hearts to be moved as theirs were, and as the prodigal's father was in Luke 15:20 when he *"saw him and had compassion, and ran and fell on his neck and kissed him."* His feet followed the moving of his heart. He was a man who was triply moved: first of all, it was inward, then outward, and finally toward. Naomi was left in no doubt that these women felt for her. She saw their reaction, and wasn't put off by it. How important it is to react in the right way. Did she not sense a welcoming spirit? And was there not a meeting of hearts as she heard their question, and responded to it?

Is this Naomi?

Did the women ask their question because they were moved by how much her once recognisable features had been altered, and at her evident decline? "Is this Naomi?" They voiced their concern, as if to say, "Is it really you, Naomi?" By replying, *"Do not call me Naomi, call me Mara,"* she very pointedly asked them not to see sweetness in her, but bitterness. It was her way of acknowledging that the old identity had gone and had been replaced by a new name that reflected her years of estrangement. Remembering that she is an illustration of Israel as a nation, we can see that the question lingered more than seven hundred years later until Jeremiah asked in Lamentations 2:15, *"Is this the city that is called the perfection of beauty, the joy of the whole earth?"* And it resurfaced again when the Saviour came into that great city of Jerusalem and *"all the city was moved, saying, 'Who is this?'"*[2] The One who is *"great"*[3] was there and *"the city of the great King"*[4] didn't know Him! It was *"the city of our God"* and *"God was in her palaces"*; it was not only of God, He was in it, and the same should be true of churches of God. The people of Israel refused to own Him as God or acknowledge that His greatness is:

- infinite, because His deity is eternal and unsearchable;[5]
- ultimate, because He is incomparable;[6]
- intimate, because it is communicable.[7]

We have no such difficulty for He makes Himself known to us and continues to share His greatness with us through a deepening relationship with Him as *"our great God and Saviour Jesus Christ,"*[8] as *"great High Priest,"* and as the *"great Shepherd of the sheep."*[9] We can say, like Jeremiah, "His compassions fail not. They are new every morning; great is Your faithfulness."[10] He also gives *"songs in the night"*[11] and great comfort by helping believers to say, *"the night also is Yours."*[12]

the Almighty ... the LORD ... the LORD ... the Almighty

In response to their concerned openness with her, she referred twice to Jehovah and twice called Him Shaddai, while openly confessing all four as having a negative connotation for her. By renaming herself Mara, she testified that bitterness had replaced pleasantness: her sweetness and beauty had evaporated in Moab, but very graciously no one called her by her choice of name. Instead she was called by 'pleasantness' at least a dozen times in the remainder of the book, and we can be assured that this was of God, otherwise her sense of bitterness would have continued in Bethlehem. There were no negative reminders, and no raking up or casting up of the past. Repentance cleared the record, and personal bitterness didn't become communal!

Had anyone asked, "Naomi, did you come home with repentance?" she probably would have said, "Yes, definitely." This is what these verses are all about – a repentant woman who was searching her heart and, in the bitterness of her soul, trying to admit what was going on inside as she sought to become right with God and with His people. By calling her by her real name, it was as if she was being reminded, "Naomi, you are forgiven." As you read this, you may be looking back and wishing that certain things had never happened in your life, too. Friend, God says, "Are you repentant? You're forgiven and it is gone."

Individual bitterness

In a very personal way, Esau had his own 'Mara' experience when he heard that his father, Isaac, had blessed Jacob, and *"he cried with an exceedingly great and bitter cry."*[13] Once kindled, this bitterness quickly became deeply rooted in Esau and turned into hatred and murderous intent that took twenty years to resolve. He certainly proved that *"The heart knows its own bitterness,"*[14] and we need to fear the deadly effects of Mara experiences, especially when we feel justified in harbouring them.

Collective bitterness

Bitterness is self-destructive, and potentially of others too. If, individually, it has to be feared, collectively, its contagion has to be dreaded. The bitter water at Marah in Exodus 15:23 was the children of Israel's first test after they had crossed the Red Sea, and it showed what bitterness can do. Having sung with Moses in verse 1, they complained against him in verse 24, and his immediate response was to call on God for the answer. The urgent action of casting a tree (*'ets* – a stick, as in 2 Kings 6:6) into the water removed the danger and made it sweet. When David wrote, *"Behold, how good [tōb –* "joyful" as in Ecclesiastes 7:14] *and how pleasant [nā'īm] it is for brethren to dwell together in unity,"*[15] he was thinking of the pleasantness that belongs to Naomi's name.

Sadly, bitterness can rob God's people of their joy, and Moses gave a very pointed warning about this that was particularly relevant to Naomi: *"that there may not be among you man or woman or family or tribe, whose heart turns away today from the Lord our God, to go and serve the gods of these nations, and that there may not be among you a root bearing bitterness or wormwood."*[16] There is nothing to suggest that she and her family served other gods in Moab, but they had exchanged God's land for a land of gods. Moses' words are echoed in Hebrews 12:15 where the warning is applied to how one person's bitterness can contaminate the assembly: *"Looking carefully ... lest any root of bitterness springing up cause trouble, and by this many become defiled."* The good thing is, in Exodus the people didn't remain at Marah, they moved on to the refreshment of Elim. Naomi must learn to do the same, and so must we. God hadn't called her back for her to hold on to where she had been!

She had used the name of the LORD in her appeals to Orpah and Ruth in verses 8 and 9, and referred twice to Him as *"the Almighty"* and twice as *"the LORD"* when describing her trials. Instead of El Shaddai being strongly for her, she felt He had been strongly against her, and she spoke about His open hand (*yad*) being against her. She may have been blaming Him, but, in her own way, perhaps she was acknowledging His right to make *"the way of transgressors ... hard."*[17] Ruth's positive awareness of the LORD in verse 17, and Naomi's lack of response seems to indicate that He had withdrawn from her. Isaiah and Joel combined both names when they said, *"for the day of the LORD is at hand! It will come as destruction from the Almighty."*[18]

The psalmist added a third name when he wrote, '*He who dwells in the secret place of the Most High shall abide under the shadow of the Almighty. I will say of the LORD," He is my refuge and my fortress, my God [Elohim], in Him I will trust."*[19] They knew Him as strong in chastening, but also in comforting; strong to destroy, but also to defend. Without realising it, Naomi needed a greater sense of God.

full ... empty

"I went out full, and the LORD has brought me home." If Naomi had stopped there, she would never have said a truer word, but she spoiled it by inferring, 'He poured me out, He has spoken against me, and He has broken me in pieces.' As far as she was concerned, He had witnessed against her wayward existence in Moab and punished her by turning her fullness to emptiness. She was right when she said, *"I went out."* At least she was honest and didn't try to claim that the Lord took her out and she went back. Going out was her doing; coming back was His! It was an admission of her condition before Him, of how she felt inside, so with repentance and godly sorrow she acknowledged the impact He had on her during those ten barren years. If only we would confess to the place that 'I' has in our troubles! She had gone out 'whole' and came back 'worthless.' But He had not simply brought her back, He had brought her *"home"* and that was the most important thing for her to recognise.

She knew she was home. Do we? Is your church really your home? It should be. Or does a sense of emptiness deprive you of your enjoyment of feeling at home in it? The One who said, *"none shall appear before Me empty"*[20] is able to fill *"empty pitchers"* with light[21] and *"empty vessels"* with oil.[22] Like Paul, we can say, *"I know how to be abased, and I know how to abound."*[23] One thing is certain, and we can learn this from Naomi, it is much better to go back empty to the full place than try to get full in the empty place!

they came to Bethlehem

There are many in the Scriptures who walked together. Among the earliest partnerships, Genesis 5:24 says, *"Enoch walked with God; and he was not, for God took him."* It gives the impression that one day they walked and just kept going. The Partner never changed, only the scenery! Abraham walked with Isaac to Moriah, like the Father and His Son going to Calvary, and all they knew was that they were going to wherever God wanted to take them. It was like a Calvary walk. Afterwards, Eliezer and Rebekah walked together as if being examples of our walking by the Spirit,[24] like a post-Pentecost and pre-Rapture walk. Other couplings include Joshua and Caleb, Ezra and Nehemiah, Joshua and Zerubbabel, Haggai and Zechariah, Paul and Barnabas, and the company of disciples whom the Saviour sent out *"two by two."*[25] All of them were coupled in a trustworthy fellowship with each other, and together with Him. A dear sister once told me that she had never had a close confidante, yet God often brings fellow-saints together for dependable confidentiality.

Naomi and Ruth were another of God's great couplings, and this was shown, not only by leaving Moab together, but in the timing of their arrival in Bethlehem for *"they came at the beginning of barley harvest."* Barley was the first crop to be reaped[26] and harvesting began immediately after the Passover, which was held on the 14th day of the month Abib (also called Nisan), and followed by the Feast of Firstfruits. The first was the great foreshadowing of the Saviour's suffering and death in the lamb; the second pointed forward to the joy of His resurrection in the wave sheaf. The chapter closes with a wonderful contrast to the way it opened. Returning replaces leaving, harvest replaces hunger, and the scene is set for a new beginning. It was as if God said to them, "Naomi and Ruth, this is a new beginning for you both." How aptly they depicted E.H. Swinstead's poem:

> There's a way back to God from the dark paths of sin;
> There's a door that is open and you may go in:
> At Calvary's cross is where you begin,
> When you come as a sinner to Jesus.

Paul combines the Lord Jesus Christ's fulfilment of these two memorable feasts in Philippians 3:10, and calls each of us to enter into their deep meaning by saying, *"that I may know Him and the power of His resurrection, and the fellowship of His sufferings."*

By the grace of God, many a drunkard was rescued through the ministry of the old Water Street Mission in New York. Sam Hadley was one who stumbled into it and was wonderfully saved as the result of hearing about the Saviour. He became so attached and involved in it that he ultimately became its Superintendent. When Charles Alexander visited the Mission, Sam Hadley took him to streets in Lower Manhattan to let him see the kind of circumstances in which men and women were living, to show him the effects of their depravity. After a lengthy walk, they reached the point where they parted and, being musically minded, Charles Alexander could hear the uneven gait of Sam Hadley walking in the other direction for he had an artificial limb. Suddenly it stopped, and when Alexander turned around he saw Sam Hadley leaning against a lamppost and hurried back, assuming that Hadley was sick. He reached him only to discover that he was pounding the lamppost with his fist and repeating, "O God, the sin of this city is breaking my heart. O God, the sin of this city is breaking my heart." In a very sensitive way he was entering into the fellowship of Christ's sufferings by showing how his heart was touched by the sin and needs of others, and longing for their deliverance just as he had known it from his past.

For Naomi and Ruth, their past was behind them too. As a returning Jew, it meant reconnecting with what she had forfeited during these empty years of her life. Coming back probably meant she was seeing it more meaningfully second time around and, like some brought up in a Christian home, she knew the reality of coming back to it for herself. For a Moabitess, as a Gentile, it meant being introduced to the truth of redemption and all that flows from it. It was a heart-searching reintroduction for Naomi, but for Ruth it must have felt like a heart-warming introduction to the service of God and she must have wondered what it was all about. Apart from sensing the people's appreciation of the Passover, the wave sheaf indicated that God had priority.

O, wonder to myself I am
That I can view the dying Lamb;
Can scan the wondrous mystery o'er
And not be moved to love Him more.
(Joseph Denham Smith)

He was first, and the remainder was for the people's on-going satisfaction as they entered into their God-given blessing from the harvest. They had come into Bethlehem when its people were moved, not only in the sense that it was for them on their arrival, but by commemorating the Passover lamb and seeing the sheaf of the firstfruits offered to God. While this meant renewal for Naomi, it was entirely new for Ruth, yet for both of them Moab was over, Bethlehem was before them, and the Land of Israel in all its fulness was theirs to be enjoyed.

The Targum says, "They came to Bethlehem on the day in which the children of Israel began to mow the sheaf of barley which was to be waved before the Lord." This was called the *"sheaf of the firstfruits,"* and the festival was held on the day after the Sabbath following Passover,[27] on the first day of the week that pointed forward to His resurrection, and it was announcing that God was given first place. It must have been a heart-searching reintroduction for Naomi and a heart-warming welcome

295

for Ruth who would learn the guiding principle - *"Honour the LORD with your possessions, and with the firstfruits of all your increase."*[28] Besides being the symbol of putting God first, the wave sheaf was the proof of more to come for the satisfaction of His people, not only of barley but also of the wheat.

These two crops were treated quite differently. Wheat was the preferred grain: its fineness enjoyed by the people and accepted by God for meal offerings on His altar.[29] Barley is a rougher grain and its Hebrew name, *s^e'orāh*, is related to the word *sa'ar*, which means rough or hairy. It was looked upon as a second-class grain, and considered poorer than wheat. This distinction is apparent in 1 Kings 4:22 and 28 where *"fine flour"* was brought to Solomon while *"barley"* was brought for the horses.

There are vivid scriptural examples of people being associated with its poverty, and Revelation 6:6 shows that it was considered being worth only one-third the value of wheat. In Numbers chapter 5:15, a unique meal offering of barley was associated with a woman whose morality was being questioned. Unlike the meal offering of fine flour in Leviticus 1, it had no oil and no frankincense on it, because it could never foreshadow the fruit of the Holy Spirit and the fragrance of Christ. These suitably belonged to the fineness of the wheat[30] as it represented *"the meekness and gentleness of Christ"*[31] in His righteous manhood, but were absent from the coarser barley that belonged to the offering of jealousy and the possible presence of sin.

Another example is found in the days of Elisha when he was brought twenty loaves of barley following a time of famine and, like the Lord's feeding of the multitude, they *"ate and had some left over."*[32] Then came the greatest feeding of all, when the Man who is the answer to the finest of the wheat took five barley loaves, gave thanks, distributed them: *"So when they were filled, He said to His disciples, 'Gather up the fragments that remain.'"*[33]

John is the only one who quotes Andrew's comment to the Lord: *"There is a lad here who has five barley loaves and two small fish,"* and we would well imagine Him thanking the lad and saying, 'I know what it's like for I was a Boy from a poor home too.' But He had come from much farther away, and with divine compassion He saw the gathering *"like sheep not having a shepherd."*[34] Who better to meet their need at Passover time than the Lamb who would take away the sin of the world on a later Passover and give Himself as the Good Shepherd. In answer to feeding the five thousand from Galilee and having twelve baskets remaining, and to feeding the four thousand from Tyre and Sidon and having seven large baskets left over, He went to the cross to demonstrate that He alone can meet the need of both Jew and Gentile.

In another portrayal of this, Naomi and Ruth came at a time that pointed to the poverty of Christ, and Ruth had no idea that she would feature in the ancestry of the Man of whom Scripture says, *"that though He was rich, yet for your sakes He became poor, that you through His poverty might become rich."*[35] He has been cut off in His death, raised in His glorious resurrection, and He has brought us into *"the beginning of the barley harvest."*

Her story, as we have already noted, was set against the background of *"the days when the judges ruled,"* one of whom was Gideon who lacked confidence when God wanted to use him against the Midianites. To reassure him, God sent him down to the enemy's camp where he overheard *"a man telling a dream to his companion"* about *"a loaf of barley bread"* that *"tumbled into the camp of Midian,"*[36] and the companion interpreted it as Gideon being the victor. At that moment, his fear fled, his faith was fanned, and worship replaced his worry. Seeing himself in the imagery of the barley loaf, he realised that God wanted to use the poverty of his inadequacy, and there's a lesson for all of us here. God would rather use the servant who feels inadequate than trust the battle to someone who feels up to the task.

Ruth's journey began with faith and ended in sight, she journeyed in hope and arrived at home. In these, she is such a graphic portrayal of the

Christian's walk with the Lord. It also begins with faith and ends in sight; it begins with hope, and it ends at home! What a beginning! *"For by grace you have been saved through faith"*[37]; and we enjoy having fellowship with our Saviour, *"whom having not seen you love."*[38] However, He will come in fulfilment of our hope by which we await the *"glorious appearing of our great God and Saviour Jesus Christ."*[39] But our hope goes beyond that of seeing Him for John gives this wonderful assurance that *"when He is revealed, we shall be like Him, for we shall see Him as He is. And everyone who has this hope in Him purifies himself, just as He is pure."*[40] Ruth had hope, but ours is an incomparable hope: we will be *"at home with the Lord,"*[41] we will see Him, and we will be like Him. No wonder Paul says, *"Now hope does not disappoint."*[42] And if hope doesn't disappoint, neither will home! Our Bethlehemite is waiting to see the fulfilment of *"the hope of His calling."*[43] What a day that will be, when His hope and ours are simultaneously fulfilled at His coming!

BARLEY CAKES

The Midianite is in the land,
And Israel's hard bestead.
There's poverty on every hand,
And scarcity of bread:
But brawny Gideon bears at night
The threshing of his floor,
And by the winepress, out of sight,
Conceals his precious store.

How well his honest heart esteems
The food his God has given!
A plain unleavened cake he deems
Fit for a guest from Heaven.
Here is a man whom God can tell,
'Go thou in this thy might.'
Yes, Midian's tents shall prove how well
A 'barley cake' can fight!

A lesson learn from Gideon's floor:
Nutritious food for you
Is in the Word; abundance more
Than ever Canaan grew.
And if you wish to serve the Lord
(For still His foes assail),
If you would wish to use the Sword,
First learn to use the Flail!
(J.M.S. Tait)

3.7 BOAZ THE MAN OF GOD

"There was a relative of Naomi's husband, a man of great wealth, of the family of Elimelech. His name was Boaz. So Ruth the Moabitess said to Naomi, "Please let me go to the field, and glean heads of grain after him in whose sight I may find favour." And she said to her, "Go, my daughter." Then she left, and went and gleaned in the field after the reapers. And she happened to come to the part of the field belonging to Boaz, who was of the family of Elimelech. Now behold, Boaz came from Bethlehem, and said to the reapers, "The LORD be with you!" And they answered him, "The LORD bless you!" Then Boaz said to his servant who was in charge of the reapers, "Whose young woman is this?"

So the servant who was in charge of the reapers answered and said, "It is the young Moabite woman who came back with Naomi from the country of Moab. And she said, 'Please let me glean and gather after the reapers among the sheaves.' So she came and has continued from morning until now, though she rested a little in the house." Then Boaz said to Ruth, "You will listen, my daughter, will you not? Do not go to glean in another field, nor go from here, but stay close by my young women. Let your eyes be on the field which they reap, and go after them. Have I not commanded the young men not to touch you? And when you are thirsty, go to the vessels and drink from what the young men have drawn." So she fell on her face, bowed down to the ground, and said to him, "Why have I found favour in your eyes, that you should take notice of me, since I am a foreigner?" (Ruth 2:1-10).

* * *

It's not always easy to gauge someone's godliness, but there was something about the deportment of Boaz when he came into the field. Everyone was busy, yet they suddenly knew he was there, as he greeted them with, *"The LORD be with you!"* In a mutual sense of God's presence, they replied: *"The LORD bless you!"* It's a well-known adage that you don't get a second chance to create a first impression, and this was the first impression that Boaz made on the young foreigner from Moab. These were the first words she heard from him, and they let her know that the LORD had priority in his life. What a marvellous introduction to the spirituality of this man! Evidently, he set the tone and work ethic of his workforce, and Ruth would discover that it would be equally apparent in his conversations with her. As a man of God, he conducted himself and his work in a godly way, and did everything to safeguard his workers from discovering that if something is ethically wrong it can't be spiritually right. This work environment must have been way beyond anything Ruth ever anticipated when she said to Naomi on the old dirt road, *"your people shall be my people, and your God, my God."*

A horticultural grower was concerned at the abnormally slow growth of his plants and made all sorts of checks to find out the cause: insufficient feeding, a problem with hydroponics, pest control, etc. Everything was as it should be, and finally the cause was discovered. It was ventilation: the atmosphere was wrong. In his Bethlehem field, Boaz made sure that the atmosphere was right both for and among his workers, and he immediately ensured it was right for Ruth too. From the outset, he was a man for whom it was worth working and who set an example, even to present-day Christians, that we should *"work heartily, as for the Lord and not for men"*[1] and that the assembly's atmosphere must be right.

It was like this in the days of Nehemiah when they were building the wall. A variety of people gave an ideal example of unity in diversity: men and women, perfumers and goldsmiths, people and high priest, all with *"a mind to work."*[2] This is a fitting description of the mindset Boaz fostered among his reapers, and it filtered down to the gleaners, including Ruth. We could hardly read Nehemiah 3 and miss the constant repetition of the word *"next."* It seems rather ordinary, but it was an integral part of Nehemiah's strategy. Far from being like people waiting in line, where the call, 'Next," refers to whoever happens to follow, in wall-building it meant something much more meaningful. These were not independent contributors. For them, "Next" was a call to blend with those on either side. Stonework must be carefully placed, and interlocking, and the work would show the inter-relationship of the workers.

The little word *'al* can simply mean "after," but in Leviticus 5:13 some versions speak of atonement being made *"for"* the person's sin. Other versions say *"touching"* or *"concerning,"* and we can readily understand the proximity intended by *'al.* However, the implications were very real for Nehemiah's builders. Each set must combine with those on their left and right to show that they are not only "next," but "for" and "touching" and "concerned" with their work. Side by side, shoulder-to-shoulder, it meant integration, until, firstly, *"the wall was joined together up to half its height."* As the workers, so the work: it was "joined together" in a real demonstration of equality. Everyone pulled their weight. There wasn't a bit of wall at one height and another bit at a different height. Men and women worked together in such a fashion that the whole thing was level. Isn't that how it should be for us too?

Complainers don't make good builders for their tendency is for the tongue to be in sympathy with an active mind and inactive hands to be in sympathy with their over-active tongues. Building is the ideal means of showing the equality or inequality of work rate, and it may be worth trying to deduce soberly before the Lord if an assembly would be better or worse off if everyone worked at your personal level. Building for God should mean togetherness; and pulling our weight is better than dragging our feet, and yet it's possible to be in a church where a core pulls its weight and a fringe drags its feet. Before the Lord, which group are we in? If you are on the fringe, please take this as a word from the Lord. He wants to draw you into the core to be a builder and worker among His people.

Nehemiah had a deep appreciation of doing what God wanted him to do, and so did Boaz. Naomi had heard that God had visited His people by giving them bread and a field of barley ready to be reaped was the evidence that He had. He had blessed, and also had arranged for Boaz to be a blessing. Leviticus 19:9 and 10 was a word from God to him: *"When you reap the harvest of your land, you shall not wholly reap the corners of your field, nor shall you gather the gleanings of your harvest ... you shall leave them for the poor and the stranger."* This made Ruth doubly qualified, but what about Naomi? A caring God provided for her by adding, *"When you reap your harvest in your field, and forget a sheaf in the field, you shall not go back to get it; it shall be for the stranger, the fatherless, and the widow, that the LORD your God may bless you in all the work of your hands."*[3] So Naomi could have been in that field as well, for there was provision for the widow as well as the stranger to be blessed through Boaz.

Whether she had tutored Ruth regarding the stranger's entitlement and the forgotten sheaf, we don't know, but Boaz certainly turned the law of the unintentional into intentional grace by ordering extra bundles for her. It's not something that fits with life on the farm nowadays for it wouldn't be good farming practice to forget a bale, or a sheaf in earlier days, for some sharp-eyed observer who could benefit. However, under the law, the widow could be blessed through man's forgetfulness, while an intentionally mindful God was watching the widow by watching the forgotten sheaf. Nevertheless, even though the sheaf had been left behind through forgetfulness, Boaz and others like him left it where it stood through their mindfulness for the law of God. By so doing, it became a provision of grace. How beautiful! He had promised Abraham that He would bless others by blessing him,[4] but His promise to Boaz was that he would be blessed by blessing others. It's worth noting that while blessing could come through being forgetful under law, we are under grace and blessing comes by remembering.

Acts 20:35 - "*I have shown you in every way, by labouring like this, that you must support the weak. And remember the words of the Lord Jesus, that He said, 'It is more blessed to give than to receive.'*"

Galatians 2:10 - "*They desired only that we should remember the poor, the very thing which I also was eager to do.*"

2 Peter 1:13 - "*Yes, I think it is right, as long as I am in this tent, to stir you up by reminding you ...*"

Hebrews 13:2 - "*Do not forget to entertain strangers ...*"

Hebrews 13:16 - "*But do not forget to do good and to share, for with such sacrifices God is well pleased.*"

As Boaz greeted his workers, he noticed a figure he didn't recognise and immediately turned to his servant who was "*in charge*" of the reapers. This is interesting. The man wasn't described as a manager or by rank. He was approached on the basis of his relationship to Boaz and to the workers. He was "*hannitstsab 'al*" or "set over," which tells us that Boaz had appointed a man who was in touch with him and his workers. He proved this by what he knew about Ruth: he knew where she came from and who brought her; he knew why she had come, and he had noted her commitment, so he was a servant and observant!

There's no doubt that he had been promoted, but he didn't lose his servant status in the process, and neither do we. It's a poor response to divine recognition if a brother appointed as an elder sees it as a promotion in rank rather than of personal relationship. All servants will not be elders, but all elders should be servants. Boaz's right-hand man was his "next" in line, and so he asked him, "*Whose young woman is this?*" He didn't ask, "Who is this young woman?" These are two very different questions. In fact, they are two different kinds of question. His way of asking showed that he was interested in possession not pedigree. Position and status can be valued as well-earned in life, and well-handled too, but are worth very little if we are not among those of whom Paul said, *"The Lord knows those who are His."*5

Boaz was like Eliezer when Abraham sent him to bring a bride home for Isaac. When he met Rebekah at the well and asked, *"Whose daughter are you?"*6 he wanted to know her possession. Likewise, when David came to Elah and conquered Goliath, Saul was so keen to find out *"Whose son is this youth?"*7 he asked the question three times. David's answer was very humble for a young man who had just rid the king and his army of a terrorising giant: *"I am the son of your servant Jesse the Bethlehemite."* There it is again: "your servant," and, presenting himself as the nameless son of the Bethlehemite, making himself of no reputation. No wonder God called him *"a man after My own heart."*8 Jesus was the true 'house of bread-ite' and His servants should take character from Him.

Ruth belonged to Moab. She was a Moabite by birth and a Moabite by nature, but she became a Bethlehemite by grace and favour and knew that it's better to be poor in Bethlehem than rich in Moab. When the servant witnessed to how busily she had gleaned, he mentioned that she had *"rested a little in the house."* As lord of the harvest, Boaz had provided a shack - it may even have been a tent for workers to go to eat and to shelter. It was a place of rest and refreshment and at some point perhaps in the heat of noon Ruth went there to rest, which was far better than trying to find rest in the house of her husband. Wycliffe points out that the Septuagint translation says, "She has not rested (even) a little in the field."

When Naomi told both girls that the Lord would deal kindly with them and give them rest, it was a rather hollow and meaningless assurance, but it was meaningful in this little place in the house of bread. Boaz wanted to set her mind at rest too, and his request must have sounded more like a statement than a question: *"You will listen, my daughter, will you not?"* Then he added, *"Do not go to glean in another field, nor go from here, but stay close to my young women. Let your eyes be on the field which they reap, and go after them."*

In fixing her direction, he fixed her position, but it was for her to fix her attention on what was his and have communion with those who were his: *"my young women ... my young men ... my harvest."* As the story progressed, he also spoke of *"my town"* and *"my people,"* but the sweetest of all was at the beginning when he called her *"my daughter"* and at the end when he owned her as *"my wife."* By asking her to focus on what was his, and on those who were his, he wanted her to feel included and to know that he had expectations of her. The Lord Jesus has done much more for us. He is interested in our position and says, *"Abide in Me, and I in you. As the branch cannot bear fruit of itself, unless it abides in the vine, neither can you, unless you abide in Me."*[9] He has fixed our position, and is worthy of our lifelong direction, affection, attention and communion.

Boaz cautioned her against being distracted and going elsewhere to *"another field."* For us as disciples of the Lord Jesus Christ, there also is the lure of another field. He said, *"The field is the world,"*[10] and although we are in it we are not of it.[11] He has set our direction. For this reason, He has given us rest to keep us at rest by graciously urging us, *"Do not love the world or the things in the world."*[12] He has set our affection. He also leaves us in no doubt that *"the lust of the flesh, the lust of the eye, and the pride of life – is not of the Father."*[13] He has set our attention. We are told in Proverbs that *"The righteous should choose his friends carefully,"*[14] and Psalm 119 directs us to say, *"I am a companion of all who fear You."* He has set our communion.

Ruth had been called into the godly atmosphere of Boaz's field, and he commanded the young men not to touch her. As a man of God, he was rich in morality and his young men were expected to be the same. They were under orders not to touch her, so she was safeguarded from being plagued by them. The New Testament lifts up the same kind of example for believers in Paul's advice to Timothy to treat older women as mothers and the younger woman as sisters. This is part of the New Testament's protection for young men towards young women, that no worldly code of conduct will be brought into the service of God, and nothing contrary to the mind of God to challenge the morality of the Word of God. The moral climate of our world is geared to distract young Christians and tempt them to accept its norms as theirs, but the Lord Jesus is looking for purity and has the ability to conquer the power of fleshly desires in us.

Ruth was encouraged by the man who would become her redeemer, but, young Christian, you are being encouraged by the Man who is your Redeemer. He has already paid for you, so that allows Him to say, *"You were bought at a price, therefore glorify God in your body."* If an Old Testament redeemer could say it to Ruth, then your Redeemer has far more right to say it to you, so that the purity of young people will be kept intact for Jesus' sake.

The reason He redeemed you is that God will confirm His purpose by saying, *"But know that the LORD has set apart for Himself him who is godly."*[15] Perhaps, as you read this, He actually wants to say to you, "You will listen, will you not?" He is making an appeal for you to commit yourself to Him and be separated to Him. It's often called being sanctified, and this means being set apart as holy. This is how the English Standard Version translates Paul's appeal in 2 Timothy 2:21 – *"Therefore, if anyone cleanses himself from what is dishonourable he will be a vessel for honourable use, set apart as holy, useful to the master of the house, ready for every good work."* To be practical about it, cleansing ourselves means saying "No" to sin. To Peter, this meant abstaining;[16] to Paul, it meant killing off the impulse and the action;[17] to us, it means both.

God wants our fleshly desires, and tendencies, and habits to be put to death for, if we don't kill them, they will kill off your walk with the Lord and your work for Him. Boaz had Ruth's interests and wellbeing at heart when he asked her to listen, and what he said didn't come across to her as an ultimatum. He called her *"my daughter"* and that was special. Years later,

David included the word for daughter when he prayed, *"Keep me as the apple of Your eye,"* which can be translated as "Guard me as the pupil, daughter of the eye." God has designed our eyes in such a way that the pupils are protected by surrounding bone structure, our eyebrows, eyelids, eyelashes, and by tears. It's in such tenderness that God protects us and makes His appeal.

If ever anyone met an appeal with a proper response, it was Ruth for *"she fell on her face and bowed down to the ground."* At that moment, she took her place among the greats of the Bible. Abraham heard the voice of God and fell on his face in obedience.[18] Ezekiel received the vision from the throne of God and fell on his face in wonder and worship.[19] Daniel saw and heard the vision of future events and fell on his face in reverence and in godly fear.[20] In her first day of gleaning, and first response to the man who would mean more and more to her as the days went by, Ruth set an example of humility for us all. Following it, we bow before a worthier Redeemer.

From her lowly position, Boaz filled her horizon. Does the Lord Jesus Christ do that for me? Does He fill your horizon? The beginning of Romans 1 says He should. He is *"of the seed of David according to the flesh, and declared to be the Son of God with power."* John 1:18 tells us that *"No one has seen God at any time. The only begotten Son, who is in the bosom of the Father, He has declared Him."* Uniquely, Jesus is the exposition, the full explanation or the exegesis of God. When Paul referred to the One who is *"declared to be the Son of God with power,"* it's very fitting that the Spirit of God gave him a different word, and from it we get our word "horizon." The Son fills His Father's horizon, and we are blessed in having the opportunity to let Him fill our vision too. Rainbows often appear as vertical full circles to hill climbers and as horizontal circles that aeroplane passengers can see in the clouds below. The spectacle is known as 'a glory' and, remarkably, the climber's image and the image of the aeroplane appears in the middle of the circle.

As we close this chapter, please let me ask you if your Redeemer is your glory? Maybe you are wondering how you can reach that point. Take the lowly place and let Him fill your horizon and, like John the Baptist, say, *"He must increase, but I must decrease."*[21] Our highest place is lying low at our Redeemer's feet.

Be thou my vision, O Lord of my heart;
Naught be all else to me, save that thou art -
Thou my best thought, by day or by night;
Waking or sleeping, thy presence my light.

Be thou my wisdom, and thou my true word;
I ever with thee and thou with me, Lord.
Thou my great Father; thine own may I be,
Thou in me dwelling and I one with thee.

Riches I heed not, nor vain, empty praise;
Thou mine inheritance, now and always;
Thou and thou only first in my heart,
High King of heaven, my treasure thou art.

High King of heaven, my victory won,
May I reach heaven's joys, O bright heaven's sun!
Heart of my own heart, whatever befall,
Still be my vision, O Ruler of all.
(Dallan Forgaill (530-598)
(Adapted Eleanor Henrietta Hull (1860-1935))

3.8 IN HIS FIELD

"So she gleaned in the field until evening, and beat out what she had gleaned, and it was about an ephah of barley" (Ruth 2:17).

* * *

The most momentous hours this world has ever known were nine o'clock in the morning and three o'clock in the afternoon. Outside Jerusalem on Calvary's Hill at nine o clock in the morning, soldiers hammered nails through the Lord Jesus' hands and feet, raised the cross and jolted it into a socket in the ground. It wasn't by chance: His timing was perfect, and when it came to three o'clock in the afternoon the Saviour said, "It is finished!" His sufferings were over.

The world didn't know it then, but these hours combined the cruelty of men and the kindness of God: their hatred and His love, their wilfulness and His will. In such a brutal way, men fulfilled what He had been writing about for centuries, and then confirmed through Peter on the Day of Pentecost: *"Him, being delivered by the determined purpose and foreknowledge of God, you have taken by lawless hands, have crucified, and put to death."*[1] There are no accidents with God, and men unknowingly complied with His timetable of morning and evening!

God loves painting pictures. In Genesis, His creation was woven around the daily timing of *"evening ['ereb] and morning [boqer]."*[2] Annually, in commemoration of Exodus 12, the Passover lamb was killed at evening as the introduction to the Feasts of Jehovah and as a constant reminder to the people of Israel's redemption from bondage in Egypt. In Exodus 29, the timing of each day's service in the tabernacle was built around *"One lamb you shall offer in the morning [from boqer], and the other lamb you shall offer in the evening [from 'ereb]."*

This was God's way of ensuring that His people's daily walk was regulated by the prominence of the lamb. The conduct of each day began with the offering of the morning lamb, and God was left with the evening lamb burning before Him in the silence of each night. In the context of these lambs, God made it known: *"I will meet with the children of Israel, and the tabernacle shall be sanctified by My glory."*[3]

Thus God completes the triplet of creation, redemption and sanctification by referring to morning and evening. In His divine artistry, was He not painting vivid portrayals of what He would achieve through the cross of His Son? Was He not anticipating the cross-centeredness of our new creation in Christ,[4] our redemption,[5] and our sanctification,[6] so that all we have from Him, and are for Him, is through the Lamb?

Ruth's Evening and Morning

When Ruth went looking for work, she was looking for more than a barley field. God had planted a thought in her heart that guided her feet for she wanted to find someone who would show grace. God honoured her desire, yet the record simply says, *"And she happened to come to the part of the field belonging to Boaz."* We could be inclined to interpret this as 'accidentally by accident,' but closer thought will help us to see it was by appointment and not by accident. It was as if she lived out Solomon's thoughts generations before he was alive: *"Keep your heart with all diligence ... Let your eyes look straight ahead ... Ponder the path of your feet."*[7]

There's no doubt that Ruth's heart, eyes and feet were in unison, but this doesn't explain how *"she happened to come"* to the field that was owned by a close relative, though this latter part had probably never entered her mind. No, for all unknown to her was the loftier thought that she had found grace in the eyes of God, and He was seeing her at the centre of her future grandson's promise, *"The steps of a good (wo)man are ordered by the LORD."*[8] This helps us to understand *wayyiqer miqrehā*– she happened to come. Some older versions say, *"her hap was to light on"* (ASV, RV), while the NIV translates the phrase as, *"As it turned out."* But who made it turn out so favourably? Ruth was yet to discover that the One who called her from Moab, who gave her the right words to say when Orpah turned back, was the One now leading her forward into far greater things.

The truth is that just as Naomi was able to acknowledge that *"the LORD brought me home,"* so Ruth ultimately would realise that God had brought this about for her. He was working out His purpose, and it's interesting that both words in *wayyiqer miqrehā* are linked to the thought of framing timbers. As we know, roof trusses don't just happen, they are planned; and bringing them together is by choice, not chance. In bringing Ruth to this field, God was intentionally laying the beams that would structure her future. Her life was under construction, and soon she would sense that her choice was within His choice.

How blessed we are when our hearts, eyes and feet conjoin and cause us to know that things happen when we allow God to order our steps and frame His plan for us. It's by His leading we also recognise His grace in bringing our thoughts and ways into alignment with His own, and find that our lives are being constructed according to His plan. It was by gleaning that Ruth found out more about this mighty man of wealth, and it's by patient and prayerful gleaning that we also deepen our bond with the Lord Jesus Christ. There's something so valuable in having someone ask, as Naomi asked Ruth, *"Where have you gleaned today?"*[9] It was gleaning that kept her going, and kept her sharing what she gathered, and it's like that for us too.

Fellow-Christian, beware the danger of not gleaning daily from your Bible!

Bit by bit, God led her to experience a deepening and more reliant bond with Boaz that illustrates the kind of relationship we are able to have with our Saviour. His call to us is, *"Take My yoke upon you and learn from Me,"*[10] but there's no learning without gleaning. For Ruth, that meant being in the field day after day. That's where she found him; and for us it means being in the Word every day for that's where we glean and enjoy communion with Christ. The same unchanging God who was in control in her life wants to be in control of our lives today, tomorrow, and every day, but we need to turn up for work!

Until evening

Evening brings us back to the word 'ereb, the time when the lamb was placed on the altar, and to a time that would be fixed in a godly Jew's mind. What a way to conclude the day, with thoughts of the lamb! But Ruth's day wasn't finished. With her gleaning over, it was time to *"beat out what she had gleaned,"*[11] and the gleaner became the beater. This was when the stalks revealed their fruitfulness, and the quantity of grain she took home after separating it from the chaff.

Her diligent effort reminds us of what it took for gleaning and beating to be turned into feeding and sets a good example for our daily reading that we meditate on it until we derive nourishment and satisfaction from it. We could put it this way: there should always be something of the "evening" in the character of what we draw from studying the Scriptures. All our consideration should lead us to the Lamb, for our thoughts will never mature until they converge with His.

Ruth's whole aim was to carry home the finished product of her gleaning, and not devote unnecessary effort on carrying straw. This is particularly relevant to those who share in the ministry of preaching and teaching. Long hours go into gathering our thoughts while preparing a message, yet its presentation will be much shorter. We do well to catch the essence of Old Testament men like Malachi who passed on what they called *"The burden of the word of the LORD."* Naomi was fed by Ruth's burden, not with bulky straw. How noticeable it is that chapters 2 and 3 end with Naomi's response to what she had brought, and both times she spoke about *"This man"* or *"the man."* It was the best of all conclusions. During the day, Ruth's eyes were fixed on the field; at night, they were fixed on the man. What a goal for preachers of God's Word! Our messages should be chaff-free.

The one who permitted and enabled Ruth's burden became the focus of their conversation, not the good barley. How much more Christ-exalting when a message prompts God's people to speak of their Redeemer rather than merely to say, "Good message." It's of necessity that the speaker prepares by gathering thoughts from the Word, but its presentation should cause our brothers and sisters to gather thoughts of the Lord. Sadly, we need much of the Spirit's help to separate the chaff for books and songbooks in Christian bookshops are not always chaff-free. God's people deserve to hear *"the word of the message,"*[12] but they won't know until the message has been delivered whether the speaker had his hands full of roasted grain or bales of straw!

At home on the farm, there's a well-known saying when building a dry-stone wall: "Don't lift the same stone twice." The aim is lift it and place it, and the stone will tell you by sound and feel that it's where it should be. This was never in Ruth's mind. She must have handled the same grain at least four or five times: gleaning, beating, carrying, milling and cooking. She well and truly made it her own. Should we ever think that the counsel of His will is finished with us when we glean? Far from it! There's much more to it that that. We may be blessed in gleaning, even publicly at the feet and in fellowship with others, but beating is a more private matter. Meditation is a deeply personal exercise, and it's vital that each of us learns to think proper thoughts of God, His Son, and of His Word.

Just as every infant masters the art of feeding, and leaving behind the early stages of being spoon-fed, the child of God must develop his or her early pickings by beating, carrying, milling and preparing what he or she has gleaned. When we come to Christ, we are like Ruth. We pick things up about Him like a stalk here and there; gradually learning about Him, being attracted to Him, wanting to be fed and satisfied by Him. We gather something and enjoy handling it for the first time, then we handle it again as we think it over, and this leads on to meditative thoughts for worship that we give to God.

In the process of making it our own, it may become something we want to pass on to others privately by letter or in conversation; or publicly in Sunday School, Bible Class or in a church gathering. By whatever opportunity the Lord gives, we can share Paul's mutual desire, *"that I may come to you with joy by the will of God, and may be refreshed together with you,"*[13] and someone might encourage you by assuring you that *"the hearts of the saints have been refreshed by you."*[14] They may not have watched you gleaning and gathering, but they will hear the evidence that you did.

Boaz watched Ruth as she gleaned. We can imagine why he kept his eye on the reapers, but he showed an added concern for her. Having thanked him for his grace he expressed it still further by inviting her, *"Come here, and eat of the bread, and dip your piece of bread in the vinegar."* Allowing her to sit with reapers was one way of showing acceptance, but to be within hand's reach of him was like a foreshadowing of Christians knowing they are *"accepted in the Beloved."*[15] She was among workers who began their day by saying to Boaz, "The LORD bless you!" but now he was blessing her. He had already provided water to quench her thirst, but now she had the added benefit of the vinegar, which was refreshing in the heat of the day. He had told her to "dip" her bread into it, which was his way of saying, "Immerse it. Plunge it in. Don't just slightly moisten it. Get the full benefit, and be refreshed."

Then his hand reached out to her with a handful of parched grain. It had been gathered and beaten out, separated from the chaff and roasted. He had handled it and wanted to share it personally with her. It's the only time in the Old Testament where the word *tsābat* is used and it was reserved for the lord of the harvest reaching out to a stranger. This was grain that had passed through the fire, and she took it from his hand. She gleaned with her own hands, and gathered what other hands let fall for her,[16] but no one else in the field ever put something into her hand. He gave it to her and it was like eating out of his hand. Ruth enjoyed what she gleaned for herself. She was blessed when others left handfuls for her, but getting something from his hand was best of all.

Is there a sequel to this for us? Oh, yes! We enjoy what we glean from the Word, and often are blessed by what others share from their study of it, but there's nothing like receiving a word from the Lord. In all your reading and study of God's Word, gather all you can and let others give all they can, but never stop there. Ask for new thoughts that are from Him for nothing compares with the experience of Jesus putting something into your hand. Be comfortable in His presence and wait until you are eating out of His hand. He is the answer to the roasted grain, because it speaks of the intensity of the cross and all He endured in those three hours of darkness from midday to three o'clock in the afternoon, when at evening He said, "It is finished!" This is where we began our Christian walk, isn't it?

I stood one day at Calvary
Where Jesus bled and died,
I never knew He loved me so,
For me was crucified;
And as I stood there in my sin,
His love reached down to me,
And O the shame that filled my soul
That day at Calvary!
(*Walter H. Huntley*)

Boaz put so much into her hand that she couldn't finish it for *"she ate and was satisfied, and kept some back."*[17] She had gathered an ephah of barley, between twenty and twenty-five pounds in weight, and Naomi must have wondered at such productive gleaning. But no gleaner ever gleaned roasted barley. It was the proof of sitting with him. She showed no reluctance in reaching out to his giving hand. When Christ reaches out to you are you prepared to reach out to Him? He always gives more than we need, and never gives short measure.

My brother and sister, in whatever way the Lord calls you to share something from His Word, others will know when you have been sitting with Him. When it happens, the proof will always be there. Again, it's how we started. When God saved us, He *"made us alive together with Christ ... and raised us up together, and made us to sit together in the heavenly places in Christ Jesus."*[18] We are already with Him. We are within hand's reach of Him, so we should let others see, not only what we are in Christ, but where we are in Christ. Naomi could tell that Ruth had been with Boaz, and others should see that we have been with Jesus.

The word *qāliy* is translated as "parched grain" six times in the Old Testament, but the closely associated *qālāh* is translated as "base, despised, and seem vile," while David applied it to himself when he spoke of being *"lightly esteemed."*[19] The first reference to parched grain is found in Leviticus 23:14 in connection with the wave sheaf of the feast of firstfruits: *"You shall eat neither bread nor parched grain nor fresh grain until the same day that you have brought an offering to your God."* We also read in Joshua 5:11 that, when he led the people over Jordan into Gilgal, they ate *"unleavened bread and parched grain"*[20] on the day after the Passover; so the parched grain, the lamb and the wave sheaf were closely linked.

This leads us to conclude that Boaz had honoured God by keeping the Passover and offering his wave sheaf before giving Ruth a handful of parched grain. This was a very meaningful way of showing to the young Gentile that she had been brought into the grace that comes by honouring the law. There seems to be a precious lesson here for us, too. The roasted grain wasn't eaten in association with the lamb, which portrayed the death of Christ, but following the wave sheaf that spoke of His resurrection. It wasn't linked to the grief of the One who was despised, humiliated on a cross as if he were evil, and lightly esteemed, but with the triumph of His ascension in glory. This is so significant for it means we feed on the sufficiency of His sufferings in the light of owning the power of His resurrection. As He gives us thoughts, consideration of His anguish doesn't leave us in mourning, but rather lifts us upward to worship God for the Victor. In our equivalent of the roasted grain, we lovingly dwell on His grief, but He puts His glory into our hands. Just as Boaz did with Ruth, Jesus wants to put them into your hand and into your home. As dear William Blane said so ably of Him:

Man of slighted Nazareth,
King who wore the thorny wreath,
Son obedient unto death,
He shall bear the glory.

* * *

It is coming, it is coming, sure and bright,
Through His grace;
That day when faith shall turn to sight
In yon place.
Where we'll tread the golden street
And at last fit praise repeat,
While we cast crowns at His feet
Face to face.

The face where Mary's sorrow drew forth tears,
We shall see;
At the feet that journeyed for us all those years
We shall be.
Feet that never rested yet,
Face that ever steadfast set,
'Till He paid our dreadful debt
On the tree.

Now 'tis finished, He's in glory, and we wait,
Where He's been.
Till His own hand leads us through the heavenly gate
Of yon scene.
Every step through desert sands,
He had trod and understands,
'Tis on strong and tender hands
That we lean.

Oh, the grace that made His holy head once bow,
Death to meet;
Ne'er forgets us in the glory where He now
Has His seat;
'Tis the love that made Him die,
Sought us, found us, keeps us nigh,
Will be rapture by and by
At His feet.
(Miss Ora Rowan)

3.9 AT HIS FEET

"So she lay at his feet until morning, and she arose before one could recognize another. Then he said, "Do not let it be known that the woman came to the threshing floor." Also he said, "Bring the shawl that is on you and hold it." And when she held it, he measured six ephahs of barley, and laid it on her. Then she went into the city" (Ruth 3:14,15).

* * *

So far, the chapters open and close with remarkable contrasts, and this chapter continues this process. Chapter 1 begins with Elimelech and others leaving Bethlehem in a time of famine and ends with his widow and Ruth returning there in a time of plenty. Chapter 2 introduces us to Boaz who stayed in Bethlehem in spite of the famine and concludes with Ruth working for him in his harvest fields. Now, chapter 3 begins with the promise of Ruth the poor stranger finding rest, and closes with him not finding rest until she is assured of a rich redeemer. In the purpose of God, she is moving on from being the gleaner who enjoyed looking for provision to become the partner who enjoyed loving the provider. So this *"rest"* is linked to finding a husband in accordance with God's law, and Naomi's dependence on Boaz fulfilling the right of redemption and marriage.[1]

My daughter, shall I not seek security for you ...?

This *"security"* is very different from the *"rest"* Naomi had in mind in chapter 1:9 when she urged Ruth and Orpah to *"find rest, each in the house of her husband."* Moab was incapable of giving *"rest"* that would allow it to *"be well"* with her. Naomi had learned the hard way that true happiness belonged to being among God's people, and He was about to make things *"well"* for Ruth by bringing her to the feet of the man who was *"cheerful,"*[2] which encourages us to think she was about to enter into the joy of her lord. Both words are based on the same Hebrew word, *yātab*, and Ruth was about to discover that her wellbeing, joy and contentment were all bound up in him. Successive chapters show their developing bond. In chapter 2, she entered into his work in the field. In chapter 3, she entered into his rest at his feet. And chapter 4 will see her entering into his home. What a wonderful progression! In the field, she saw loose stalks and bound sheaves, but at his feet she saw the garnered harvest in its entirety. As Christians, we have the joy of being given *"rest"* and of continuing to find it as we serve Him. Ruth also had a developing rest, and we see this in verse 18 when Naomi urged her to *"sit still"* for she considered Boaz as being the resting place for her.

Boaz was the key to both doors, to redemption and rest, and Naomi could see the possibility of a complete new future for Ruth in him. She was so fully acquainted with his whereabouts that she could advise Ruth to be involved in what he was doing *"tonight."* No reaper is named, Ruth is the only named gleaner, and Boaz himself is the winnower. Winnowing separates the barley and wheat from the chaff and, in Israel, an evening breeze comes in from the sea and he would see the benefit of this as he tossed the grain into the wind for it to remove the light chaff. For maximum benefit, the threshing floor would be located on an exposed place outside the village on the side of a hill or at its top. To reach it Ruth had to *"go down"* the hills on which Bethlehem stands.

This is confirmed in chapter 4:1 where it says, *"Boaz went up to the gate"* after parting from Ruth at the threshing floor. Threshing floors are among God's landmarks that pointed to Calvary, as we will see in chapter 14. Grain is one of God's beaten things, and different instruments fulfil a range of work: the flail for grain, the mortar for manna, the hammer for gold, the press for olives, and the feet for grapes. How meaningfully He implemented each one to produce feeding, adorning, enlightening and rejoicing, and all are fulfilled in Christ for the enriching of our lives.

Therefore wash yourself ... anoint ... put on your best garment and go

Coming into his presence called for preparation, and approaching his feet called for more personal examination than being in the field. There was a proper way to approach the lord of the harvest: not with the stench of the day's sweat or in old working clothes. By removing the filthiness of the flesh, bearing a fragrance, and looking her best, Ruth had no other motive but to do her utmost for him. We see her readiness, her reverence and her rest, as a bride prepared for marriage.

She washed

Her purity was of first importance for she wanted to be appealing. Naturally speaking, it was pointless to wash before going to the dusty, cloudy atmosphere of the threshing floor, but Ruth washed herself[3] for the person not the place. By doing this, she gave the right spiritual lesson for those who want to live in the unclouded atmosphere of the Christ of the cross. Having fellowship with Him, first of all, means being fully bathed – *leloumenos* from *louō*, washed all over[4] because of the Word.[5]

She anointed

This was her sanctity, since she wanted to be appropriate, but her purity was the essential foundation of her sanctity. There can't be sanctification without purification, and it's vital we know that being sanctified flows from being purified. Defilement can never be anointed![6] Nor can it be covered up. Fragrance can't adorn filth, just as faith can't condone the flesh. Naturally, perfume can be applied to an unwashed skin, but it's scent will be compromised by the admixture. Sanctity depends on purity, and God's holiness demands that His will cannot use what His Word hasn't washed!

She put on

This was her dignity for she wanted his approval. It meant setting aside the widow's foreign garb of Moab and the working clothes of the field and wearing what many versions call her "best clothes."[7] Garments in Scripture often refer to testimony. Ruth had a good one, and she wanted to be at her best for him. As we thought in the seventh chapter of our study in Jude, this particular word for *"garment"* (*kasalmāh* from *salmāh* and *simlāh)* means 'a dress that takes shape from what is under it.' The word is used in Psalm 104:2 where the psalmist spoke to God as the One *"who cover Yourself with light as with a garment."* As we thought then, he was speaking of God's pre-bodily form and thinking of a garment taking shape, not from His body, but from His Being. Apart altogether from what she was wearing under her shawl, from a spiritual point of view, Ruth was at Boaz's feet in her "best garment," for even the darkness of night couldn't hide the light of her inner character that shaped and commended her testimony to him. He was touched by what he saw in her, and she was touched by what she saw in him.

We speak about having contacts, and of people having contact with us, but what does it really mean to be 'in touch,' and with what are they 'in touch'?

Hopefully, it's not only with the 'outer me,' otherwise the benefit will be poor and short-lived. It's in touching others and in them being in touch with our *"inner man"* (Eph.3:16) that they will be in touch and be touched by Christ-likeness. If friends come to us for advice, let it be the Wonderful Counsellor they reach for and not our limited counselling. When they come in their times of sorrow, let it be the Comforter who reaches out to them and not merely the hand of our limited consolation. It's equally important when correction or judgment is needed, and this includes assembly matters, fragile situations call for Christlike care and not for uncaring Christians. Loved ones should always know that they are being helped by those whose garment of testimony resembles the Lord's in that it takes shape from what there is of Him in us.

She went down

This was her humility for she wanted his acceptance. The gleaner of the field was still in lowly deference at his feet. Just as sanctity is repelled by impurity, humility is repelled by pride. Haughtiness is no companion of holiness, and those who are high-minded never fill the lowly place. There was nothing haughty about Ruth. All Boaz's acts of kindness in the field hadn't made her the slightest bit pompous or obnoxious. As he had humbled himself to care for her, so she humbled herself to be with him. God never ceases to be the High and Lofty One,[8] and we should never cease to be *"clothed with humility."*[9]

She came softly

This was her propriety. There was no flamboyant entrance; no noisy or clumsy access. She came secretly and silently,[10] and never drew attention to herself or advertised what she was doing. She knew how to approach him, and the lessons pour out of her to help us see how to do the right thing in the right way. All four parts of her preparation contributed to this. There was softness in her spirit long before there was softness in her steps. It was good that she came, but how she came was better. We should know and show that spiritual service is not all about "me." Drawing near to God calls for spiritual caution.

Perhaps it's worth asking ourselves, "If we were to come like Old Testament offerers, would we be allowed in?" Reverence is vital, and so is standing in awe. The psalmist had it right when he said, *"Let all the inhabitants of the world stand in awe of Him."*[11] We draw near to pour out our hearts in prayer, but it's not a wake; and we draw near to worship and celebrate, yet it's not unruly. We should never allow a sense of familiarity to creep into our approach to God. Better to say, and mean it, *"I will go softly all my years."*[12] Jacob showed similar caution in Genesis 33:14 when he promised Esau that he would *"lead on slowly"* out of consideration for the children and livestock. Christ-like gentleness calls for reverence and deference in His followers, leaders, and preachers.Followers must learn the proper approach, and so must leaders and preachers. Humility is the hallmark of each and will save them from all sorts of hurt and harm, not least where pride can mar not only the approach, but also the outcome. Such was the case for a preacher whose apparently proud approach caused an elderly sister to observe, "If you had gone up the way you came down, you would have come down the way you went up!"

Did God gently rebuke Naomi when Ruth said, *"All that you say to me I will do"*? It was like an echo of His people's promise at Sinai[13] and should have been a reminder of her national obligation to covenant law and love. Ruth's pledge was acceptable conduct for the threshing floor, and a fitting pointer to the One who would say, *"I have finished the work which You have given Me to do."*[14]

where he lies ... lie down

Repeating the same Hebrew verb implied making the place of his rest her rest, of finding his rest and entering into it by doing what he had done. What an exemplary flow there is in verses 3-7: *"go down ... lie down ... went down ... lay down"*! She claimed the place of his wife by sharing his blanket, but being at his feet signified that she didn't yet have this status. There was no immoral standard implied in her action, and no damage done to their reputations. Their behaviour was consistent with a godly line. As lord of the harvest, Boaz was rejoicing in his harvest. His work was over and he had cause to rest in it with joy. In this we see something of the One who said, *"It is finished!"* and who endured everything *"for the joy that was set before Him."*[15]

Once again, it was as if she were entering into the joy of her lord,[16] but he was startled when he suddenly awoke and found her there. His question was different from what he asked on her first day in the field. Then, it was, *"Whose young woman is this?"* But now it was simply, *"Who are you?"* He was more interested in "Who?" than "Whose?" because she had spread part of his blanket over her to indicate her wish for marriage. Her response confirmed this: *"Spread your wings over your servant, for you are a redeemer."*[17] Adam Clarke says in his commentary:

"The wing is the emblem of protection ... The meaning is, Take me to thee for wife; and so the Targum translated it, Let thy name be called on thy handmaid to take me for wife, because thou art the redeemer; i.e., thou art the go'ēl, the kinsman, to whom the right of redemption belongs. Even to this present day, when a Jew marries a woman, he throws the skirt or end of his tallith over her, to signify that he has taken her under his protection."

He had already used the plural form of the word to her in chapter 2:12 – *"The LORD ... under whose wings you have come for refuge."* Now he realised she was looking for his redeeming wing to cover her and that, in effect, she was saying, "Be my kinsman-redeemer and marry me." She was a common gleaner, but she gave her double acknowledgement of what she was to him as *"maidservant"* in verse 9, and it was met with his double acknowledgement of what she was to him as *"my daughter"* in verses 10 and 11. How enlightening this is for she didn't say, 'Your daughter', and he didn't say, 'My maidservant'! He conferred on her the honour and affection of a higher relationship, because he recognised her submission to God's law and her expectation of a godly man fulfilling it. He knew her background when he spoke with her in the field, but he knew her character and conduct when he spoke to her at his feet.

Lie down until morning

She had laboured in his field *"until evening"*[18] and lay at his feet *"until morning"*; action had been replaced by affection, and the public place had been replaced by the secret of his presence. She walked and sat and lay with him. Now her spirit was settled on his word *"until the morning,"* knowing that he would settle the matter of her redemption. Ours is, too, as we wait to see *"the Bright and Morning Star,"* and *"a morning without clouds."*[19] She had entered into his work in the field, and now she entered into his rest at his feet, but this wasn't an idle rest. Her rest was in his word, partly on his assurance of timing, but also in the content of his promise, *"I will do for you all that you request."*[20] This was a valued part of a threefold confirmation of their compatibility:

* Firstly, she sensed the assurance of a matching commitment that echoed what she said to Naomi in verse 5, *"All that you say to me I will do."*

* Secondly, he assured her of their matching character. He was a man of great "wealth," and he chose the same Hebrew word to describe her word when he said she was "virtuous."[21]

* Thirdly, they shared matching conduct for she knew he was "kindly" to

her,[22] and he praised her for her "kindness" to him.[23]

In partnership, they symbolise the mutual fellowship of joy and blessing that co-exists between the Saviour and believers as they reflect the resemblance of the bride to the Bridegroom, the growth of the body with the Head, and the stability of the church with its Builder.

Bring ... and hold

From the first day until now, Boaz had much to give, and so it proved on that special morning when he told her, *"Bring the shawl that is on you and hold it."* She had kept it on in the cool of the night, but now what had surrounded her was about to be wrapped around the six measures of his blessing. It was worth holding, and, once filled, he laid it on her. On the face of it, this simply means he placed it on her as she prepared to carry it home, but the word *shiyth* can also suggest that he attired or dressed her with his gift. What a response to having dressed herself the previous night. Another consideration here is the impact this had on Naomi. For her to see how richly Boaz had provided for Ruth, and to know he had intentionally told her not to go *"empty-handed to your mother-in-law,"* would emphasise that he had no desire for her ever to know the emptiness she felt on her return from Moab.

She had used the word *reykām* to describe the great void she felt in her life, and, by enriching her through Ruth, he ensured she would never feel such emptiness again. There is no word for "handed" in the Hebrew text, so he emphasised his care by using only the word *reykām*. Job was accused by one of his so-called comforters, *"You have sent widows away empty,"*[24] which was far from true. With a similar heart for the widow, Boaz made sure that Naomi shared in Ruth's fulness. It's all a wonderful picture of Israel being brought into the riches of God's blessing on Gentiles through the Christ, as we thought in chapter 1.

There is much in this that depicts the blessing we enjoy by having close communion with the Lord Jesus Christ. If we spend time with Him, we will have something to give to others. We shouldn't depend on getting fulfilment from working for Him when waiting on Him is such a blessing. Finding encouragement from what we do for Him is fine, but there's nothing more uplifting or rewarding than receiving satisfaction directly from Him. There is blessing to be found at his feet, and no one ever leaves poorer than when they came. Like Ruth, we will discover that we leave more behind than what we receive for it is *"of His fulness we have all received"*[25] and we will never exhaust *"the unsearchable riches of Christ."*[26]

In giving of His riches, He wants to attire us, so that the evidence of our witness is attributed to Him and not to ourselves. Ruth knew better than anyone that, even on her first day, what she took home wasn't all the result of her gleaning, even though she carried it home in the evening. But this day was completely different: what she carried was all of grace, and she took it home in the morning. No gleaner ever did that! She also took it home intact: none of it was lost on the way. What a way to go home! It's only as we think of our own blessings in Christ that we reflect what Ruth did by holding her shawl. She left him that morning as the lord of the harvest, but the next time she would see him would be as her bridegroom, and it's like this for us too. We work for the Lord of the harvest, and are waiting for our Bridegroom, whose word to each of us is, *"Only hold fast what you have until I come."*[27]

SOFTLY
"...and she came softly" (Ruth 3:7)

Softly, softly through the cornfield, past the heap of grain stacked high
 To the spot where he was sleeping, softly, softly, Ruth drew nigh.
 Washed and purified beforehand, sanctified with garments meet,
  She came nearer, softly, softly, to lie down beside his feet.

 Softly, softly to my Saviour as He hung on Calvary's tree,
  With my load of sin and sorrow, which He bore instead of me.
  One glad day I hastened softly at His pierced feet to fall,
 And acknowledged Him as Sovereign, gladly yielding Him my all.

  For the sake of my dear Saviour I would wash myself again,
  And now sanctified completely I am free from every stain.
  With His garments of salvation I am waiting, dignified,
   To surrender all to Jesus, my Redeemer crucified.

  Softly, softly, I would worship, at Your feet I humbly bow,
 Blessed Bridegroom mould and fill me with Your Holy Spirit now.
    (Danny Mawhinney)

3.10 UNTIL

"Now the two of them went until they came to Bethlehem" (Ruth 1:19).

"So she stayed close by the young women of Boaz, to glean until the end of barley harvest and wheat harvest; and she dwelt with her mother-in-law" (Ruth 2:23).

"Then she said, 'Sit still, my daughter, until you know how the matter will turn out; for the man will not rest until he has concluded the matter this day'" (Ruth 3:18).

* * *

God has glorious expectations locked into the word "until," and Scripture shows that it has been His marker for blessing from earliest days. Take Genesis 49:10, for example, where the coming of the Lord Jesus Christ is prophesied: *"The sceptre shall not depart from Judah, nor a lawgiver from between His feet, until Shiloh comes; and to Him shall be the obedience of the people."* In the glorious anticipation of the Incarnate Christ's coming back to reign on earth as the Messiah after the rapture of the church and the dark days of the great tribulation, the remnant of Israel will enjoy the fulfilment of God's purpose for them in this "until."

The theme is still about Him in the Passover of Exodus 12:6 when God told His people to take the lamb, *"Now you shall keep it until the fourteenth day of the same month. Then the whole assembly of the congregation of Israel shall kill it at twilight."* The One who prophesied the incarnation of Christ and His ultimate rule is now prophesying His crucifixion. He has moved our attention from the Man of the glory of Shiloh to the suffering Lamb of God. When we step in to Leviticus 23 and read through God's calendar of future events, He begins with the Passover and follows it with the Feast of Firstfruits. It's in this lovely portion of Israel's annual ceremony that God says to them in verse 14, *"You shall eat neither bread nor parched grain nor fresh grain until the same day that you have brought an offering to your God."* Now the "until" of the Incarnation, that became the "until" of the crucifixion, has become the "until" of the resurrection! These were deliberate and precise prophecies from God painted by Him in the landscape of Old Testament writings to portray what He will achieve in His Son.

The implications of the "until" are no less significant in the Book of Ruth. God is on the march. The three chapters that precede the marriage of Ruth to Boaz all end with an "until," and we can think of them as follows:

 • at the end of chapter one, there's an anticipation of the place;
 • at the end of chapter two, it's the anticipation of provision;
 • at the end of chapter three, it's the anticipation of a partner.

Chapter 1 was a leaving process, chapter two was a learning process, and chapter three was a longing process. Coming to Bethlehem with Naomi meant all three for Ruth. They went on "until" they came to the place where God's providence, His purpose and His provision could be experienced, and their arrival coincided with the beginning of barley harvest. The timing was perfect for reaping the barley harvest began at Passover time in conjunction with the lamb that was from God for His people and the sheaf of the firstfruits that was from the people for God. How wonderfully He put the lamb and the sheaf together to symbolise that Jew and Gentile need the death and resurrection of Christ to unite them with Himself. We all went away from Him in Adam, and then Israel went away from Him as a nation; so Ruth represents us coming as lost sinners to our Redeemer, and Naomi is the picture of the remnant of Israel coming to receive His salvation. Both are vividly depicted in the treasury of Romans 11's goldmine, as we thought of them in our introduction in Chapter 1.

In 2007, Mahmoud Ahmadinejad the former president of Iran made an announcement that the USA, Great Britain and Israel will disappear from the world map. Well, he could be right on the first two, but he's definitely not right on the last. It's impossible, for her Redeemer has still to come, and the fulfilment of Naomi's return has still to be achieved in the deliverance of the remnant of Israel. Well might we borrow God's triumphant words from Isaiah 46:11, *"indeed I have spoken it; I will also bring it to pass. I have purposed it; I also will do it."*

Until the end

When Naomi said to Ruth, at the end of chapter 2, *"It is good, my daughter, that you go out with his young women, and that people do not meet you in any other field,"* Ruth knew that her place was set *"until the end of barley harvest and wheat harvest."* But the big difference was that she knew he had called it *"my harvest,"* so she was serving the lord of the harvest. What she didn't know, of course, was that although she was only a worker at the beginning of Boaz's barley harvest, she would be his wife before wheat harvest began.

These were two different crops. Unlike barley harvest, which began at Passover, Exodus 34:22 indicates that wheat harvest was associated with Pentecost: *"And you shall observe the Feast of Weeks, of the firstfruits of wheat harvest."* The Saviour's death on the cross was at Passover time and identified with His poverty, but Pentecost was associated with wheat harvest that points to His riches. If those who are *"born of the Spirit"*[1] also *"walk by the Spirit,"*[2] God will ensure that the sequel to Psalm 81:16 will be theirs. His word to His people was, *"He would have fed them also with the finest of wheat; and with honey from the rock I would have satisfied you."*

333

God's rich feeding always relates to fulness, fatness and sweetness, and in these lies the secret of being edified and satisfied. Just as coming to Christ guaranteed our leaving process, leaving our sinful and worldly ways, walking by the Spirit will guarantee our learning process. It's our anticipated provision, but we don't get it all at once. If the cross of Christ has brought a life-giving step, we will show it by allowing the Spirit of Christ to bring a life-changing walk. We met *"Christ our Passover"*[3] in our poverty, but we walk with Him in His riches *"until"* Christ is formed in us.[4] As we do, God will ensure that, *"He who has begun a good work in you will complete it until the day of Jesus Christ."*[5] He will do this if we adopt Paul's desire for Timothy, that he would *"keep the commandment, without spot, without reproach, until the appearing of our Lord Jesus Christ."*[6] Ruth served *"until,"* from *"the beginning"*[7] to *"the end,"*[8] and she knew the poverty of the barley and the fineness of the wheat by walking with the man who had said, *"my harvest."* Will we do that too?

Naomi had missed ten Passovers, so she couldn't claim that she had maintained fellowship with the lamb. The unmissable fact was she preferred bread! That's the lesson, and it teaches us we can't go away from God and keep having fellowship with Christ. Some claim they maintain a close relationship with the Lord Jesus, even while living in a sinful relationship with a partner. It's like living in Moab and claiming to being in fellowship with the lamb. As Jeremiah said, *"The heart is deceitful above all things,"*[9] and there are professing Christians who prove this to be true. Naomi knew there was only one remedy: she had to return to Bethlehem to be reconnected with God and with the lamb.

In God's goodness, there's a remedy for us, too: like lamenting Jeremiah, we need to say from deep conviction, *"Let us search out and examine our ways, and turn back to the LORD; let us lift our hearts and hands to God in heaven."*[10] He knows how real we are, and how unreal! That's why Jeremiah went on to say, *"You have covered Yourself with a cloud, that prayer should not pass through."* Christian, when you feel that the heavens are like brass[11] you can't also claim *"His heavens shall also drop dew."*[12] Evidence of His Spirit's presence never coexists with the absence of prayer contact with God, and the only answer is *"search ... examine ... turn."*

Naomi had missed the joy and satisfaction of these for ten years; but worse by far, the people of Israel have missed their sequel for two thousand years. At the darkest Passover time ever, they failed to see what Pilate, the Gentile governor saw. Having examined the Lamb of God, he reached his verdict and pronounced, *"I find no fault in Him."*[13] In response, they condemned Him and themselves, not only by saying, *"Crucify Him, crucify Him,"* but by adding, *"His blood be on us and on our children."*[14]

Little did they know that by their permission the blood of the Passover Lamb would be shed in His crucifixion to fulfil Exodus 12, and that he would be cut off and lifted up in glorious resurrection as fulfilment of the wave sheaf in Leviticus 23. Oh, by what strange means we are caused to say to God, *"Surely the wrath of man shall praise You."*[15] In their blindness, they failed to reap the blessings that belong to the poverty of Christ depicted in *"the beginning of barley harvest"*; and were consigned to miss the further outpouring of His riches at Pentecost at *"the end of ... wheat harvest."* How triumphantly our Sheaf of the firstfruits went home! He has *"risen from the dead, and has become the firstfruits of those who have fallen asleep. For since by man came death, by Man also came the resurrection of the dead. For as in Adam all die, even so in Christ all shall be made alive. But each one in his own order: Christ the firstfruits, afterward those who are Christ's at His coming."* Harvest day is coming, and as we wait for it we can make truth out of what Eliphaz said to Job for believers will go home *"like sheaves gathered in season."*[16]

As each year passes, our prayer should be that we are growing more fully into conformity to Christ, and the greatest spiritual benefit we can be to each other is that we help one another to grow into the likeness of Christ. It's not merely helping what they do for Him, but assisting what they are for Him! Developing His character is what matters, but obtaining His depends on abstaining from our own. Paul made this link when he wrote, *"Therefore, having these promises, beloved, let us cleanse ourselves from all filthiness of the flesh and spirit, perfecting holiness in the fear of God."*[17] It takes a lot of honesty to answer Paul's question, *"For what man knows the things of a man except the spirit of the man which is in him?"*[18] There may be "things" in the recesses of our spirit that no one sees except the Lord, and we may need Him as the Carpenter to smooth our rough edges until He shapes us inwardly to His likeness.

But it's not wholly in the shaping of character; it's also in the developing of conduct. Blind spots exist, and each of us can say, 'I can be very tolerant of me.' That's easy. We can be adept at excusing ourselves, yet be intolerant of others. The spirit needs to change, so that our conduct changes. A lot rests on our spirit, including in how we conduct ourselves in gatherings of the Lord's people. At the beginning of Galatians 6, Paul urges churches to welcome back someone who has recovered from a fault, and he was looking for something deeper than an outward expression of acceptance. By saying, *"restore such a one in a spirit of gentleness,"* he emphasised that conduct and character go together, and he emphasised the solution in the final verse of his letter: *"Brethren, the grace of the Lord Jesus Christ be with your spirit."* Yes, we need the riches of His grace to be an ingredient of the finest of the wheat!

Until you know

Naomi's could sense that something was unfolding for Ruth, and this caused her good advice to continue at the end of chapter 3. *"Sit still, my daughter, until you know how the matter will turn out; for the man will not rest until he has concluded the matter this day."* Her word Sh^{e}biy had strong implications that Ruth should feel settled there, as if she were married to the spot, and well might she for she had absolute trust in "the man." Does this depict the bond of trust there is between you and our Lord Jesus Christ, or is there a danger that you will be unsettled and not wait for Him to conclude whatever matter weighs on your mind?

The word *"until"* appears ten or eleven times in the Book of Ruth, depending upon which English version you read, and we find it twice in this verse. It's as if the whole book hangs on these *"untils."* They were deep experiences for her, and the two we are now looking at speak to us, not of the living process or learning process, but of the longing process that had come into her heart. She knew that God had made provision in His Law[19] for a close relative of her husband to marry her, and she quietly rested on this. Did that mean sitting idle and doing nothing? No, for the second *"until"* tells us that she was fully prepared to show that her definition of sitting still didn't mean an attitude of indolence, but one of dependence. It was no haphazard longing, and neither is ours. Those who belong to *"the Man Christ Jesus"*[20] are perfectly settled and waiting, and will continue to do so *"until the redemption of the purchased possession."*[21]

Far greater than Ruth's, our waiting time will be worth it. If she could be content to *"sit still,"* believing that her *"until"* would pass and, ultimately, she would stand at his side, how much more should we? God assures us in His Word that we have the certainty of Christ's return, and this caused James to say, *"Therefore be patient, brethren, until the coming of the Lord."* Ruth lived in the presence and power of each *"until,"* but believers in our Lord Jesus Christ live in the promise of each "until" that God has given us. Today, like Ruth, we "sit still," settled in the sure hope of His coming, but soon we also shall stand as a bride at the side of our Bridegroom: *"For in just a little while, He who is coming will come and will not delay."*[22] He *"was offered once to bear the sins of many. To those who eagerly wait for Him He will appear a second time, apart from sin, for salvation."*[23]

Soon the watching will be over,
And the waiting time be past,
Earthly praying will be ended;
We shall meet our Lord at last.
(Miss I. Hickling)

* * *

My heart can sing when I pause to remember
A heartache here is but a stepping stone
Along a trail that's winding always upward,
This troubled world is not my final home.

But until then my heart will go on singing,
Until then with joy I'll carry on,
Until the day my eyes behold the city,
Until the day God calls me home.
(Stuart Hamblen)

3.11 BOAZ THE BRIDEGROOM

"Now it is true that I am a close relative; however, there is a relative closer than I" (Ruth 3:12).

Now Boaz went up to the gate and sat down there; and behold, the close relative of whom Boaz had spoken came by. So Boaz said, "Come aside, friend, sit down here." So he came aside and sat down.And he took ten men of the elders of the city, and said, "Sit down here." So they sat down. Then he said to the close relative, "Naomi, who has come back from the country of Moab, sold the piece of land which belonged to our brother Elimelech. And I thought to inform you, saying, 'Buy it back in the presence of the inhabitants and the elders of my people. If you will redeem it, redeem it; but if you will not redeem it, then tell me, that I may know; for there is no one but you to redeem it, and I am next after you.'" And he said, "I will redeem it."

Then Boaz said, "On the day you buy the field from the hand of Naomi, you must also buy it from Ruth the Moabitess, the wife of the dead, to perpetuate the name of the dead through his inheritance." And the close relative said, "I cannot redeem it for myself, lest I ruin my own inheritance. You redeem my right of redemption for yourself, for I cannot redeem it."

Now this was the custom in former times in Israel concerning redeeming and exchanging, to confirm anything: one man took off his sandal and gave it to the other, and this was a confirmation in Israel. Therefore the close relative said to Boaz, "Buy it for yourself." So he took off his sandal. And Boaz said to the elders and all the people, "You are witnesses this day that I have bought all that was Elimelech's, and all that was Chilion's and Mahlon's, from the hand of Naomi.

Moreover, Ruth the Moabitess, the widow of Mahlon, I have acquired as my wife, to perpetuate the name of the dead through his inheritance, that the name of the dead may not be cut off from among his brethren and from his position at the gate. You are witnesses this day" (Ruth 4:1-10).

* * *

It was in the main store in Madras, South India, while a package was being wrapped for me, a member of staff at another counter was reading a small book. He was so engrossed that he didn't know he was being watched. Evidently, he was reading some Hindu scriptures for, as he turned each page, he lifted the book to his lips and kissed it, and the thought flashed through my mind: "I wish I loved my Bible as much as that man appears to love his book."

Ruth's story is one good reason for loving God's Word for it is a treasure within a treasury, and reflects a characteristic harmony that has been given by its Inspirer. It opens without a king[1] and closes with a king; it begins with death, and it ends in birth; it starts with division, and finishes in union. We have already thought of how chapter 1 opens with famine and ends with plenty; chapter 2 starts with barley harvest and finishes with wheat harvest; chapter 3 opens with Boaz at rest and concludes with Ruth at rest. In that chapter, she went down. Chapter 4 says, *"Boaz went up."* There's something about the way God does things that makes us stand in awe and recognise that, no matter who the author is on earth, His hand is behind the penmanship. It would be strange if chapter 4 were any different, and it's not, for it begins with ten witnesses and ends with ten generations. The amazing balance is everywhere!

Verse 1 of chapter 4 doesn't tell us that *"Boaz went up"* simply to stand as a contrast to what we read in chapter 3 that *"she went down."* There's more to it than that. The world 'ālāh means to ascend, but is very closely associated to the word 'ōlāh which refers to the burnt offering in Leviticus. The ascending of the burnt offering was more than upward; it was Godward, and wholly for God. This captures the deeper intention in the heart and mind of Boaz as he went up. Ten other men went up to the gate that morning, but only Boaz went up for God, yet he wasn't aware that he was going up to fulfil a key part of the purpose of God. Yes, he knew that he was going up to honour the provision made in the law for a redeemer, but he had no idea that God saw his going up as a step toward fulfilling His provision of the Redeemer under grace.

In Exodus 24, we are told four times that Moses *"went up,"* and chapter 19:3 says, *"Moses went up to God."* The people should have been so gripped by the sight of the ascending, receding figure, and every heart should have been acknowledging, "He's going up for me." Ruth could have said the same, and, thankfully, so can we. Luke 2 adds its own remarkable commentary of how the twelve-year-old Jesus *"went up"* to Jerusalem with His parents for the Passover. What a scene! The Lamb, *"Christ, our Passover"*[2] was there! But a greater day was coming for which *"He went on,"*[3] then *"He, bearing His cross, went out,"*[4] and three days later *"He went up."*[5] It was the greatest going up of all, for the One who had offered Himself on the cross was the true ascending Offering going home.

The Purpose of the Gate

The gate was a place of discussion and debate, where decisions were made, and Boaz knew that local matters of justice and judgment would be settled there, including important issues like redemption. The practice was steeped in history, the first scriptural example being Sodom in the opening verse of Genesis 19, but its spiritual connotation is presented in chapter 28:17 where Jacob woke from his dream at Bethel and announced, *"How awesome is this place! This is none other than the house of God, and this is the gate of heaven!"* Apart from being the place of access, it also implies a place of divine authority that calls for submission to its claims and control, and a place of opportunity. It was there that Jacob took his stone pillow and upended it as a pillar.

This imagery is captured in 1 Timothy 3:15 for present-day application to disciples walking together and having their behaviour governed *"in the house of God, which is the church of the living God, the pillar and ground of the truth."* This is made clear in the previous verses, which apply to godly conditions being applied in very practical ways in our homes and in His house. Those who love Jesus *"the door"*[6] as their access to salvation shouldn't struggle to comply with subjection at "the gate" for service.

Job also spoke of his ministry at the gate,[7] and it still does our hearts good to sense the range of pastoral care that should be available at "the gate." It wasn't just a men's meeting, this was a place where whatever was relevant to everyone and everything was considered. Job's list of those present included young men, the aged, princes and nobles, and he made an impact on the poor, the fatherless, the widow, the blind, and the lame. He could do all that at the gate. He was the ideal role model for the ideal overseers' meeting!

Another telling example comes from the occasion when Jeremiah was left to sink in the dungeon and Ebed-Melech pleaded with the king who *"was sitting at the Gate of Benjamin."*[8] This may seem an unimportant detail until we recall that when Benjamin was born his mother, Rachel, wanted to call him Ben-Oni: son of my sorrow. If Rachel's will had been carried out, Ebed-Melech would have gone to see the king at the Gate of Ben-Oni, the son of my sorrow, but Jacob's intervention meant he went to the Gate of the son of the right hand, the place of victory and triumph.

Boaz came to the gate believing it was a place of divine ministry. It wasn't a talking shop, but a place where the voice of God was heard and where His confirmation was given through what was discussed and decided. Once there, he *"sat down"* to wait for the close relative (from *yāshab*), just as Ruth was able to *"sit still"* (also from *yāshab*) to wait for him to settle his right to redeem:

"According to the principle of levirate marriage, the next brother (or, as we note later, kinsman) was expected to marry the childless widow of his deceased brother. The first child of the second marriage was accounted to the deceased brother, and that child carried on the family name and inherited the property as if he had been the child of the deceased man" *(The Wycliffe Bible Commentary).*

Boaz's call to him was probably from familiarity for, although some versions translate it as *"Come, my friend"* or *"Come over here, my friend,"* his phrase, *peloniy 'almoniy*, can mean *"such a one"* (JND), *"such and such,"*[9] or *"so and so."* With this low-key welcome, Boaz ensured there was neither tension nor rivalry and gave him the opportunity, but not the obligation, to redeem the land and Ruth.

There was no conflict or animosity between them, just as there's none between the law and grace. The law is holy, spiritual, righteous and good,[10] and so is grace for they both came from the heart of God. But the law had limitations and so did the close relative with whom Boaz spoke. Initially, the man said, *"I will redeem it,"* but when he discovered that he also had to redeem Ruth his answer became, *"I cannot redeem it for myself, lest I ruin my own inheritance."* The Keil & Delitzsch Commentary explains this:

"The redemption would cost money, since the yearly produce of the field would have to be paid for up to the year of Jubilee. Now, if he acquired the field by redemption as his own property, he would have increased by so much his own possessions. But if he should marry Ruth, the field so redeemed would belong to the son whom he would beget through her, and he would therefore have parted with the money that he had paid for the redemption merely for the son of Ruth, so that he would have withdrawn a certain amount of capital from his own possession, and to that extent have detracted from its worth."

He wasn't prepared for this, so Boaz triumphed in grace.

Ten men of the elders of the city

God sometimes works with tens. Chapter 1 speaks about ten years; chapter 4 about ten witnesses. The number often is symbolic of responsibility and irresponsibility. For example, going away from Bethlehem for ten years was irresponsible, but bringing ten men was responsible. Ten commandments were given In Exodus 20 to govern the lives of men and women on earth and to show them the difference between the irresponsible and the responsible. The ten men at the gate were there to verify the agreement made by Boaz and the other man, and they probably formed a quorum, just as a minyan is adopted among present-day Jews. This is not the only time that God used witnesses. The most outstanding example is in Romans 8 in the matter of adoption.

"It is only when we understand how serious and complicated a step Roman adoption was that we really understand the depth of meaning in this passage. Roman adoption was always rendered more serious and more difficult by the *patria potestas*. The *patria potestas* was the father's power over his family; that power was absolute; it was actually the absolute power of disposal and control, and in the early days it was actually the power of life and death. In regard to his father a Roman son never came of age. No matter how old he was, he was still under the *patria potestas*, in the absolute possession, and under the absolute control, of his father. Obviously this made adoption into another family a very difficult and a very serious step. In adoption a person had to pass from one *patria potestas* to another. He had to pass out of the possession and control of one father into the equally absolute possession and control of another. There were two steps.

The first was known as *mancipatio*, and it was carried out by a symbolic sale in which copper and scales were symbolically used. Three times the symbolism of sale was carried out. Twice the father symbolically sold his son, and twice he bought him back; and the third time he did not buy him back, and thus the *patria potestas* was held to be broken. After the sale there was a ceremony called *vindicatio*. The adopting father went to the *praetor*, one of the Roman magistrates, and presented a legal case for the transference of the person to be adopted into his *patria potestas*. When all this was completed then the adoption was complete. Clearly this was a serious and impressive step. But it was the consequences of adoption which are most significant for the picture that is in Paul's mind. There were four main consequences.

1.The adopted person lost all rights in his old family, and gained all the rights of a fully legitimate son in his new family. In the most literal sense, and in the most binding legal way, he got a new father.

2.It followed that he became an heir to his new father's estate. Even if other sons were afterwards born, who were real blood relations, it did not affect his rights. He was inalienably co-heir with them.

3.In law, the old life of the adopted person was completely wiped out. For instance, legally all debts were cancelled; they were wiped out as if they had never been. The adopted person was regarded as a new person entering into a new life with which the past had nothing to do.

4.In the eyes of the law the adopted person was literally and absolutely the son of his new father...

He uses still another picture from Roman adoption. He says that God's Spirit witnesses with our spirit that we really are children of God. The adoption process was carried out in the presence of seven witnesses. Now, suppose the adopting father died, and then suppose that there was some dispute about the right of the adopted son to inherit, one or more of the seven witnesses stepped forward and swore that the adoption was genuine and true. Thus the right of the inheritance was guaranteed and he entered into his inheritance. So Paul is saying, it is the Holy Spirit Himself who is the witness to our adoption into the family of God ... It was Paul's picture that when a man became a Christian he entered into the very family of God. He did nothing to earn it; he did nothing to deserve it; God, the great Father in His amazing love and mercy, has taken the lost, helpless, poverty-stricken, debt-laden sinner and adopted him into His own family, so that the debts are cancelled and the unearned love and glory inherited." (William Barclay on Romans).

Boaz prefigured the Lord Jesus Christ in different ways throughout this process. Firstly, by fulfilling the requirements of the law, he pointed forward to the One who would *"exalt the law and make it honorable."*[11] Secondly, he was willing to have Ruth as his bride within his inheritance, and we see this perfectly expressed in Ephesians 1:18-19, *"that you may know what is the hope of His calling, what are the riches of the glory of His inheritance in the saints, and what is the exceeding greatness of His power toward us who believe."* The cross of our Redeemer has guaranteed "His hope ... His inheritance ... and ... His power" for Himself, while guaranteeing *"our hope,"*[12] *"our inheritance,"*[13] and *"power"* for us.[14] Through the blood of His cross our Redeemer has paid the full price to secure an inheritance for Himself and for every believer. All the wealth of His goodness, grace and glory are ours; and we are *"heirs of God and joint heirs with Christ."*[15] Sir John Bowring, former governor of Hong Kong put it well when he said:

> In the cross of Christ I glory,
> Tow'ring o'er the wrecks of time;
> All the light of sacred story
> Gathers round its head sublime.

The house of him who had his sandal removed

On hearing the outcome of the discussion between Boaz and the other relative, Ruth could have exercised her right to go up to the gate to confront the unwilling redeemer, but she didn't. She preferred to "sit still" by faith and, with Naomi's help, decided she didn't need to react as she was entitled by the law to disgrace him from head to foot:

"But if the man does not want to take his brother's wife, then let his brother's wife go up to the gate to the elders, and say, 'My husband's brother refuses to raise up a name to his brother in Israel; he will not perform the duty of my husband's brother.' Then the elders of his city shall call him and speak to him. But if he stands firm and says, 'I do not want to take her,' then his brother's wife shall come to him in the presence of the elders, remove his sandal from his foot, spit in his face, and answer and say, 'So shall it be done to the man who will not build up his brother's house.'"

Under this provision, other disappointed women would have called for a threefold face-to-face response, but Ruth had no desire to go up to the gate to speak her mind, to spit in his face or pull off his sandal. She hadn't come to Bethlehem looking for law, but for grace, and grace didn't retaliate. Instead, she rested through faith on what God would provide by grace. What a lovely picture she gave of sinners hearing God's word in Ephesians 2:8 – *"For by grace you have been saved through faith, and that not of yourselves, it is the gift of God."* The truth is that she didn't need to be there for the man suddenly bent down and took off his sandal and handed it to Boaz. It literally means that he plucked it off, as swiftly as a soldier unsheathing his sword.[16] It was a practice in Israel that, when a man decided that a property was not a place where he wanted to set his foot, he would take off his sandal as an indication of surrendering his right, of renouncing his claim, and of voluntarily losing his title.

The man who forfeited his right to Boaz is like the law yielding to the greater claims of grace, not that he typified a weak law, but rather a law that was weak through the flesh. In this, he proves Romans 8:3 and 4, *"For what the law could not do in that it was weak through the flesh, God did by sending His own Son in the likeness of sinful flesh, on account of sin: He condemned sin in the flesh, that the righteous requirement of the law might be fulfilled in us who do not walk according to the flesh but according to the Spirit."* God's law never retaliates against His grace, like those who are weak through the flesh, but acknowledges its limitations and surrenders. Nor was it the law that abused Him with the unclean insult of spitting in His face,[17] but ungodly Jews who broke their own law in the weakness of their own flesh. The contrast could hardly be greater: in grace, Ruth never spat on an unwilling redeemer's face, yet those who were weak through the flesh spat on the willing Redeemer's face!

As we triumph in our Saviour's rightful claim on His redeemed, it's good that we ask if our lives prove that previous claimants have lost their claim. Have all our rights been fully surrendered to Christ? Are we the kind of people who have plucked off our sandal or do we resemble those whose sandals are firmly stuck to their feet like a sword wedged in its scabbard? Figuratively speaking, our sandal can be in only one of two places: on our feet or in His hand. Which will it be? Will we surrender our right to self by saying, *"it is no longer I who live, but Christ lives in me"?*[18] Will we forsake our right to the world, and its right to us, since our boast is *"in the cross of our Lord Jesus Christ, by whom the world has been crucified to me, and I to the world"?*[19] And will we show that the adversary's rights have been severed, because we have turned *"from darkness to light, and from the power of Satan to God"?*[20]

As those who are waiting to meet our Redeemer, let's encourage one another to be men and women who have yielded our rights to Him. It should be our custom[21] to surrender, but have we given Him our sandal?

I have acquired as my wife

Boaz was a man of great wealth, yet through redemption he chose not to be bride-less, and by obtaining his bride he anticipated *"that the name of the dead may not be cut off from among his brethren."* This was his thoughtful, considerate retrospective look – honouring the names of Elimelech, Chilion and Mahlon – yet the prospective look that God had was all unknown to him, that the Name above all names ultimately would come from the line of Ruth, his bride. But he was bride-less no more, and neither is our Lord Jesus Christ. Through the seal of His Redemption, He has purchased His bride and we can never be lost!

As chapter 4 nears its end, Naomi took Ruth's newborn infant, Obed the servant, and laid him on her bosom. She took him to her heart. Isn't that the implication? She held him at the centre of her affections. Oh, there was no sign of Marah now! No, it was with joy she became his "nurse," in her language the word *'omeneth* belongs to *'āman*, as if she were saying 'Amen' to the wonder of God's purpose. Praise God, the day is coming when Israel will say it too. At last, they will take their Messiah to heart and rejoice that His goodness and grace have brought them into greater riches than they ever knew under law.

The day when Jesus stood alone
And felt the hearts of men like stone,
And knew He came but to atone
That day "He held His peace."

They witnessed falsely to His word,
They bound Him with a cruel cord,
And mockingly proclaimed Him Lord;
"But Jesus held His peace."

They spat upon Him in the face,
They dragged Him on from place to place,
They heaped upon Him all disgrace;
    "But Jesus held His peace."

My friend, have you for far much less,
With rage, which you called righteousness,
Resented slights with great distress?
    Your Saviour "held His peace."
        (L.S.P.)[22]

3.12 NOT LEFT WITHOUT A REDEEMER

"Then the women said to Naomi, "Blessed be the LORD, who has not left you this day without a redeemer, and may his name be renowned in Israel" (Ruth 4:14 ESV).

* * *

We thank God for verses that leap out from the page of Scripture and fix themselves in our minds, and then allow us to begin the process of dividing them into segments, like peeling an orange and squeezing as much juice from them as possible. Ruth 4:14 is such a verse, as long as we honour its place in its context.

In earlier days, while involved with carpet manufacturing something glinted in the pile of a sample and caught my eye. To my surprise, it was a diamond. Wondering whether it was of any value, I went to a nearby jeweller to hear his opinion. "Yes," he said, "it's a valuable diamond, but it would be of more value in its setting." I have never forgotten that, because it's equally applicable when we come to verses of Scripture. No matter what verse it is from which we derive particular pleasure, as soon as we re-evaluate it in its setting we automatically discover a resonance it never had on its own that radiates a spectrum of divine light borrowed from its surroundings in God's Word.

It's like this with the Lord's call in Matthew 11:28, isn't it? *"Come unto*

Me, all you who labour and are heavy laden, and I will give you rest." What a marvellous verse! Many have responded to His words and tucked them away in their hearts to do them good for a lifetime, but put them in their setting and we will discover how much they increase in value. Listen to the wider range of His message, and notice how He called on God before calling on men: an upward plea before the outward:

"I thank You, Father, Lord of heaven and earth, that You have hidden these things from the wise and prudent and have revealed them to babes. Even so, Father, for so it seemed good in Your sight. All these things have been delivered to Me by my Father, and no one knows the Son except the Father. Nor does anyone know the Father except the Son, and the one to whom the Son wills to reveal Him."

It's then He called, *"Come to Me."* Now we can see how the context enhances the content of His call, as the attributes of the Caller give reasons for a response from the called. First of all, there's His own relationship with God as His Father. Secondly, He showed the relevance of His call to everyday folk who wouldn't see themselves as being included in *"the wise and prudent,"* and how this expresses the Father's will. Thirdly, as Speaker, He confirmed His co-equality with God and helped those to whom He spoke to sense that He alone has the authority to reveal the Father and call them into a true relationship with Him. The purpose of God had been safely confined to the hands of Him whom He sent, and they can be safely in them, too, by coming. By emphasising what is God-centred and Christ-centred His man-centred words have greater appeal, and all this lies behind verse 28. Suddenly, the diamond sparkles in a way it never did on its own, because of the greater breadth and depth of what the Lord Jesus was saying.

It's the same with Hebrews 13 verse 8: *"Jesus Christ is the same yesterday, today, and forever."* This is another tremendous verse, yet it also sparkles in a way that it doesn't when isolated from the surrounding text. Having commended the stability of leaders who ministered the unchanging Word of God in verse 7, the contrast is made in verse 9 with a warning against being carried along by many shades of teaching that are foreign to the Word. The secret of true spiritual stability is found in being stabilised by grace, which is only to be found in the changeless Jesus of verse 8. Once again, the verse is made to sparkle in its setting between the verses on either side.

The whole Book of Ruth is like this; and we do well to see chapter 4:14, not only in the context of the Book of Ruth itself, but in its Bible-wide setting. This will help us to see how the gleam of all Scripture shines into it through its setting, so that the facets of the diamond radiate with refracted light that draws us even more fully to the Saviour than the single verse does on its own. *"Blessed be the LORD, who has not left you this day without a redeemer,"* is a word from the Lord that we can take with us and rejoice in forever. But let's explore it through the avenue of the book's four chapters, and then see the whole book in the overall setting of its Bible-wide context of God's revelation. When we do this, we will recognise that it has a consistent representation of the gospel, and a consistent presentation of God that draws us in even more closely than the single verse did. In matchless wisdom, God is proving the interdependence of all Scripture, which we thought about at the beginning of Chapter 1's introduction, and opening up the wider foreshadowing of His coming Redeemer and the wonder of His redemption.

In Exodus 12, the blood-stained doorways of God's people meant that they would open their doors in the morning and go forward in the liberty and victory of the lamb and never go back. Prior to that, God had said very clearly in Exodus 8:23, *"I will make a difference between My people and your* [Pharaoh's] *people,"* and He didn't simply mean that there would be a division between them. It was much more than a distinction or a line of demarcation, He was announcing their deliverance by assuring them He had *"set redemption"* (RV margin). To begin with, this meant they were saved from plagues that caused harm and death in Egypt, including a darkness that brought everything to a standstill in their homes. *"But all the children of Israel had light in their dwellings."*[1]

Finally, in the Passover, God's people could testify, *"He struck the Egyptians and delivered our households"*[2]; and they mourned, *"for there was not a house where there was not one dead."*[3] The Passover brought light and life: similarly, before writing about *"The Lamb of God who takes away the sin of the world,"*[4] John said of Him, *"In Him was life, and the life was the light of men."*[5] He had come that God might set redemption through His blood and make a division between believer and unbeliever, and an eternal distinction between those who are saved and those who are lost.

God drew a definite line at Calvary, as did David when he came to the Vale of Elah, the valley of the tree, and stood at Ephes Dammim, which literally means the boundary of bloodshed. At such a significant landmark, David defeated Goliath to prefigure his greater Son who went to Calvary's tree to set His own boundary of bloodshed and *"destroy him who had the power of death, that is the devil."*[6] This is the great triumph of the gospel of Christ: through repentance and conversion we cross the boundary line that He set in His death and find refuge in His redemption.

When you think of the realm of great Bible events, there are three in particular that are given unique divine approval. The first is in the book of Genesis in the time of the flood when God showed His displeasure in the catastrophe that took place, yet demonstrated His grace at the same time in calling eight souls into the ark to know His safekeeping and blessing. It took the buffeting of the deluge for them, just as Christ endured the buffeting of the cross for us while God's waves and billows swept over Him. In the deepest way of all, He faced the full blast described in Psalm 42:7, *"All Your waves and billows have gone over me,"* and Psalm 88:7, *"Your wrath lies heavy upon me, and You have afflicted me with all Your waves."* How grateful we are that it was in that storm He made peace for us through the blood of His cross.[7]

In Genesis, the ark was the means of a new beginning with these eight people – Noah and his wife, their three sons and their wives – just as in

the Gospels God gave a greater new beginning through another eight –
Zacharias, Elizabeth, and John the Baptist; Mary, Joseph and Jesus; Simeon
and Anna.

Between these two great times of divine intervention, we find the momentous story of Ruth and the accompanying similarity of bringing her
centre stage among eight named characters: Elimelech, Naomi, Mahlon
and Chilion, Orpah and Ruth, Boaz and Obed. So there are three outstanding
God-given events:

- In Genesis, a new beginning through judgment;
- In Ruth, a new beginning through a Gentile;
- In the gospel, a new beginning through Jesus.

– and the number eight is consistently associated with a new beginning in
each one, just as we also would find if we began to explore scriptures that
speak about the eighth day.

Spiritual decline always begins by losing sight of God; and there's something
very precious about keeping our eyes on Him. For the right reasons, His
eyes are in every place, but it's not such a good thing when ours do the same
for the wrong reasons! We want our eyes to be on Him and the evidence
of Elimelech and Naomi and their boys having lost sight of God was seen
when they went to dwell in the land of Moab. Some Bible versions say they
went to "sojourn," which means they went there to be inhabitants, and
they "remained" or became committed to it. It's as if they transferred their
citizenship and, declining what was His, walked away from Him.

When we look at the journey Ruth took toward Bethlehem, she stands in
stark contrast to her husband and in-laws in the journey they took away
from it. Her vision was very God-centred, while theirs was self-centred, and
we need to ask ourselves which of these two journeys we are on. Our Bibles
also tell the story of another young woman, Esther, who lived in a climate

where God wasn't mentioned, and it was in that environment she courted the attention of a wealthy Gentile. Ruth's experience was so different: God was mentioned more than twenty times; recognised as Jehovah, Elohim and Shaddai, and it was in that climate she prepared to marry a wealthy Jew.

There's a balance going on in the Book of Ruth that indicates something of the majestic workings of God, and we can see this as Ruth is being drawn towards Bethlehem in the company of her mother-in-law. On the outward journey away from God there were four; on the homeward journey, Naomi was the only one left. It's as if there was only a remnant coming home, and isn't this a picture of how it's going to be at the last? Zechariah tells us about Jerusalem in chapter 14:2 that, *"Half of the city shall go into captivity, but the remnant of the people shall not be cut off from the city."* Immediately, he adds, *"Then the LORD will go forth."*

How tragic that half will give up just before He arrives, and the other half wonderfully delivered by their Messiah-Redeemer when He comes to make Himself known on the earth. There are divisions in Ruth's story, too, for we discover two women in the first chapter, one of one whom reneged and couldn't be redeemed; and in the last chapter we meet two men, one of whom reneged and couldn't be the redeemer. Reading these tragedies highlights the present possibility of beloved fellow-believers who lose heart and give up when they would be blessed by going on. How real the Lord's question is, and how heart-searching, *"Do you also want to go away?"*[8]

Ruth was bound to have heard of the land of Israel because there were times when the people of Moab must have spoken to one another about what was going on in Israel, not least in the days of Ehud who slew their king. The people of Moab must have been impacted in a way that would have its knock-on effect on young women like Ruth. After all, the God of Israel had not only made Himself known, He had exposed the impotence of their gods.

During the Normandy Landings in 1944, a young soldier in one of the vessels found his mind being lifted from the battle as the words of this poem formulated in his mind.

> He has fixed the set proportion of the ocean and the land
> According to the detail of His plan;
> He has measured out the waters in the hollow of His hand
> And meted out the heaven with a span.
>
> But although that arm is power in the infinite expanse,
> That same unerring hand is in control
> To determine and to govern in my every circumstance –
> And to claim supreme submission in my soul.
> *(R.G. Fear)*

Naomi had a very different thought in mind as she anticipated arriving in Bethlehem and spoke about that omnipotent hand having *"gone out against her."* I wonder where we are with the hand of our omnipotent God. Can you say like Ezra, *"I was encouraged, as the hand of the LORD my God was upon me,"*[9] and tell others like Nehemiah, *"And I told them of the hand of my God which had been good upon me"*?[10] Are you assured, as they were, of His approving and commending hand; or do you feel like Naomi that His disapproving and condemning hand is against you? Ruth must have felt the haunting, pathetic echo of these words – *"gone out against"* – yet it was at her mother-in-law's side she was about to discover that same unerring hand was in control to determine and to govern in her every circumstance, and to claim supreme submission in her soul.

This is the secret of knowing the hand that reaches and touches and confers His blessing. Naomi's return was one of mixed feelings, and maybe you can relate to her because of some regret in your life. Ruth was different. She was an outstanding example of someone who wholeheartedly and unreservedly says, *"The blessing of the LORD makes one rich, and He adds no sorrow with it."*[11] And we can say it, too, and add, *"This I know, because God is for me."*[12]

If we were studying Paul's letter to the Romans, we would enjoy the privilege of thinking about the glory of God. Were we considering the letter to the Hebrews, we would be led into the majesty of His greatness. Moving forward and reading Peter's first letter, we would be treated to his rich appreciation of His grace. Ruth's little book makes no mention of His glory, nor is there any reference to His greatness, but, like Peter, grace is everywhere. The marvel is, that as we absorb the proofs of kindness and favour in its four chapters, we sense that the glory of God and greatness of God are stamped on each one for they depict something so grand in its great and glorious message of redemption.

Orpah came so near to it, and turned back. Leaving home, as Ruth did, she came to a point in the journey where Naomi's appeal became her way of escape; the way to God and freedom apparently lost forever. Whatever seed may have been sown, at last bore no fruit. If we borrow the imagery of the parable of the sower, Orpah was like those who answer to the wayside, the stony places or among thorns.[13] As she accompanied Naomi and Ruth, she may have looked like a ripening stalk, but there was no grain and she returned to her ungodly place not harvested.

Naomi knew the route as she retraced her steps. She had travelled it ten years earlier, and memories must have flooded back as she recalled going in the opposite direction with her husband and sons. The northern route would have taken them past Jericho, the place of the first victory of faith that the people of God ever knew in the land, then across the Jordan into the land of Moab. Ultimately, on its plains, they would be in the region where God told Moses to speak to the children of Israel about crossing over the Jordan.[14] It was a day when, as Hebrews, they fulfilled the root meaning of their name, which includes the thought of crossing over. Sadly, Elimelech and family had crossed over in the opposite direction. They had left, not entered. They had gone out, not come in. They displeased God, not pleased Him. Now, ten years later, Naomi was going in the right direction: crossing over – a Hebrew in the land, but motivated by looking for grain.

Ruth was at her side, drawn by a power far greater than Naomi, and she had a longing in her heart: she was looking for grace. In chapter 1, she was a widow; in chapter 2, a worker; in chapter 3, she was waiting at her redeemer's feet; and in chapter 4, she was a wife. She had known what it was to be a foreigner; she knew what it was to be in the field; she has known what it was to be at Boaz's feet, but she would never be satisfied until at last she knew what it was to be in his family. She met him as proprietor in chapter 2, as lord of the harvest in chapter 3, and finally as her redeemer and bridegroom in chapter 4. What tremendous progress, and what an example she is of the journey we have made to our Redeemer!

> "My Redeemer, oh what beauties in that lovely name appear
> None but Jesus in his glory shall the honoured title wear."

Yes, He wears it, and He shares it with us. How thankful we are that the Spirit of God brings this message to us: *"Blessed be the LORD, who has not left you this day without a Redeemer."* Can you imagine being without your Redeemer? He is the personification of love, and He alone causes us to say that He is the *"Son of God who loved me and gave Himself for me."*[15] We look at the book of Ruth and call it a love story, but the word "love" appears only once, and we find it in chapter 4:15. It's not the love of God, it's not the love of Ruth for Boaz or his for her, it's her love for Naomi, yet the whole story is one of God's redeeming love, and the love of a redeemer and his bride. How wonderfully it all points to our Redeemer of whom Paul says, *"Christ also loved the church and gave Himself for her."*[16]

With its close association to Calvary's incomparable demonstration of the Saviour's love, we may find it intriguing that the word "love" doesn't appear at all in the Acts of the Apostles, yet the evidence of love is on every page. Similarly, the letter to the Hebrews make no mention of light, yet the One who is the brightness of God's glory in chapter 1:3 shines right through its thirteen chapters. When we reach the end of the book of the Acts, we won't find the word "disciple" in the remaining twenty-two books of the Bible, yet the theme of all the letters is discipleship.

Yes, our verse is like a diamond in the cameo we thought of in the opening paragraph of our introduction, but now it's ablaze with colour as it reflects the valuable theme of redemption that's traced in the little book of Ruth. More than that, all the great truths of the gospel associated with redemption in the Epistle to the Romans come with dazzling power and shine their light into it, and so does the light of the Person who is the brightness of God's glory in Hebrews. Everything combines to assure Jew and Gentile alike that God has provided a Redeemer. Ruth's short message reminds us that, just as Naomi brought her to God and His land, so the law is our tutor to bring us as Gentiles to Christ.[17]

She also points us in the direction of seeing that, as Naomi was brought into the joy of Ruth's redeemer, so also the Jewish nation will be brought to know Christ as their Redeemer when He comes to Zion.[18] The writer to the Hebrews adds to this by saying, *"God having provided some better thing for us, that apart from us they should not be made perfect."*[19] At last, they will be broken in heart before the Man of the cross, and He will acknowledge their return by saying, *"they will look on Me whom they pierced."*[20]

Ruth helped Naomi and Naomi helped Ruth for the Jew brought a message to the Gentile, and through the Gentile God had a message for the Jew. What a story for through it we see the Lord Jesus as the answer to:

- the lamb of Passover at the time of the barley harvest;[21]
- the wave sheaf for the day of his resurrection;[22]
- the handful of parched corn;[23]
- the Bethlehemite;[24]
- Lord of the harvest;[25]
- the Redeemer;[26]
- the Beloved.[27]

– and, more than any, we are able to say, *"Blessed be the LORD, who has not left us this day without a Redeemer."*

> Oh, my Redeemer, how can I be silent
> When Thou art bestowing such blessings on me?
> Surely Thy mercy has followed me ever,
> My heart is o'erflowing, I'm happy in Thee.
>
> Safe in Thy watch-care no evil can harm me,
> Thou chargest Thine angels my guardians to be;
> And so I go onward, upheld and protected,
> Believing Thy promise and trusting in Thee.
>
> Oh, my Redeemer, how can I be silent
> When Thou art so precious, Thy presence so near?
> I will exalt Thee, and tell of Thy goodness,
> My voice in the morning, O Lord, thou shalt hear.
>
> I will exalt Thee, for Thou art my Saviour,
> Thy word is a light and a lamp unto me.
> And so I go onward through shadow and sunshine,
> Believing Thy promise and trusting in Thee.
> *(Fanny J. Crosby)*

3.13 VARIATION ON A THEME

"And Naomi said to her two daughters-in-law, "Go, return each to her mother's house. The LORD deal kindly with you, as you have dealt with the dead and with me" (Ruth 1:8).

"Then Naomi said to her daughter-in-law, "Blessed be he of the LORD, who has not forsaken His kindness to the living and the dead!" And Naomi said to her, "This man is a relation of ours, one of our close relatives" (Ruth 2:20).

"Then he said, "Blessed are you of the LORD, my daughter! For you have shown more kindness at the end than at the beginning, in that you did not go after young men, whether poor or rich" (Ruth 3:10).

* * *

Great composers have produced famous works that were skilfully built on musical themes and have paid tribute to the original scores while showing their own mastery of them. As we read and re-read the four chapters of Ruth, we trace a theme written by a divine hand, the melody of which is taken up and expressed in a variety of ways by different individuals. Although it can be heard through Naomi, it flows more loudly from Ruth, while the echo chiefly resounds from Boaz himself. The theme is 'Grace', and we follow its harmony in the way God dealt so graciously with them.

Grace! 'Tis a charming sound,
Harmonious to the ear;
Heaven with the echo shall resound,
And all the earth shall hear.

May grace, free grace, inspire
Our souls with strength divine;
May all our thoughts to God aspire,
And grace in service shine.
(Dr. P. Doddridge)

As we come to the end of our study, we will have exalted the God of all grace if we have highlighted how grace sometimes permits man's will when it is the servant of what He has decreed in His will. To put it briefly, all four chapters show His grace to and through each of the three main characters to foreshow:

· Through Naomi, His grace to the beleaguered remnant of Israel in a coming day;
· Through Ruth, His grace to the Gentiles through the cross;
· Through Boaz, His grace in a redeeming Saviour.

It's wonderful to see that Naomi was able to assure Ruth that *"the LORD has not forsaken His kindness"*[1] for that was a huge recovery from having falsely assured both her and Orpah that He would *"deal kindly"*[2] with them if they went back to Moab. On both occasions, she used forms of the word *chesed* that spoke of His lovingkindness, but it was only on the second that she could link it to saying, *"Blessed be he of the LORD."*[3] Could she have "blessed" him if they had gone back to their gods? Not possible! She had chosen the word *bārak*, which, apart from giving praise, reveals an attitude of heart depicted by kneeling down, as when the psalmist said, *"Oh come, let us worship and bow down; let us kneel before the LORD our Maker."*[4]

Moab had been a place of estrangement for her, just as Babylon had been for the people of Israel and as their present state of national unbelief is concerned. However, the year of His redeemed will come,[5] and they will say, *"Come, and let us return to the LORD; for He has torn, but He will heal us; He has stricken, but He will bind us up."*[6] Only then, when God proclaims *"the year of My redeemed has come,"*[7] will they discover that *"the LORD has not forsaken His kindness,"* and be able to say of Christ their Redeemer, *"Blessed be He of the LORD."*

The Grace of God Seen in Boaz by Ruth

It didn't take Ruth long to find what she wanted. She was looking for grace, and used the word *chēn*,[8] which she found in Boaz who showed it to her in ever-increasing measure. There was every likelihood that Boaz was influenced by his mother Rahab's experience of God's love for the stranger, and that Ruth came into the mainstream of this influence. The day was still a long way off from when Solomon would write, *"Let your father and mother be glad, and let her who bore you rejoice,"*[9] yet Ruth was bound to see that Boaz had learned how to treat the stranger.

Let's follow her and catch her deepening awareness of how gracious he was. It's as if God is giving us a glimpse of the most gracious Man who gives us *"grace for grace"*[10] for she found it in his ...

Presence

Having already found it in receiving his permission to keep gleaning in his field, her thoughts raced as she wondered, *"Why have I found favour [chēn] in your eyes, that you should take notice of me, since I am a foreigner?"*[11] Why was he paying any attention to a stranger? Why was he showing any regard for her? The only answer was, "Grace." It was comforting grace; it was communicating grace for she sensed it in the way he spoke; and it was undeserved grace for she wasn't one of his maidservants, yet it was inclusive grace for he made her feel included.[12]

Provision

Was he being restrictive when he set the boundary of her gleaning? No, this was the provision of grace. It was the assurance that all she needed was there. Thankfully, she understood this and didn't interpret it as being limiting. This was proved in later provision that came from his hand and from the hands of the reapers until he gave her the greatest amount of all at the end of the harvest. How carefully God was painting His picture of the One through whom we can say, *"of His fulness we have all received."*

Protection

Gleaning is backbreaking work, and Boaz knew she would tire and be thirsty. Grace anticipated this, not only by anticipating her need, but by appointing others to meet it and insisting they took no advantage of her. Grace was interested in her: not only in her being satisfied, but in being protected. This reminds that the Lord Jesus Christ is *"the Saviour of the body,"*[13] and as such is its Preserver. Like Boaz, He has ensured that we are refreshed for we *"all were made to drink of one Spirit"*[14] and, like the people of Israel, we are constantly refreshed in Christ.[15]

Promise

Naomi's earlier desire for Boaz, *"Blessed be he of the LORD"*, was echoed when he said to Ruth, *"Blessed are you of the LORD,"*[16] but he didn't stop there. Grace stilled her fears and strengthened her hope by telling her, *"do not fear"*, and assuring her, *"But if he is not willing to redeem you, then, as the LORD lives, I will redeem you."*[17] Thus she was assured by the willingness of grace. She had told him earlier, *"All that you say to me I will do,"*[18] and his reply was, *"I will do for you all that you request."*[19] This was covenanting grace and, resting on his promise, she took him at his word, *"Lie down until morning.*"[20]

Principles

A man of promise needs to be principled, and Naomi knew that he was. As a man of his word, he wouldn't loosen his grip on grace or on his expressions of it. Nor would he give false impressions, so he was an example of the truthfulness of grace. He didn't hide the fact that there was a closer claimant, and he was completely honest and principled with him too. When the Lord said, *"I have given them Your word,"*[21] He was able to do it because *"truth is in Jesus"*[22] and He is *"full of grace and truth."*[23] He has nothing to offer except *"the true grace of God,"*[24] and we live by His principles.

The Grace of God Seen in Ruth by Boaz

Boaz never witnessed the faith Ruth expressed in response to God's grace, but it may have been part of what he meant by saying, *"It has been fully reported to me, all that you have done for your mother-in-law since the death of your husband, and how you have left your father and your mother and the land of your birth, and have come to a people whom you did not know before."*[25] He never saw her fortitude when she made her pledge to Naomi at the parting of the ways with Orpah. Neither had he heard her say to Naomi, *"Please let me go,"* or to the servant, *"Please let me glean,"* but the servant let him know about her gracious ways. Her kindly caring, deciding, seeking and pleading were all witnesses of grace, and she showed the humility of grace when *"she fell on her face"*[26] before him. So he saw in her what she saw in him, and what an example this is to us who should *"be clothed with humility, for God resists the proud, but gives grace to the humble."*[27] We see it in Christ, and He should see it in us.

Having concluded our walk through Ruth's four delightful chapters, both she and Naomi are prominent from first to last. Boaz, on the other hand, is not seen in chapter 1 at all: unknown and unseen, except by God who caused the story to begin and have it written for our good. Chapter 1 is like looking at His plan to bring Jew and Gentile to Himself, while chapters 2, 3 and 4 reveal how He makes that plan unfold. There's an unseen Man, unknown in the emptiness of the human heart, and it's only by the mercy of God that our past estrangement is graciously overcome as He brings us on the journey of repentance to Himself. It's then that we make this grand discovery that He has His own Lord of the harvest for us to meet, and Redeemer to meet our need. In his own wonderful way, Boaz is an Old Testament voice saying, *"But when it pleased God, who separated me from my mother's womb and called me through His grace, to reveal His Son in me, that I might preach Him among the Gentiles."*[28]

Having said that, we also see ourselves in chapter 1, as lost strangers being led by an unseen hand from our lost-ness toward the wealth of our unknown Redeemer. We are introduced to His Bethlehemite, into whose hands God has entrusted the unique ministry of being the One who reveals and declares Him.[29] It will do us good to see ourselves in Ruth and Christ in Boaz, and, by relating all that he was to her and she to him, grow in our daily appreciation of being redeemed until we stand at His side as our Bridegroom. Safely Home, at last!

Standing somewhere in the shadows you'll find Jesus
He's the Friend who always cares and understands;
Standing somewhere in the shadows you will find Him
And you'll know Him by the nailprints in His hands.
He's the only One, yes, He's the only one,
Let Him have His way until the day is done.
When he speaks, you know, the clouds will have to go,
All because He loves you so.
(E.J. Rollings)

* * *

Through waves and clouds and storms,
He gently clears the way;
Wait thou His time, so shall this night
Soon end in joyous day.

What though thou rulest not,
Yet heav'n, and earth, and hell
Proclaim, God sitteth on the throne,
And ruleth all things well.

Leave to His sov'reign sway
To choose and to command.
So shalt thou wond'ring own His way,
How wise, how strong His hand!

Far, far above thy thought
His counsel shall appear,
When fully He the work hath wrought,
That caused thy needless fear.
(Paul Gerhardt)

3.14 LIKENESS TO CHRIST

"There was a relative of Naomi's husband, a man of great wealth, of the family of Elimelech. His name was Boaz. Now behold, Boaz came from Bethlehem, and said to the reapers, "The LORD be with you!" And they answered him, "The LORD bless you!" (Ruth 2:1,4).

* * *

Boaz shines among Old Testament individuals whose character was commendably Christlike. As we think about him, we may even decide, not only commendably but uniquely. Even so, the New Testament is silent about him, apart from being included in Matthew and Luke's genealogies of the Saviour. Hebrews 11 speaks of Rahab from a generation before him, and David from three generations after, yet, as we will discover, Boaz undoubtedly belongs to faith's unnamed legion.Scripture is far from silent about those in whom God saw Christ-likeness. Abraham rejoiced to see His day,[1] and God called him, *"My friend"*[2]; Moses esteemed *"the reproach of Christ greater riches than the treasures in Egypt,"*[3] and God called him, *"My servant"*[4]; David in the Spirit called Him *'Lord,'*[5] and God said that he was *"a man after My own heart."*[6] "My friend," "My servant," and "My own heart," but He called none of them "My Son." They bore similarities, but none of them was equal to Him. God asked a vital question in Isaiah 46:5 – *"To whom will you liken Me, and make Me equal and compare Me, that we should be alike?"* In comparison to the deities of idolatry, the answer is "No one" or "Nothing";

in comparison to true Deity, the answer is "Christ."

Paul gives the reason for this in Colossians 2:9 – *"For in Him dwells all the fulness of the Godhead bodily"* – so He is the incomparable Christ of the incomparable God. His nature is eternally unique, yet He graciously allows His servants, past and present, to share His likeness. Many did in Old Testament days, and we can in New Testament days. In the opening of his second letter, Peter assures us that *"His divine power has given to us all things that pertain to life and godliness, through the knowledge of Him who called us by glory and virtue, by which have been given to us exceedingly great and precious promises, that through these you may be partakers of the divine nature."* Presently, we can be like Him, and John assures us that, eternally, *"we shall be like Him,"*[7] but neither now nor then shall we be equal with Him. He remains incomparable!

> Lord, You are the Lamb that God provided;
> Lord, You are the Life, the Truth, the Way;
> Lord, You are the brightness of God's glory
> And no one in my life compares with You.
>
> Lord, I want to know more of Your riches;
> Lord, I want to show Your glory, too;
> Lord, I want to radiate Your beauties
> Till others say that none compares with You.
> *(A. McIlree)*

The man's name ... is Boaz

Would you have been surprised if the Book of Ruth had been called the Book of Boaz? His name is mentioned twenty-one times in English versions (twenty times in the Hebrew), while Ruth is mentioned only twelve, so we could say that her story is all about him, even though Naomi is referred to nineteen times. This seemed to be the case, even for her, for at the end of her first day's work she told Naomi, *"The man's name with whom I worked today is Boaz."*[8] Later, at the end of another day, *"she told her all that the man had done for her,"*[9] and when it came to the matter of being redeemed she was settled in knowing, *"the man will not rest until he has concluded the matter this day."*[10] It was all about him! And isn't it the same for us? We are saved through *"the gospel of Christ,"*[11] fed with *"the word of Christ,"*[12] for us to live *"is Christ,"*[13] and finally we shall be *"with Christ."*[14] Yes, it's all about the Man! But do we know what our Redeemer is really like? Ruth certainly knew what hers was like.

The Unseen

There is no mention of Boaz in chapter 1, and his absence speaks of the unseen Christ. Just as Elimelech and family had vanished from the sight of those in Bethlehem, so Boaz had vanished from theirs, yet God's eyes were fixed on him as He waited to bring him centre stage in the lives of Ruth and Naomi. As their story started to unfold, as we thought in chapter 1, they typified God's dealings with His people, Israel, who would be brought to redemption through the One who alone is the answer to the unseen Passover lamb of the barley harvest and the unseen wave sheaf that foreshadowed His death and resurrection. Through these and His glorious ascension, the One who stood in the shadows of the Old Testament took His place as the Lamb on the middle cross and as the Lamb who is in the midst of the throne that He might become centre-stage in our lives too.

A Man of Great Wealth

This is the first thing we are told about him, but Ruth had no idea of how he would share his riches or of how she would enter into them. After all, it didn't cost him much for her to glean or to gain from the un-reaped corners of the field, [15] but she knew what it meant to her as a poor stranger. The difference between her poverty and his "wealth" was found in little things, but gradually this changed until she knew the full blessing of belonging to Him. During this process, she discovered that his wealth went much deeper than material for he was a man of *chayil*, which meant strength of character and virtue. He was wealthy in his nature, in his manner, in other words a man of real substance and ability. Being rich in different ways meant that she would be enriched in different ways as she drew on all that he meant to her. In this, she pointed forward to all that we are in Christ as we draw from the riches of His goodness,[16] the riches of his glory,[17] and the riches of His grace.[18] So our Man of great wealth is greater than Boaz for, not only does He cause us to go from *"strength to strength"* – *mēchayil 'el chayil*,[19] but from *"glory to glory"*[20] and *"grace upon grace,"*[21] and these enrich our sense of belonging.

> And every virtue we possess,
> And every victory won,
> And every thought of holiness,
> Are His alone.
> *(Miss H. Auber)*

A Man of Faith

Proof of this was seen when Elimelech and family showed their unfaithfulness by leaving Bethlehem because of the famine and Boaz decided to stay. His field was precious to him: and because it was, he depended on it by faith as strongly as Eleazar defended his by faith in 2 Samuel 23:9,10. Just as Eleazar's sword became inseparably one in his hand, Boaz's faith was inseparably one in his heart, and Ruth was blessed in this as we are so much more fully in the One who is the Author and Finisher of our faith.[22] He is its beginning and its end, its cause and its completion, its Captain and its consummation.

Unlike Elimelech who was an example of Israel's unfaithfulness, it would never be said of Boaz that *"Then [he] despised the pleasant land, having no faith in his promise."*[23] He must have endured those years of famine, and would have been thankful had he been able to glean what he could and survive when the pickings were so sparse. Being faithful in God's land, even when it wasn't yielding its pleasantness, meant more to him than being unfaithful in Moab's land. Ruth was blessed by his faithfulness to God and would have no reason to question his faithfulness to her. How much more can we say this of the Man who is in the presence of God for us! He is the ultimate faithful Servant. *"If we are faithless, He remains faithful."*[24] He is faithful to us, having shown Himself to be faithful to Him who appointed Him as the Apostle and High Priest of our confession. We have no need to question our faithful Saviour for He has already shown Himself to be the faithful Servant, the faithful Son: Jesus, *"the same yesterday, today, and forever."*[25]

A Man of Strength

In these three chapters, there isn't the slightest indication of weakness in Boaz. Strong in faith, strong in his resolve, strong in his principles, strong in his consideration of others, strong in his protection of Ruth: he was altogether a man of strength. There was no weakness of doubt or uncertainty, of wavering, selfishness, or of poor reputation. God was his mainstay, and he was strong in Him. Outside of Ruth's four chapters we find God's evaluation of Boaz alluded to in His temple. Two pillars stood side by side. What would God call them? Moses and Aaron? Joshua and Caleb? No, He called them Jachin and Boaz[26]: combining "He shall establish" with "In him is strength."

They were good names for pillars and, although there's no indication they were named after people, they were good names for men. Boaz the man of strength was an appropriate reflection of God's choice of a pillar for he remained like a pillar in Bethlehem while Elimelech became like a log in Moab! What caused his weakness? Well, it was lack of faith. And what caused his lack of faith? Would it not have been a lack of prayer? By parallel reasoning, we conclude that Boaz was a man of strength, because he was a man of faith; and a man of faith, because he was a man of prayer. Thankfully, our Man of strength was the model Man of prayer, and still is for He *"also makes intercession for us."*[27]

A Man of Grace

There was no one like Boaz, and Ruth was impressed by his grace. She responded to him by finding grace in his eyes as the man of wealth[28]; she received from him by hearing it in his voice and finding it in his hands as the lord of the harvest[29]; she rested in him by finding grace at his feet as her redeemer[30]; and she related to him by finding grace at his side as her bridegroom.[31] She found grace that was visible, audible and tangible and, as we reach out to our gracious Saviour, we are blessed in knowing that we have all these in Him.

> Thus Wisdom's words discover
> His glory and His grace,
> The everlasting Lover
> Of our unworthy race.
> His gracious eye surveyed us
> Ere stars were seen above;
> In wisdom He has made us
> And died for us in love.
> *(William Cowper)*

A Man of Provision

As soon as Boaz heard that his servant had given Ruth permission to glean, he made sure that this would increase by authorising her provision. By doing this, he also made sure that there would be no thought of her going hungry. He was a true Bethlehemite, a man from the house of bread, but he could never say, *"I am the bread of life."*[32] This is the unique claim of our

Man of provision: the eternal "I AM," and our lifelong feeding! Feeding is what He does; the "I AM" is who He is. And day-by-day we are finding that His garment takes shape from what is underneath.

A Man of Rest

During Naomi's unsettled years in Moab, Boaz was resting: not physically, but spiritually. In the threshing floor, he rested physically at the end of a tiring work, but inwardly he both rested and rejoiced in the satisfaction of a finished work. The Saviour was like this, too, but to an infinitely greater degree. The cross was His threshing floor, like Ornan's on Moriah in the landscape of Calvary. Physically, He was *"marred more than any man"*[33]; but spiritually, He entered into the satisfaction of completing redemption's work and saying, *"It is finished!"*[34] Having secured rest for Himself, He also secured it for everyone who hears His call, *"Come to Me, all you who labour and are heavy laden, and I will give you rest."*[35]

The Lord of the Harvest

Boaz was in no doubt as to who was the true Lord of the harvest, and all his workers knew that. There was mutual recognition of this as they responded, *"The LORD bless you,"* to his greeting, *"The LORD be with you!"* It was under his lordship that the spiritual climate of the field was set for all who gathered, gleaned, and gained. Familiar with every stage of crop management, he would have mastered an understanding of ploughing, sowing, reaping, and winnowing: identified with dirt and dust from beginning to end. He also would have a good knowledge of his seed and of his land. One evident feature of his work was that we meet him in the field, in the threshing floor, and in the gate, but never in his home until it is implied when he took Ruth to be his wife.

In Matthew 9:37 and 38, the Lord Jesus Christ told His disciples, *"The harvest truly is plentiful, but the labourers are few. Therefore pray the Lord of the harvest to send out labourers into His harvest."* As the last Adam, the Lord from heaven became the Lord of the harvest; identified with *"the man of dust"*[36] from beginning to end. In keeping with Boaz's claim that the harvest was *"my harvest,"*[37] Jesus announced a harvest that was *"His harvest,"* and, better than any, He knows the quality of the *"good soil"* and of the *"good seed."*[38] He also knows what the harvest ingathering will be. On earth, He definitely sowed with tears, but when He returns He will come again with rejoicing, bringing His sheaves with Him, in the fullest demonstration of Psalm 126:6. Boaz was a lovely example of Solomon's advice in Proverbs 24:27 – *"Prepare your outside work, make it fit for yourself in the field; and afterward build your house"* – and the Lord Jesus lovelier still!

The Faithful Witness

Ruth's introduction to the people of God was through unfaithful witnesses, but coming to Bethlehem changed all that. There she heard Boaz witness to all she had done for her mother-in-law, but it meant more to her that Naomi could testify to the closeness of his family relationship. Best of all was when he became witness to what others thought of Ruth: *"all the people of my town know that you are a virtuous woman."*[39] Did she hear rightly? Did he say she was a woman of *chayil*? Yes, he thought of her what Naomi said of him: a man of wealth – of *chayil*! So both of them were chayil-like.

When Jesus met with Nicodemus in John 3, He invited him into the inner certainty of His witness being linked with the Holy Spirit's by telling him, *"Most assuredly, I say to you, We speak what We know and testify what We have seen, and you do not receive Our witness."*[40] His faithful presentation of the gospel confirmed that what is "of God" and what is "of the Spirit" is made known only through "Our witness." Similarly, when He addressed the seven churches in The Revelation, He did so as *"the faithful witness."*[41] He neither minimised nor exaggerated what he saw. It was balanced insight for good or ill, because what He is in His Being determined how He saw them in their belonging. Seven churches heard His assessment knowing it was from *"the*

Amen, the Faithful and True Witness."[42] It wouldn't go unnoticed that He witnessed to others what He thought of Antipas by calling him *"My faithful witness."*[43] If only he could say that of us all!

Redeemer

Completely unknown in chapter 1, the full purpose of Boaz remaining in Bethlehem wasn't clear until chapter 4 where he became the one who had the right to redeem. While working in the field, Ruth began to glean more than ears of barley as she observed the multi-faceted wealth of Boaz. As each of these eight features gradually dawned on her, she was brought into the heartfelt longing of one settled desire: she wanted to be redeemed. In his heart was the corresponding desire that was equally of God: he wanted to redeem, and she became his purchased possession.

From earliest days of gleaning an appreciation of Christ, God has brought us into a deeper awareness of His redemption, beginning with the dawning of our salvation *"through His blood"*[44] and ending with *"the redemption of our body"*[45] when He returns to the air for His church. With greater longing than Ruth, we wait for our Redeemer to come from a much higher gate, the gate of heaven; waiting, waiting, waiting *"until the redemption of the purchased possession, to the praise of His glory."*[46] Amen. Come, Lord Jesus!

Bridegroom

A Gentile bride for a man in his ten-fold likeness to Christ: what could be better? There is only one answer: being the bride of the Man who is Christ. Our spiritual journey began when we came in our sinfulness as strangers to the Lamb, and it will end when He takes us home in our sinlessness to be *"the bride, the wife of the Lamb."*[47] What a Saviour! Incomparable! No wonder John the Baptist made it so clear that he was not the Christ.[48] In John chapter 3, John said, *"I am not"* – *"Egō ouk eimi"*; and in chapter 4, Jesus said, *"I AM"* – *"Egō eimi."* John's faithful ministry led to proclaiming

Jesus as *"the Lamb of God"*[49] and as *"the Son of God"*[50]; and to saying of Him, *"He who has the bride is the bridegroom."*[51]

We may search the Old Testament in vain for anyone with a greater range of likeness to Christ than Boaz. He was such a Christlike man of wealth, faith, grace, strength, provision and rest, lord of the harvest, faithful witness, redeemer and bridegroom; but we have Christ. Ruth was blessed through a godly man, but we are blessed through the Man who is God.

It doesn't go unnoticed that this little book began with funerals and ends with a wedding, and, as we absorb its message, our hearts are drawn to worship the God who had such a bright end in view, even when departure and death seemed to dominate the picture. In a greater way, we look at the rejection, death and burial of our Saviour and take greater note that God has a brighter prospect in view for those who know Him. The day is coming when we will hear *"as it were, the voice of a great multitude, as the sound of many waters, and as the sound of mighty thunderings, saying, "Alleluia! For the Lord God Omnipotent reigns! Let us be glad and rejoice and give Him glory, for the marriage of the Lamb has come, and His wife has made herself ready."*[52] Well might we worship: we are going to a wedding!

Jesus, I am resting, resting in the joy of what Thou art;
I am finding out the greatness of Thy loving heart.
Thou hast bid me gaze upon Thee, as Thy beauty fills my soul,
For by Thy transforming power, Thou hast made me whole.

O how great Thy loving-kindness, vaster, broader than the sea!
O how marvellous Thy goodness lavished all on me!
Yes, I rest in Thee, Beloved, know what wealth of grace is Thine,
Know Thy certainty of promise and have made it mine.

Simply trusting Thee, Lord Jesus, I behold Thee as thou art,
And Thy love, so pure, so changeless, satisfies my heart;
Satisfies its deepest longings, meets, supplies its ev'ry need,
Compasseth me round with blessings: Thine is love indeed.

Ever lift Thy face upon me as I work and wait for Thee;
Resting 'neath Thy smile, Lord Jesus, earth's dark shadows flee.
Brightness of my Father's glory, sunshine of my Father's face,
Keep me ever trusting, resting, fill me with Thy grace.
(Jean Sophia Pigott)

3.15 MUTUAL SUPPORT

"The Preacher sought to find acceptable words; and what was written was upright—words of truth. The words of the wise are like goads, and the words of scholars are like well-driven nails, given by one Shepherd. And further, my son, be admonished by these. Of making many books there is no end. Of making many books there is no end."[1]

Solomon warns us to expect that they will never match *"The words of the wise"* or equal their God-given purpose. But how do we tell the difference? Solomon has given us three key proofs:

* They reflect the inspired Word by being delightful and truthful. They convey divine pleasure and reflect divine truth.

* They prompt us, like *goads*, to focus on divine direction; and, like *nails*, they fix thoughts in our minds that are consistent with divine instruction and on the One who truly is our *"nail in a sure place."*[2]

* The writers may be different, from differing backgrounds and experience, but they unite under the divine guidance of *one Shepherd*.

We made a very important premise in the first paragraph of our introduction to this book: The story of Ruth has found an honoured place in literature, but, right at the outset, we salute its much more highly prized place in Scripture. The romance of literature can stand on its own, needing neither background nor foreground, and most authors would derive satisfaction if their particular book gained recognition for its individuality. The Bible is never like that. The revelation of Scripture is completely different. Unlike literature's independence, the interdependence of all scriptural content reveals that background and foreground are essential to each individual part, and that Divine authorship is satisfied by its overall harmony. Ruth's contribution beautifully reflects this. In fact, if we miss the wonder of its wider application, we miss its true relevance.

The Word of Promise

The last fourteen chapters should have proved this to us, but now, with Solomon's three points in mind, we can review the book of Ruth believing that it is well able to answer two vital questions. How does it support the rest of Scripture? And how does the rest of Scripture support it? By the leading of the Holy Spirit we can trace how God never intended that any of His writers would be independent of the others, but that each and every one would contribute to the overall harmony and authority of the canon of His Word. Two lines of thought will help us to confirm how the book of Ruth meets this divine requirement. Firstly, we may ask how it fulfils the promises of God? And then, how it complies with the prophecies of God?

God-honouring and God-honoured

Take, for example, God's promise in 1 Samuel 2:30 – *"For those who honour Me, I will honour."* Although spoken by an unnamed man of God to Eli, the principle stands true and can be applied more widely than to its immediate priestly context. Had all the kings of Israel lived by it, the kingdom would have been in better shape, but they chose to discover what the man of God went on to say, that *"those who despise Me shall be lightly esteemed."* It makes a very fitting promise for us to remember and uphold in our own lives, and a warning to avoid. Ruth certainly lived by it long before it was written, and all four chapters of her story show this very clearly. Right from the start, and way before Boaz came on the scene, she was committed to honouring God. Unlike Orpah, Ruth never caused her parents to find out that she was of the give-up-and–go-back type. It was her wonderful declaration of intent that silenced Naomi and caused her to see *"that she was stedfastly minded."*[3]

Naomi's attempted dissuasion had worked with Orpah, but not with Ruth; faith overcame the obstacles, and she focused on the course that would prove that being God-honouring would lead to being God-honoured. Naomi should have been encouraging Ruth and attracting her to Ephrathah's fruitfulness, not discouraging her. Isn't it tragic when a believer does the adversary's work by giving wrong advice and attempting to deflect someone from doing what's right?

During the Summer Olympics in 2004, Vanderlei Cordeiro de Lima of Brazil was suddenly confronted by a spectator while competing in the marathon and lost his lead for the gold medal. In a spiritual sense, Paul challenged the Galatians, *"You were running well. Who hindered you from obeying the truth?"*[4] Peter also was concerned when he warned, *"Beware lest you fall from your own stedfastness, being led away by the error of the wicked."*[5] Ruth was tested at this very early stage and, before setting foot in Bethlehem, learned what sort of advice to resist and which to accept. It was a necessary part of learning, by the inner strengthening of the call of God, how to make stedfastness her own, and never fall from it.

Spiritually speaking, none of us can run in the strength of someone else's stedfastness. We have to make it our own, and by whatever degree we possess it, we go forward or fall back, either helped by *"the way of the upright"*[6] or hindered by *"the way of the wicked."* There is no doubt that shallow belief needs no more than the shallow reasoning of shallow opposition to make it lose ground, and even more so in these days when shallow conviction and understanding of God's Word is so prevalent. Solomon's advice still stands: *"The righteous should choose his friends carefully, for the way of the wicked leads them astray."*[7]

If Ruth was "stedfastly minded" in chapter 1, she was even more so by the time she took the initiative at the beginning of chapter 2 to *"go to the field, and glean ears of corn after him in whose sight I shall find grace."*[8] How noticeable it is that the choice of place and character of the person were her own and not Naomi's, yet she was the one who knew both! There's a real lesson here: our choices are in safe hands when they are part of being "stedfastly minded." She had heard from Naomi that the LORD had visited His people by giving them bread, and instinctively knew that her empty hands of faith could be filled only by the full hand of God's grace.

So her trust was in the LORD before she began to know that Boaz was the one through whom His full hand would fill hers. Little did she know, though shortly she would begin to discover it, that God was giving her early proof through Boaz that, *"Those who honour Me, I will honour."* So she was doubly honoured: for her own faithfulness, but always through the faithful man who began to fill her hand, her conversation, and her life. Whether by her own handfuls in gleaning, in additional handfuls from reapers in their giving or by receiving directly from the hand of Boaz himself, in every handful she held she traced his hand and the hand of their faithful God.

This was evident from the beginning of the harvest in chapter 2 to its end in chapter 3. It continued as God honoured her by honouring Boaz when he redeemed her at the gate and she became his bride in chapter 4. Overall, Ruth would have had ample opportunity to speak of *"the good hand of my God upon me."*[9] But what was the secret of Ruth's honouring and being honoured? The answer lies in another of God's great promises: *"Trust in the LORD with all your heart, and lean not on your own understanding; in all your ways acknowledge Him, and He shall direct your paths."*[10]

All Your Heart ... All Your Ways

These are the vital signs of being God-honouring. Many make a profession of committing their lives to Jesus Christ, and it has become part of the language of modern evangelism, while bearing no resemblance to New Testament definitions. Mind you, it rather demonstrates how readily easy-believism is followed by easy-discipleship. It's profession without conviction, salvation without conversion, and confession without true commitment. It may be claimed to be heartfelt, but is it life-changing? Ruth's conversion from ungodly Moab to godly Bethlehem came with her own heartfelt version of commitment, which indicated she knew it was life-giving, life-changing and lifelong.

* *"Do not urge me to leave you or turn back from following you;* A clean break from the past – its ways, its company, and its gods – that no longer held any appeal.

* *for where you go, I will go, and where you lodge, I will lodge. Your people shall be my people, and your God, my God.* This took care of the present with a real change of direction and devotion that governed her decisions.

* *Where you die, I will die, and there will I be buried. Thus may the LORD do to me, and worse, if anything but death parts you and me.* This was her sense of the future – a life-changing call from God, and a lifelong call to God.

It was no flash in the pan. No, it changed her heart and her ways. More than that, the change affected "all her heart," and she became an early example of Hebrews 4:12, in that the thoughts and intentions of her heart were changed to such an extent that they shaped "all her ways." Her allegiance, diligence and obedience were above reproach, and demonstrate what Paul meant when he closed his first letter to the church in Thessalonica with this longing for them, *"Now may the God of peace Himself sanctify you completely; and may your whole spirit, soul, and body be preserved blameless at the coming of our Lord Jesus Christ.*"[11]

Oh, this is the key to becoming God-honouring: it takes a work of God, not merely a work of our will. Like our salvation, our sanctification begins with Him; with the Holy one helping us to be holy. This allows Him to change what we are, before allowing Him to change what we do. It's one thing to desire Ruth's outwardly manifested triplet of changed direction, devotion and decision-making, but quite another to desire God's inner working that sets us apart in spirit, soul, and body. If the inward is in His hands, the outward will follow. But – and it's a big but – if we attempt to have the outward triplet without the reality of the inner, we will fail.

Ruth's reputation proves this. It didn't take long for her stedfastness to close Naomi's mouth in chapter 1, nor did it take long for her to open the foreman's mouth in chapter 2. By the time we come to chapter 3:11, Boaz was in no doubt that he could voice the general opinion of her: *"all the people of my town know that you are a virtuous woman."* Initially, they saw how God-honouring she was; ultimately, they saw how God-honoured she was. What a testimony! They saw what he saw. Now then: what about us? Do we ever spend enough time seeing in each other what our Redeemer sees in us? This is not always so, is it? Sadly, right from the days of the early churches, God had to speak through James, the Lord's brother, about the damaging use of the tongue, and warn them through Paul, *"If you bite and devour one another, beware lest you be consumed by one another."*[12] As those who are saved by redeeming grace, bought with His precious blood, and bound together by Calvary's ties, we should see what our Saviour sees in us – with *all our hearts* and in *all our ways!*

The Word of Prophecy

We also noted in the introduction how closely the book of Ruth foreshadows God's purpose for Jew and Gentile, as outlined by Paul in his letter to the Romans. This in itself gives remarkable credence to Ruth's story and helps us to recognise its meaningful place in Scripture. Far from being a fable or mere allegory, it sits comfortably among other Old Testament teaching such as the portrayal of the cross of Christ in Abraham's willingness to offer Isaac in Genesis 22, and the overall presentation of the tabernacle in Exodus, *"which is a parable for the time now present."*[13] Examples are many, including the opportunity to consider Boaz among other delightful individuals who foreshadow Christ in all the Scriptures. But there's also the collective aspect of seeing the remnant of the nation of Israel represented in Naomi, and God's purpose for Gentiles prefigured in His dealings with Ruth.

His Reward is With Him

Nestling among the many Old Testament prophecies regarding Israel's Messianic deliverance, God assured them through Isaiah 62:11, *"Say to the daughter of Zion, 'Surely your salvation is coming; behold, His reward is with Him, and His work before Him.'"* There is no doubt that Naomi was rewarded for the change of heart that brought her into the blessing of coming back to Bethlehem, and a future day will see the nation being blessed by coming to Christ. He will bring them into new covenant blessing with a complete change of heart and changed ways. What a testimony they will become to the nations when God gives "His reward," performs "His work," and fulfils His word. The process is detailed for us in Ezekiel 36:23-28:

"And I will sanctify My great name, which has been profaned among the nations, which you have profaned in their midst; and the nations shall know that I am the LORD," says the LORD GOD, "when I am hallowed in you before their eyes. For I will take you from among the nations, gather you out of all countries, and bring you into your own land. *SANCTIFICATION*

Then I will sprinkle clean water on you, and you shall be clean; I will cleanse you from all your filthiness and from all your idols. *PURIFICATION*

I will give you a new heart and put a new spirit within you; I will take the heart of stone out of your flesh and give you a heart of flesh. **CONVERSION**

I will put My Spirit within you and cause you to walk in My statutes, and you will keep My judgments and do them. Then you shall dwell in the land that I gave to your fathers; you shall be My people, and I will be your God." **COMMUNION**

Like Naomi, they will come from their places of foreign gods, turn from their disobedience to Mosaic law and submit themselves to the blessing of Messianic law, which will be written, *"not on tablets of stone but on tablets of flesh, that is, of the heart."* In this they will reflect the present-day believer's experience of 2 Corinthians 3:3, just as Hebrews 8:10 corresponds with Hebrews 10:16 with God putting His laws into renewed minds to be learned and in renewed hearts to be loved.

The Reward of the Inheritance

Among the choice things Boaz ever said to Ruth was his expressed desire on their first day of meeting: *"The LORD repay your work, and a full reward be given you by the LORD God of Israel, under whose wings you have come for refuge."*[14] What work did he mean? Was it her effort as a gleaner? No, it was for her actions as a seeker: faithfulness to her mother-in-law, forsaking her own father and mother, for leaving her homeland and coming to the people of God. But Boaz recognised the deeper motivation underlying all that: the reward wasn't simply for her doing, but for what he saw in her being. By speaking so freely to her of the revered Names of Jehovah and of Jehovah Elohim, he indicated that he already knew she had come under His wings for refuge (Heb. from *chāsāh*), which suggests fleeing to Him for protection. No god could have given this in Moab, yet she was assured that the God of Israel not only could, but would.

Under His wings I am safely abiding;
Though the night deepens and tempests are wild,
Still I can trust Him, I know He will keep me;
He has redeemed me, and I am His child.

Under His wings—what a refuge in sorrow!
How the heart yearningly turns to His rest!
Often when earth has no balm for my healing,
There I find comfort, and there I am blest.
(William Orcutt Cushing)

Ruth's greatest honour came through her redeemer and in her bridal union with him, but the truth is that she was wonderfully blessed in the inheritance that meant everything to Boaz. And is it not even more so with Christ and us? Our deliverance was designed in eternity past – when God *"chose us in Him before the foundation of the world"*[15] – and designed for eternity to come. With great anticipation, we wait for His return and for Him to *"present her to Himself a glorious church"*[16] when we shall be *"before the presence of His glory with exceeding joy."*[17] The glory is all His, shared with every born-again believer through His death on the cross, through which *"It was fitting for [God], for whom are all things and by whom are all things, in bringing many sons to glory, to make the captain of their salvation perfect through sufferings."*[18]

God's purpose, in offering His Son and bringing many sons to glory, is perfectly in keeping with His nature, and means that the perfect and perfecting work is all His too. Fellow-believer, *"He who has begun a good work in you will complete it until the day of Jesus Christ."*[19] You did not bring yourself to Him for salvation. It was His work – *"This is the work of God, that you believe in Him whom He sent."*[20] Nor is the work of daily sanctification your own. It also is His – *"For it is God who works in you both to will and to do for His good pleasure."*[21]

You may say, 'But in the previous verse Paul said that we should *"work out*

[our] *own salvation with fear and trembling.*"' But note the preposition he used. He said we have to work "out" our salvation, which we do by the help of the Holy Spirit, and didn't say we have to work "for" it. In the true sense of working it out, we work with Paul's urging in mind: *"And whatever you do, do it heartily, as to the Lord and not to men, knowing that from the Lord you will receive the reward of the inheritance; for you serve the Lord Christ."*[22] Yes, with greater expectation than Ruth's, and according to Revelation 19:7, let us apply her story to ourselves whilst longing to hear that glorious proclamation, *"Let us be glad and rejoice and give Him glory, for the marriage of the Lamb has come, and His wife has made herself ready."*

Meanwhile, as we look for the day of eternal compensation, let us live as closely as we possibly can to the Lamb, our Redeemer. Better than Ruth, the ingathering of His harvest is coming, and so is the wedding!

If the path I travel lead me to the cross,
If the way Thou choosest bring me pain and loss,
Let the compensation daily, hourly, be
Shadowless communion, blessed Lord, with Thee.
(Margaret E. Barber)

3.16 CONCLUSION

Our theme for this series, 'Men God Moved,' accepts that God was their Mover and that divine intent lay behind each writer. We also accept that, since He knows the end from the beginning,[1] He foreknew each writer and the content of the messages He would give. This also presupposes that He knew why He wanted to speak through them, and to whom. As far as the latter is concerned, the hearers would be contemporary with the writer, and God would have intended to move them. However, His revelation has wider application, as we learn from Romans 15:4 – *"For whatever things were written before were written for our learning, that we through the patience and comfort of the Scriptures might have hope."* Well might we borrow Paul's earlier comment about Abraham in Romans 4:23 and apply it to each writer: *"Now it was not written for his sake alone ... but also for us,"* and, by taking their messages to heart, discover that we also are moved.

If the closing verse of the book of Judges points us back to years of adversity for the people of God under the hand of the enemy, the opening verse of Ruth directs us forward to their years of adversity under the hand of God. Adversity is a testing ground, and in this context the story of Boaz has something preciously common with that of Job. Boaz reacted differently to it than Elimelech, and Job's trusting approach caused him to ask his doubting wife, *"Shall we indeed accept good from the hand of God, and shall we not accept adversity?"*[2] Boaz was very much of the same mind, and his godly acceptance led him to depend on the One who would cause Solomon to write, *"A friend loves at all times, and a brother is born for adversity."*[3]

Little would Boaz have thought that Ruth (from *rāʻāh* – companion) would be the friend that God would bring into his life as his adversity turned to prosperity, yet this was the man who proved Solomon's words long before he wrote them: *"In the day of prosperity be joyful, but in the day of adversity consider."*[4] It was in the joy of his prosperity that he went to *"lie down at the end of the heap of grain,*[5] and it was there that Ruth, the friend, *"lay at his feet until morning."*[6] What a glorious picture! The Lord of the harvest was entering into the joy of it, yet God had more to reveal. She was to be the bride for the bridegroom, and his adversity was crowned with prosperity.

His story, and hers, combine in such a wonderful way to depict the Lord Jesus Christ, *"who for the joy that was set before Him endured the cross."*[7] In the full anticipation of His prosperity He faced the ultimate adversity and, as the result, we bow at His feet – our present Lord of the harvest, and future Bridegroom!

Ruth's story probably stands among the most easily read, understood and enjoyed portions of God's Word, and one by which we are most easily moved. The evidence of God's grace is hall-marked in her meteoric rise from obscurity in Moab to featuring so prominently in the kingly line through which our Lord Jesus Christ was born. A barren place yielded a woman from whom David the king would come, just as the next book yielded a barren woman through whom Samuel the prophet would come. Such are the ways of God! However, Ruth's singleness of heart and prominence don't mean that we should view her in isolation, even though the divine plan elevated her from gleaning to glory. God has many great characters in His Word, men and women who stood out from the rest, yet never separated from them, for his purposes always go far beyond the individual, even when they tower above their fellows.

Gleaners must have reapers and a master. Leaders must have followers. Kings must have subjects, and bridegrooms must have brides. Moses could never function without Aaron, the prophet must have a priest, and neither could operate without a people. In the wisdom of God, it's ever the case that individuality is at its best in a community, and interdependence is designed to achieve much more than independence.

From Genesis to Malachi, the Old Testament was richly blessed with men and women through whom their generations proved that *"As for God, His way is perfect,"*[8] yet servants, prophets, priests and kings all point to a greater Man of whom we can say, "As for God, He is perfect." He verified this Himself when He said, *"I am the way"*[9] by which He combined who He is, the eternal "I AM," with what He has for us, "the way." It was from all these books that the risen Saviour spoke to the two on their way home to Emmaus, and caused their hearts to burn.[10]

If ever a book was designed to warm the heart, it's the book of Ruth, for its four chapters convey the unlikely union of a Bethlehemite and a Moabite and foreshadow the bridal bond between Christ and His church, between the Son of God from heaven and sinners on earth. With such a lofty eternal theme locked within its brevity, we thank God for moving one of His servants to write it – many authorities suggest it was Samuel – and for moving us through it. In Ruth, it kindles thoughts of ourselves; in Boaz, it ignites thoughts of Christ. May He, like the bridegroom in the Song of Songs, put in His hand by the hole of the door, and our hearts be moved for Him.[11]

> Burn in me, Fire of God,
> Burn till my heart is pure;
> Burn till Your life shines out in me,
> Steadfast and strong and sure.

> Burn in me, Fire of God,
> Spare not for price nor pain;
> Burn till all dross of earth consume,
> Only Your gold remain.

Burn in me, Fire of God,
Burn till Your eye can see
Jesus' own image, strong and sure
Formed by Your grace in me!
(Margaret Clarkson)

FOOTNOTES

3.1 INTRODUCTION

(1) Rom.11:33 (2) Acts 13:22 (3) Ruth 4:22 (4) Ruth 1:13 (5) See also Isa.66:8; Jer.31:31-34; Zech.12:10 (6) Jn 4:22 (7) Prov.30:27 (8) 1 Sam.8:19 (9) Jn 19:15 (10) 1 Cor.15:57; 2 Cor.2:14; Heb.2:14; 1 Jn 3:8 (11) Ps.115:3 (12) Gen.49:10, RV (13) Hos.13:11 (14) 1 Sam.17 (15) Acts 13:22 (16) Rom.1:3 (17) Matt.1:1 (18) Job 13:7 ASV & RV (19) Eph.2:13; Col.1:13 (20) 1 Tim.3:16

3.2 THE TIMING

(1) Ruth 2:2 RV (2) 2 Sam.5:10 (3) Est.10:3 (4) Ezek.40:4; 43:2 (5) Ps.22:1,18; 31:5; 34:20 – see Matt.27:46; Mk.15:34; Jn 19:24; Lk.23;46; Jn 19:36 (6) Acts 2:25-35 (7) Heb.3:1 (8) Ex.18:17,18 (9) Ex.18:21 (10) Heb.9:15 (11) Heb.7:25 (12) Ex.31:10; Num.20:28 (13) Josh.2:10,11 (14) Ex.15:14,15 (15) Heb.2:14 (16) Jer.31:10-12 (17) Deut.16:16

3.3 THE DECISION

(1) Gen.8:22 (2) Num.18:27 (3) Eph.1:3 (4) Amos 8:11 (5) Amos 7:12,13 (6) 2 Kin.4:38 (7) 1 Kin.19:19 (8) 2 Kin.2:21 (9) 2 Kin.6:6 (10) Deut.11:14-17 (11) Ps.16:3 (12) Josh.19:15,16 (13) Gen.41:52 (14) Mic.5:2 (15) Matt.21:13; 23:38 (16) Rev.2:5; 3:16 (17) 1 Sam.28:6,16 (18) Ps.28:1 (19) Judg.16:20 (20) 2 Chron.32:31 (21) Jer.17:9 (22) Gen.29:35 (23) Ps.107:1 (24) Ps.32:5

(25) Gen.19:36,37 (26) Lev.23 (27) Rom.2:4; 2 Cor.7:9,10 (28) Ps.37:3 (29) Prov.2:21

3.4 THE CONSEQUENCE

(1) Gen.2:17 (2) Prov.13:15 (3) Ps.78:55-57 (4) Matt.4:4 (5) Lk.15:16,23 (6) Ps.29:10 (7) Isa.33:24 (8) Isa.1:5 (9) 1 Cor.11:30 (10) Ruth 1:3,5 (11) Is.10:22 (12) Ex.15:18 (13) Ps.10:16 (14) Lam.5:19 (15) Ruth 1:5 ESV, KJV, NIV, RV (16) Ezra 9:8 (17) Isa.37:31 (18) Rom.11:5 (19) Isa.59:20; Rom.11:26,27 (20) Zech.12:10 (21) Mic.5:5 ESV (22) Ezra 9:1,2; Neh.13:23-25 (23) Jer.48:4 (24) Josh.7:21 (25) Rev.2:4

3.5 RETURNING TO THE LAND

(1) Job 29:13 (2) Heb.10:25 (3) Ps.84:6 (4) Ruth 2:20 (5) Gen.2:24 (6) Gen.25:8; 35:29; 49:33 (7) Num.20:24; 27:13 (8) Judg.2:10 (9) 2 Sam.12:23 (10) 1 Sam.3:17; 25:22; 2 Sam.19:13; 1 Kin.2:23 (11) 2 Sam.15:21 (12) Gal.3:24

3.6 WALKING TOGETHER

(1) Mic.5:2 (2) Matt.21:10 (3) Lk.1:32 (4) Ps.48:2 (5) Ps.145:3 (6) Ps.77:13; Isa.46:5 (7) Heb.2:3 (8) Tit.2:13 (9) Heb.4:14; 10:21; 13:20 (10) Lam.3;22,23 (11) Job 35:10 (12) Ps.74:16 (13) Gen.27:34 (14) Prov.14:10 (15) Ps.133:1 (16) Deut.29:18 (17) Prov.13:15 (18) Isa.13:6; Joel 1:15 (19) Ps.91:1,2 (20) Ex.23:15 (21) Judg.7:16 (22) 2 Kin.4:3 (23) Phil.4:12 (24) Gal.5:16,18,25 (25) Lk.10:1 (26) Ex.9:31,32 (27) Lev.23:10,11 (28) Prov.3:9 (29) Lev.2:1; Num.18:12; 1 Chron.21:23 (30) 1 Chron.21:23 (31) 2 Cor.10:1 (32) 2 Kin.4:42-44 (33) Jn 6:12 (34) Mk.6:34 (35) 2 Cor.8:9 (36) Judg.7:10-15 (37) Eph.2:8 (38) 1 Pet.1:8 (39) Tit.2:13 (40) 1 Jn 3:2,3 (41) 2 Cor.5:8 ESV (42) Rom.5:5 (43) Eph.1:18

3.7 BOAZ THE MAN OF GOD

(1) Col.3:23 ESV (2) Neh.4:6 (3) Deut.24:19 (4) Gen.22:17 (5) 2 Tim.2:19 (6) Gen.24:23 (7) 1 Sam.17:55 (8) Acts 13:22 (9) Jn 15:4 (10) Matt.13:38 (11) Jn 15:19; 17:16; 1 Jn 4:5,6 (12) 1 Jn 2:15 (13) 1 Jn 2:16 (14) Prov.12:26 (15) Ps.4:3 (16) 1 Pet.2:11 (17) Rom.8:13; Col.3:5 (18) Gen.17:3 (19) Ezek.1:28; 3:23 (20) Dan.8:17 (21) Jn 3:30

3.8 IN HIS FIELD

(1) Acts 2:23 (2) Gen.1:5,8,13,19,23,31 (3) Ex.29:43 (4) 2 Cor.5:17 (5) 1 Cor.5:7 (6) 1 Thess.5:23 (7) Prov.4:23,25,26 (8) Ps.37:23 (9) Ruth 2:19 (10) Matt.11:29 (11) Ruth 2:17 (12) 1 Thess.2:13 (13) Rom.15:32 (14) Phlm.7 (15) Eph.1:6 (16) Ruth 2:16 (17) Ruth 2:14 (18) Eph.2:5,6 (19) 1 Sam.18:23 (20) Josh.5:11

3.9 AT HIS FEET

(1) Lev.25:23-28; Deut.25:5-10 (2) Ruth 3:7 (3) Ex.30:17-21; Ezek.16:9; Ps.24:3,4; 2 Cor.7:1 (4) Jn 13:10 (5) Jn 15:3 (6) 2 Sam.12:20 (7) Gen.3:21; 39:12; Ex.28:2; Eccl.9:8; S of S 4:11; Isa.61:10; Jas.1:27; Jude 23; Rev.3:4,18 (8) Isa.57:15 (9) 1 Pet.5:5 (10) Gen.33:13,14 (11) Ps.33:8 (12) Isa.38:15 RV (13) Ex.19:8; 24:3,7 (14) Jn 17:4 (15) Heb.12:2 (16) Matt.25:21 (17) Ruth 3:9 ESV (18) Ruth 2:17 (19) 2 Sam.23:4 (20) Ruth 3:11 (21) Ruth 3:11 (22) Ruth 2:13 (23) Ruth 3:10 (24) Job 22:9 (25) Jn 1:16 (26) Eph.3:8 (27) Rev.2:25 ESV

3.10 UNTIL

(1) Jn 3:6 (2) Gal.5:16 ESV (3) 1 Cor.5:7 (4) Gal.4:19 (5) Phil.1:6 (6) 1 Tim.6:14, RV (7) Ruth 1:22 (8) Ruth 2:23 (9) Jer.17:9 (10) Lam.3:40 (11) Deut.28:23 (12) Deut.33:28 (13) Jn 19:4 (14) Matt.27:25 (15) Ps.76:10 (16) Job 5:26 NIV (17) 2 Cor.7:1 (18) 1 Cor.2:11 (19) Deut.25:5; Ruth 3:13 (20) 1 Tim.2:5 (21) Eph.1:14 (22) Heb.10:37 NIV (23) Heb.9:28

3.11 BOAZ THE BRIDEGROOM

(1) Judg.21:25; Ruth 1:1 (2) 1 Cor.5:7 (3) Lk.19:28 (4) Jn 19:17 (5) Acts 1:10 (6) Jn 10:9 (7) Job 29:7 (8) Jer.38:7 (9) 1 Sam.21:2; 2 Kin.6:8 (10) Rom.7:12,14 (11) Is.42:21 (12) 1 Tim.1:1 (13) Eph.1:14 (14) 1 Cor.1:18 (15) Rom.8:17 (16) Ruth 4:8; 1 Sam.31:4 (17) Matt.26:67; Num.12:14 (18) Gal.2:20 (19) Gal.6:14 (20) Acts 26:18 (21) Ruth 4:7 (22) Guide Lamps for God's Lambs

3.12 NOT LEFT WITHOUT A REDEEMER

(1) Ex.10:23 (2) Ex.12:27 (3) Ex.12:30 (4) Jn 1:29 (5) Jn 1:4 (6) Heb.2:14 (7) Col.1:20 (8) Jn 6:67 (9) Ezra 7:28 (10) Neh.2:18 (11) Prov.10:22 (12) Ps.56:9 (13) Matt.13:4-7 (14) Num.33:50 (15) Gal.2:20 (16) Eph.5:25 (17) Gal.3:24 (18) Isa.59:20; Rom.11:26,27 (19) Heb.11:40 ESV (20) Zech.12:10 (21) Lev.23:5 (22) Lev.23:10,11 (23) Jn 17:14 (24) Mic.5:2; Matt.2:4-6 (25) Matt.9:38 (26) Gal.3:13; Rev.5:9 (27) Matt.12:18; Eph.1:6

3.13 VARIATION ON A THEME

(1) Ruth 2:20 (2) Ruth 1:8 (3) Ruth 2:20 (4) Ps.95:6 (5) Isa.63:4 (6) Hos.6:1 (7) Isa.63:4 (8) Ruth 2:2 KJV (9) Prov.23:25 (10) Jn 1:16 (11) Ruth 2:10 (12) Ruth 2:13 (13) Eph.5:23 (14) 1 Cor.12:13 ESV (15) Isa.12:3; 1 Cor.10:4 (16) Ruth 3:10 (17) Ruth 3:13 ESV (18) Ruth 3:5 (19) Ruth 3:11; Jn 14:14 (20) Ruth 3:13 (21) Jn 17:14 (22) Eph.4:21 (23) Jn. 1:14 (24) 1 Pet.5:12 (25) Ruth 2:11 (26) Ruth 2:10 (27) 1 Pet.5:5 (28) Gal.1:15,16 (29) Matt.11:27; Jn 1:18

3.14 LIKENESS TO CHRIST

(1) Jn 8:56 (2) Isa.41:8 (3) Heb.11:26 (4) Num.12:7 (5) Matt.22:43 (6) Acts 13:22 (7) 1 Jn 3:2 (8) Ruth 2:19 (9) Ruth 3:16 (10) Ruth 3:18 (11) Rom.1:16 (12) Col.3:16 (13) Phil.1:21 (14) Phil.1:23 (15) Lev.19:9 (16) Rom.2:4 (17) Rom.9:23 (18) Eph.2:7 (19) Ps.84:7 (20) 2 Cor.3:18 (21) Jn 1:16 ESV (22) Heb.12:2 (23) Ps.106:24 ESV (24) 2 Tim.2:13 (25) Heb.13:8 (26) 1 Kin.7:21 (27) Rom.8:34

(28) Ruth 2:10 RV (29) Ruth 2:13,14 RV (30) Ruth 3:7,8 (31) Ruth 4:13 (32) Jn 6:48 (33) Isa.52:14 (34) Jn 19:30 (35) Matt.11:28 (36) 1 Cor.15:48 (37) Ruth 2:21 (38) Matt.13:23,24 (39) Ruth 3:11 (40) Jn 3:11 (41) Rev.1:5 (42) Rev.3:14 (43) Rev.2:13 ESV (44) Eph.1:7 (45) Rom.8:23 (46) Eph.1:14 (47) Rev.21:9 ESV (48) Jn 1:20; 3:28 (49) Jn 1:29,36 (50) Jn 1:34 (51) Jn 3:29 (52) Rev.19:6,7

3.15 MUTUAL SUPPORT

(1) Eccl.12:10–12 (2) Isa.22:23 ASV (3) Ruth 1:18, RV (4) Gal.5:7 ESV (5) 2 Pet.3:17 (6) Prov.15:19 (7) Prov.12:26 (8) Ruth 2:2 KJV (9) Neh.2:8 (10) Prov.3:5,6 (11) 1 Thess.5:23 (12) Gal.5:15 (13) Heb.9:9 RV (14) Ruth 2:12 (15) Eph.1:4 (16) Eph.5:27 (17) Jude v.24 (18) Heb.2:10 (19) Phil.1:6 (20) Jn 6:29 (21) Phil.2:13 (22) Col.3:23,24

3.16 CONCLUSION

(1) Isa.46:10 (2) Job 2:10 (3) Prov.17:17 (4) Eccl.7:14 (5) Ruth 3:7 (6) Ruth 3:14 (7) Heb.12:2 (8) 2 Sam.22:31 (9) Jn 14:6 (10) Lk.24:32 (11) S. of S.5:4 (see RV)

ABOUT THE AUTHOR

Andy was born in Glasgow, Scotland. He came to know the Lord in 1954, and was baptized in 1958. He is married to Anna, and he lives in Kilmacolm, Scotland. They have two daughters and one son. He entered into full-time service in 1976 with the churches of God (www.churchesofgod.info). He has engaged in an itinerant ministry in western countries and has been privileged to serve the Lord in India and Myanmar (formerly Burma).

MORE BOOKS FROM ANDY MCILREE

The Five Solas of the Reformation

Five centuries after Luther nailed his Ninety-five Theses to the door of a Catholic church, is there still a need for reformation? Yes, the Reformers' 'Five Solas' - Scripture Alone, Christ Alone, Grace Alone, Faith Alone, the Glory of God Alone - should be engraved on all our hearts, and the need could hardly be greater for them to be nailed to the doors of today's shallow churches today that are in danger of "being destroyed for lack of knowledge" (Hosea 4:6).

Garments for Glory

An in-depth study of the types and shadows (pictures) of Christ in Israel's High Priest under the Levitical order of the Old Testament Tabernacle and Temple, and specifically how his work, person and clothing speak of Jesus as our Great High Priest on the throne of God. But this is far from a dry, scholarly endeavour; its meditations will make your heart soar in fresh appreciation of what God has so expertly revealed in His Word about His Son; and its challenges will help you consider afresh "how should we now live" in view of what God has shown us about Him.

ABOUT THE PUBLISHER

Hayes Press (www.hayespress.org) is a registered charity in the United Kingdom, whose primary mission is to disseminate the Word of God, mainly through literature. It is one of the largest distributors of gospel tracts and leaflets in the United Kingdom, with over 100 titles and many thousands dispatched annually. In addition to paperbacks and eBooks, Hayes Press also publishes Plus Eagles' Wings, a fun and educational Bible magazine for children, and Golden Bells, a popular daily Bible reading calendar in wall or desk formats.

If you would like to contact Hayes Press, there are a number of ways you can do so:

• By mail: c/o The Barn, Flaxlands, Royal Wootton Bassett, Wiltshire, UK SN4 8DY

• By phone: 01793 850598

• By eMail: info@hayespress.org

• via Facebook: www.facebook.com/hayespress.org

www.ingramcontent.com/pod-product-compliance
Lightning Source LLC
Chambersburg PA
CBHW051937090426
42741CB00008B/1178